Alternative Sentencing

Electronically Monitored Correctional Supervision
2nd edition

Foreword by
Congressman James A. Traficant, Jr.

Richard Enos
John E. Holman
Marnie E. Carroll

 Wyndham Hall Press
Bristol, IN 46507

First edition published in 1992.

Library of Congress Cataloging-in-Publication Data

Enos, Richard.
    Alternative sentencing : electronically monitored correctional supervision. – 2nd ed. / Richard Enos, John E. Holman, Marnie E. Carroll ; with a foreword by James A. Traficant, Jr.
        p.   cm.
    Includes bibliographical references.
    ISBN 1-55605-288-X (pbk.)
    1. Probation. 2. Alternatives to imprisonment. 3. Electronic monitoring of parolees and probationers. 4. Home detention.
    I. Homan, John E. II. Carroll, Marnie E., 1970- . III. Title.
    HV9278.A52   1999
    364.6'3–dc21   99-12970
                                                CIP

FOREWORD

Throughout my fourteen years in the U. S. House of Representatives, I have been an outspoken proponent of tough penalties against those who commit violent crimes. I authored several death penalty legislative proposals that are now the law of the land. I have also been a strong and outspoken supporter of long, mandatory sentences for repeat violent offenders and drug kingpins. I am proud of my record on crime.

I have also strongly supported numerous pieces of legislation to toughen our drug laws and to build more federal and state prisons. These were good pieces of legislation and I am glad that most of them have been enacted into law. But for years I have been disturbed and dismayed over the lack of attention given to the large number of people behind bars who are not violent offenders.

Building additional prisons is an important part of an overall national and state strategy to deal with violent crime and prison overcrowding. But it should not, and must not, be the only solution. Congress and state legislatures need to examine the very pressing issue of dealing with nonviolent offenders who do not receive life sentences.

Study after study indicates that most violent crimes are committed by those who have previously served time in a prison or in a juvenile detention facility. The fact is, the overwhelming majority of those sent to prison will some day return to society. What policy makers at the state and federal levels should be focusing their energy upon is how to reduce the level of recidivism among the majority of convicts who return to society.

I believe that the innovative prescriptions set forth by Enos, Holman, and Carroll in this book offer a compelling solution to a vexing problem. For example, I do not believe that a drug addict convicted of drug possession who is not involved in trafficking and does not have a prior record or history of violence, should be sent to prison. Drug treatment and counseling should be a mandatory part of any alternative sentencing arrangement. Some form of community service should also be considered. Electronic monitoring could and should be a method that could make alternative sentencing programs feasible.

With proper supervision, staffing and scope, alternative sentencing programs can achieve a number of previously elusive objectives at the state and federal levels. They can reduce the rate of recidivism, ease prison overcrowding, and reduce the crime rate. Rather than "letting someone off easy," alternative sentencing programs that feature electronic monitoring can result in true rehabilitation for those offenders who do not pose a threat to society and who respond to appropriate counseling and treatment.

As a former drug counselor, I know how challenging it is to deal with those who have substance abuse problems. In many instances, prison can exacerbate the problems of a drug addict and dramatically increase the likelihood that the addict, when released from prison, will continue to use drugs and perhaps be involved in violent crimes.

While electronic monitoring does not represent a magical solution to America's crime problems, it should and must be actively examined as an integral part of this nation's long-term strategy to deal with the problems of crime and prison overcrowding. If America is to address its crime and prison problems, a consensus must be reached by policy makers at the state and federal levels that certain nonviolent offenders should not be sent to prison. Once that is done, alternative sentencing and electronic monitoring must become an integral part of a multifaceted solution to a multifaceted problem.

Alternative Sentencing: Electronically Monitored Correctional Supervision (2nd edition), is a must read for any policy maker or private citizen interested in innovative solutions to one of society's most serious and compelling challenges.

James A. Traficant, Jr.
Congressman
United States House of Representatives

PREFACE

Ten years ago, when the first edition of this text was being conceived, electronic monitoring was in its infancy. The total number of offenders being electronically monitored worldwide was small and the technology was crude. Yet there was considerable interest in this "comic book" technology that seemed to promise cost savings to a criminal justice system that was struggling with overcrowded prisons. That it may also offer community integration for offenders while keeping them under close supervision was an added benefit. Electronic monitoring also piqued our growing interest in computer technology. It is not surprising that many of the early technologies originated in South Florida, the birthplace of the IBM personal computer.

During the decade of the 1990's many other flavors of correctional technology have been developed and implemented. Some have gained widespread acceptance such as boot camps and simple drug screening. Others such as ignition interlock devices that prevent a drunk driver from starting a car, and the monitoring of offenders using global positioning, have as yet to catch on. In the meantime, electronic monitoring has become a standard tool in the probation and parole officer's arsenal of supervision technology. But one thing remains constant, there is a complete lack of serious research about whether this or any other correctional technology really works.

In *Alternative Sentencing: Electronically Monitored Correctional Supervision (2nd edition)*, the authors analyze this correctional technology within the context of the probation and parole process. Electronic monitoring is presented as a technology that incorporates the ideals of rehabilitation with punitive control, an ideal currently more in vogue with a "just desserts" minded public. The authors argue that electronic monitoring is a tool of supervision that can permit an offender to avail himself or herself of rehabilitative opportunities that the community, rather than a prison, can provide. Being on house arrest is punishment; electronic monitoring effectively supervises an order of house arrest; remaining in the community allows availability for rehabilitation. In this Second Edition, the authors argue forcefully for correctional case management to supplement electronic monitoring and encourage that community rehabilitation.

The core of *Alternative Sentencing: Electronically Monitored Correctional Supervison (2nd edition)*, remains the research on the effects of electronic monitoring upon the participants of a l989 probation and parole program. The effectiveness of electronic monitoring in reducing prison overcrowding or reducing the recidivism rates of offenders subjected to it was beyond the scope of this study (there were too participants in this early program and the study did not have the luxury of long term evaluation). Instead, the authors focused on measurable indices of individual adjustment to various forms of community supervision, not only for the offender but also for the family members affected by the sentence. The results of this study suggest what criminologists have been saying for decades, an offender's positive integration with his or her community is the most significant factor in keeping them out of the criminal justice system in the future. To the extent that electronically monitored house arrest can increase the chances of that integration it will be successful.

Richard C. Grinter
Co-Founder of Program Monitoring, Inc.
International Consultant on Electronic Monitoring
and Electronic Monitoring Software

TABLE OF CONTENTS

THE HISTORICAL DEVELOPMENT
OF PROBATION

Probation refers to a judicial process by which an offender is allowed to remain in the community under the supervision of the probation department as an alternative to incarceration. It is, therefore, primarily a legal disposition of the circumstances of the offender's behavior. In this vein, Allen, Carlson, and Parks (1979), have indicated that it contains three characteristic elements: First, release of the offender back into the community; second, the release is contingent upon the imposition of certain conditions; and, third, the release is under the supervision of the probation department.

Perhaps the most helpful summation of the practice is provided by the translation of the term from its roots in Latin, which reflect the ideas of testing, proving and forgiving. In other words, probation provides an opportunity for an offender to "prove" that he or she is capable of remaining in the community, in spite of the fact that he or she has been found guilty of a crime. It offers a second chance for the community to "test" or determine whether the individual will or can obey the laws of society. A fuller definition and one of a more legal nature would designate probation as a method of responding to crimes of a less serious nature, misdemeanors and non-felonious types, and frequently, first offenses, in which the judgement rendered is a suspended sentence. The offender is assigned to the supervision of a probation officer for a specified period of time and as long as laws and probation rules are obeyed. In the event of a violation of laws or rules of probation, the original sentence can be reimposed on the offender (Larson, 1984).

There are at least three components of the practice which need to be under-scored. First, the release is conditional. Second, assuming that all conditions are fulfilled, the penalty will be served in the community. Third, the practice includes supervision. These components of probation are included as essential elements in the definition of probation used by the American Bar Association (Cole, 1992). Often a sentencing judge will impose a prison term on an offender but suspends the execution of it and places the offender on probation. Thus, with respect to the second component, the offender does not spend time in prison unless conditions prescribed or required by the court are violated.

PROBATION VERSUS PAROLE

In defining probation it is helpful to compare the concept with the practice of parole. The latter can be contrasted with probation in that the offender has been incarcerated prior to release, whereas probation is a penalty rendered by a judge rather than some form of imprisonment or a jail sentence. A second contrast occurs with respect to the location of the decision for release into the community. The release of the offender into the community, on probation, is the result of a decision made in the judicial system. By contrast, the decision to return an offender to the community, on parole, is a direct result of a decision made in the correctional organization (Cole, 1992).

Although this differentiation of parole and probation seems quite distinct when the two concepts are contrasted, serious differences do exist with respect to accountability or location of authority for the programs. In essence, the dichotomy outlined is, in theory, correct. However, in practice, it requires some qualifications even though it is the courts which supervise the probation process. Bowker (1982) contends that probation is really part of the corrections mechanism. He bases his contention on the fact that the sentence occurs after a finding of guilty. Thus, logically, it becomes a part of the corrections function. The most pragmatic view is that it is more important to understand the reality of how probation is administered than to understand the organizational part of the criminal justice system in which it is located. In short, politically speaking, the function of probation may be more important than its structural or organizational location. However, in most states, it refers to a set of procedures supervised by the judiciary in the local community.

The importance of this discussion has to do not only with defining probation but also with understanding the actual locus of control for these programs; especially, when considering alternative approaches or innovations in the practice, the impact of the programs on offenders, and the quality or effectiveness of the programs. Although state correctional structures may, in fact, be formally responsible for probation services, locally elected county judges may for all practical purposes be in charge. This has been an ongoing controversy and has significance not only with respect to corrections reform, but also regarding the lack of appropriate training of judges in corrections and the additional burdening of an overcrowded court system. Some criminal justice professionals and criminologists argue, in fact, that judges are not trained in the areas of corrections and that such programs add significant and unnecessary responsibilities to already overloaded courts. Other participants in the debate underscore the increased stigma for offenders if the program is located in corrections as opposed to the judiciary. Specifically, this perspective contends that identification of probation programs with correctional organizations would create an unnecessary and significant stigma for the offender (Cole, 1992).

One of the arguments for including probation as a part of the correctional component of criminal justice is the fact that other human service agencies used by probation are a part of the executive branch of government. Thus, some criminal justice practitioners and criminologists contend that probation officers have more direct access to such services if the probation officers themselves are a part of the corrections organizations. If that becomes the case, then it is posited that the probability is higher that such services can be, and will be, exploited to the greatest benefit of the clients. Those who support the concept of judicial control argue that the close relationship between the judge and the supervising officer is critical to the most constructive consequences of probation. Included in this perception is the idea that such a relationship between judges and probation officers engenders confidence in presentence reports and the supervision of cases. A corollary may also be that this system permits judges to appoint probation officers who will be more likely to reflect, and defer to, the community standards and political structures (Cole, 1992).

In spite of such historic differentiations of probation and parole, some states have adopted models for merging the two practices. Rationale for such models have often been more in terms of efficiency rather than in terms of philosophy and effectiveness. Still, there is considerable logic underlying such models and a strong philosophical argument could be made for this practice. However, as has been emphasized here, corrections professionals have made significant arguments for the specific administrative locations of both probation and parole. Unless the models which are used in merging the two practices are under the auspices of the probation departments and the courts, they are still subject to all of the criticisms outlined.

Thus, the differentiation of probation in theory and practice will be of critical importance throughout this book. This reflects the reality of current models and the politics with which each program must be concerned, but in this instance, particularly, the political issues with which probation departments must be involved. The issues which relate to that discussion will also be observed to have genuine impact on the use of electronic monitoring (EM) as one alternative in the probation process. Specifically, the actual control of the programs, the training of those administering them, and their perceived effects on offenders have tremendous impact on the responsibilities for introducing innovative techniques and the probabilities for the success of such programs. A treatment of the history of probation to the present time illustrates this fact and provides evidence for this assertion.

THE DEVELOPMENT OF PROBATION

The first practice of probation is usually dated as 1841 and is attributed to the efforts and actions of a wealthy Boston merchant, John Augustus. Edward Savage, a Boston police officer, is usually identified as the first official probation officer and is thought to have conducted the first presentence investigation Both probation and parole evolved as a result of major social and legal reforms throughout Western nations in the Nineteenth century. In particular, the reforms represented attempts to provide more humane treatment than was provided by fixed punishments. Probation and parole may have been the most significant contributions to new developments in penology.

Although the specific practice is often identified with the activities of Augustus, there are other historical antecedents. Although scholars do not necessarily agree upon the importance, or direct correlation, between these antecedents and the current practice, most agree that precedents exist in various aspects of English Common Law (Reid, 1981). Some scholars have pointed to the early practices of reprieves and pardons used in England as the forerunner of probation (McCarthy & McCarthy, 1991). Specifically, these practices included benefit of clergy, judicial reprieve, and recognizance. One of the earliest practices which could have lent credence to initial attempts at probation was known as "benefit of clergy." The Church claimed sole authority over the behavior of members of the clergy. Thus, all clergy crimes were adjudicated by Church courts as opposed to criminal courts (Reid, 1981). Another possible origin for probation is the suspended sentence. This was a practice which diverted offenders from prison. A second violation could lead to imprisonment (Mannle & Hirschel, 1988). Other scholars contend that such suspensions or judicial reprieves were not permanent. Rather they were used as temporary measures in circumstances such as an offender awaiting or seeking a pardon. In some cases judges resorted to such practices if they were dissatisfied with a verdict or requested additional or more specific information (Larson, 1984). The practice of releasing offenders through recognizance involved the development of an agreement between the offender and the court that the offender pledges to perform certain behaviors, particularly obeying the laws transgressed, and to follow specific procedures to insure that such transgression would not occur again. Such specific procedures might involve agreeing to appear at specified times to provide assurance of appropriate behavior, a payment of a fine, providing some form of a guarantee of monetary payment, or a bond, for any new violation or failure to appear (Larson, 1984).

In assessing the historical precedents of probation, it is essential to emphasize that while these practices from English Common Law were influential in the development of this procedure in both England and the United States, in the latter they culminated in their own unique and historically significant variations. One example was "provisional filing" of cases in Massachusetts. This practice permitted the indefinite suspension of a guilty verdict after sentence was pronounced. The sufficient conditions for this practice included extenuating circumstances, such as situations in which higher courts were expected to render opinions on similar legal questions. Approval of both defendant and prosecutor were necessary prior to the rendering of this decision (Larson, 1984). The critical historical fact with respect to these variations was a 1916 United States Supreme Court ruling which declared that these precedents did not provide grounds or means in Federal courts for indefinitely or permanently suspending a sentence. In fact, however, these innovations had gained considerable support and approval. When the innovations were themselves ruled illegal, this resulted in the passing of actual statutes authorizing probation and the suspension of a sentence. Thus, the decision by the Supreme Court to terminate practices which had emerged from English common law resulted in the creation of laws specifically permitting suspended sentences and probation (Stojkovic & Lovell, 1992). Further, it is of significance in the discussion of the historical development of probation to emphasize that the first statute authorizing the practice in the United States was passed in Massachusetts in 1898. Such laws did not emerge in England until 1907.

Although the first case for which Augustus served as a probation officer involved an adult male, the practice did not receive widespread approval until it was used by the juvenile courts. In fact, few states had such laws for the supervision of probationers by 1900. In 1899, the first juvenile court was established. It was this development which led to dramatic increases in the use of probation. Current research suggests that, even now, probation is the most common disposition for cases officially processed through the juvenile courts (Kratcoski & Kratcoski, 1979). By 1910, forty states used probation for juveniles and all states were using such programs by 1925. In contrast, it was thirty-one years later, or 1956, before all of the states had some form of adult probation (Bowker, 1982). Although the growth of adult probation was slower than the growth of juvenile probation, the outcomes were quite similar. For example, Mannle and Hirschel (1988) suggested that as high as 60 percent of all offenders sentenced to correctional treatment are placed on probation. More recently, available data from the U. S. Bureau of Justice (1995) indicates that approximately three million persons are on probation. And, probation is still the most frequent outcome for juveniles who have been officially processed through the juvenile courts.

It should also be noted that the rapid growth of the use of probation for juveniles was later paralleled in adult probation. Records indicate that by 1924 perhaps as many as 200,000 offenders a year were being placed on probation. These figures themselves can be misleading with respect to the significance and use of probation. For example, for the figures for any year, when control is provided for the short-term nature of many probated sentences, the number of persons on parole during any one year increases dramatically. Thus, the figures reported may indicate one million such individuals, when in fact, two or three times as many juvenile offenders may actually have been on probation at some time during that particular year.

The overall impact of these data cannot be overemphasized. That is, that the practice of probation is a significantly important mechanism in response to criminal offenders and continues to grow in importance. That process and growth has not been without some transformation in the practice. Further, there is evidence to suggest that recent changes or innovations are a direct result of the problematic nature of the program. For example, numerous states are experimenting with models for combining probation and parole (Clear & Cole, 1997). In addition, although the concept of "community corrections" has its own history, one might well argue that the inclusion of a variety of supervisory and rehabilitative approaches under this concept clearly demonstrates the changing nature of the probation process. The development of community corrections is definitely one of the most significant developments in the field of corrections. It certainly has had a major impact upon the practice of probation and probably upon parole as well. The fact that community corrections approaches developed within traditional probation programs without having first been created as a part of a definite philosophy may in fact explain the ambiguous or vague nature of the concept.

THE ROLE OF THE PROBATION OFFICER

The issue of the role of the probation officer is a complex one. It is not simply a matter of the supervisor versus the service-provider. Nor is the debate strictly the result of recent events. The role definition and role expectation have been dynamic and fluid. Cole (1992), traces its development through five historic phases and in doing so presents, by far, one of the best historical-analytical view of this phenomenon. In the first phase, the probation officer took a holistic approach to his or her client. That is, they were concerned about and involved with the various aspects of the daily life of the offender. These aspects included the family, employment, social life, recreation, leisure, education and religious or moral life. In addition, it was anticipated that the officers would serve as positive role models and provide appropriate moral influence upon those they supervised. This can be designated as the casework model of probation.

In the second phase, therapeutic counseling was added to the role. Casework was not eliminated but much greater emphasis was given to therapeutic responses in the structure or confines of the probation supervisor's office as opposed to the daily settings in the life of the offender. This meant that counseling was confined to the office setting; a kind of structured therapeutic milieu. This was consistent with the development of psychiatry and psychology in the first quarter of the Twentieth Century, which emphasized the importance of psychodynamic factors in understanding human behavior. This approach seemed to signal a change in that the probation officer could now be viewed as a monitor or supervisor appointed by the community to ensure that societal value systems were upheld. This change reflected new expectations that the officer would focus more on assisting offenders in resolution of specific emotional or social issues. This, of course, had significant parallels with clinical social work and clinical psychology models. Any such model, of course, permits considerable latitude on the part of the probation officer in analyzing the needs of each client and in designing the appropriate probation plan for the client. At the same time, this model assigned considerable responsibility to the individual officer with regard to accountability. Equally important was the fact that offenders were no longer considered to be passive participants in their own treatment. Rather, a part of the probation process included strategies for involving them in their own rehabilitation, reintegration and resocialization.

In the third phase, the offender was expected to take even more responsibility for the necessary social and behavioral changes necessary for his or her own successful rehabilitation, reintegration and resocialization. During the 1960's probation plans shifted from a focus on insight development to a focus on very concrete problem resolution. This may be characterized as a reality therapy approach. Correctional agencies at this time were particularly influenced by Glasser's (1965) "reality therapy" approach to psychiatry. In correctional agencies, this translated into counseling methods which incorporated into their treatment regime a variety of life coping skills such personal health, basic money management, schooling, interpersonal skills, communication, job interviewing, employment, housing and, in addition, the utilization of appropriate community and agency services via referral. This effectively ended a model which fixed upon an office-based kind of psychotherapy. The role expectations of probation officers in this new role identify what can be labeled the advocate model. In this role the probation officer serves as an advocate or one who stands in front of or with the offender in his/her daily attempts to negotiate his or her life in both the public and private sectors. As the designation implies, the officer is an advocate for the offender with public and private service providers, rather than the actual vehicle for delivering these herself or himself.

New developments in the 1970's altered this latter model and resulted in a third phase characterized by an increasing concern with respect to lowering the security risk to individuals and society embodied in the probated offender. Thus, rehabilitation and reintegration became secondary in importance to the dangers the offender was thought to provide and in reducing this threat. The model could perhaps be described as the community security monitor model. Technical parole violations were more important than the fact that an offender might be making significant progress in becoming a useful and law abiding citizen. The policing-supervising- revoking officer was the ideal model.

Finally, the decade of the 1980's can be viewed as a time in which classification with respect to the needs, risks and potential rehabilitation of the offender were predominate. This fifth phase could perhaps be identified with the legal concept of the reasonably foreseen risk. In other words, the concern with reconciling the offender and the community is a part of the probation officer's role. However, this is balanced with a vigilant concern about risks with the realistic possibilities for the offender to live successfully in the community. In the 1990's, we seem to be continuing with the approach of the 1980's.

THE PROBATION PROCESS

There are three aspects of the process or actual operation of probation which remain for discussion. These are:

1. The conditions of probation.
2. The revocation of probation.
3. The use of probation risk scales.

A consideration of these three aspect of probation essentially comprises a review of the historical development of probation as well as a description of some recent developments in the field. An understanding of these three aspects of probation is critical to any discussion of the use of a house arrest enhanced sanction, such as electronic monitoring.

CONDITIONS OF PROBATION

All probationers are given conditions or rules of their probation. The conditions or rules of their probation are determined by the courts, and are generally derived from the investigation and assessment work of the probation officer. This culminates in the development of a Presentence Investigation Report (PSI) which is presented to the judge. There are two usually two types of conditions. The first is usually referred to as standard or general conditions. The other is called specific conditions.

Standard or general conditions, as the name implies, are rules that the judiciary orders for all of its probationers. These conditions most often include:

1. Steady employment.
2. Restitution to the victim for financial or emotional losses.
3. Cooperation with the probation officer.
4. Obeying all laws.

Specific conditions are those which are ordered specifically for an individual offender and may be unique in the sense that it has applicability for this particular offender. For example, a sex offender may be specifically ordered not to live within five miles of an elementary school, attend sex offender group therapy, and participate in community service, and so forth.

The various types of conditions of probation emerge from two sources. First, such conditions can be imposed from the rules that govern the probation department to which the offender is assigned. Such rules apply to all offenders supervised by that department. Second, the court can impose conditions at its own discretion. The court can also be as innovative as it chooses in determining specific conditions for a particular client. We have seen this, for example, when a court forces a DWI offender to affix a sign to his car stating that he was convicted of that offense. The de facto nature of such specific conditions applied by various courts can only be challenged if such conditions are deemed by a higher jurisdiction to be unreasonable, have no relevance to the specific sentencing objectives, or violate the Constitutional rights of the probationer.

REVOCATION OF PROBATION

Probation can be considered to have two general outcomes: success or failure. Successful probation occurs when the offender has fulfilled or completed the probationary conditions imposed by the judicial order. The offender then becomes a free person, no longer under the control of the court. Failure occurs when the offender is judged to have violated a condition of probation. This results in probation being revoked by the court. Generally, in these instances, the end result is that the offender is remanded to a penitentiary for the remainder of his or her sentence. There are two categories of revocation violations. The first type occurs when the probationer re-offends, i.e., is arrested for a new crime. The second type of failure concerns technical violations of the probation order. For example, failure to comply with the conditions of probation imposed by the court, such as failure to report for drug screening. According to Siegel (1998), approximately seventy five (75%) percent of revocations are for re-offending or committing a new offense while on probation.

Although the probation officer reports the violation, it is the court (the judge) rather than the probation office which revokes probation. In our legal system only the courts have authority to revoke probation. Probationers whose probation is being threatened with revocation are entitled to basic due process rights. A dual-stage revocation hearing is often necessary. The initial or preliminary hearing is designed to ascertain probable cause for revocation and to determine if a full hearing is necessary. In the event of a finding of probable cause, a second hearing will be held wherein a decision of revocation will be decided. It is at the second hearing that a decision concerning revocation will made. Constitutional safeguards are required at both hearings (Tewksbury, 1997).

Three possible outcomes can emanate from a revocation hearing:

1. No violation occurred.
2. A violation occurred but a reprimand is sufficient punishment.
3. A violation occurred and the offender is to be imprisoned or punished in some other way.

In revocation hearings, probationers are afforded due process rights. For example, they are granted a hearing before an impartial committee or judge. Written notices of the hearing are required and the specific charges attendant to the hearing are promulgated. In addition, a written notice of the nature of the offense and the description of evidence of the offense must be presented. Finally, specific reasons for the revocation must be presented in writing (Holman & Quinn, 1996).

It should be noted that although probationers are afforded these rights, a hearing is significantly different from a trial. A hearing is a judicial inquiry conducted by a judge or a committee concerning the procedures applied to probationers by the probation department. Many of the technicalities of trial procedure are omitted and/or do not apply. For example, rules regarding evidence admissibility, and the right to be present. Therefore, a probationer's probationary status can be revoked even if the probationer is not present at the hearing. If revocation occurs in the absence of the probationer, a warrant for his or her arrest is issued (Cole & Smith, 1996).

PROBATION RISK SCALES

Probation risk scales, or risk assessment instruments, have evolved over the entire history of the development of probation. From the very earliest applications of probation, attempts were made to determine which offenders would be most appropriate to be released back into society, or to remain in the community, in order to be given an opportunity to prove that he or she was capable of prosocial behavior in spite of the fact that they had committed a crime (Bohm & Haley, (1996). Many of the earliest measures reflected informal efforts. Quite frequently these informal measures incorporated the prejudices of the individuals who were empowered to make decisions concerning community placements. Eventually the process became "scientific" as criminologists and professional practitioners developed and devised scales based upon empirical research techniques and statistical methods. The Wisconsin Risk Assessment System (Baird, Prestine, & Klockziem, 1989), is probably the prototype for most parole and probation risk assessment systems in use today.

Probation risk scales are presumed to be diagnostic as well as classification devices. That is to say, they are attempts to determine or predict potential of risk for flight or elopement, dangerousness, and amenability for rehabilitation. Therefore, they are very useful in making decisions about placements in community service programs aimed at offender rehabilitation. The baseline or normative points of most of these scales are derived from the performance of prior groups (cohorts) of probationers. In addition, these scales have utility value for probation departments with respect to screening clients for the highest probability of success given the least amount of restrictive supervision (Bohm & Haley, 1996; Cole & Smith, 1996). By assigning values to the variables on the scale related to a variety of characteristics of offenders that have been statistically determined to be significant, and by ranking each offender with respect to each value, an individual risk score can be determined.

Risk scales, like other sorts of psychologically derived diagnostic evaluation and testing procedures, are problematic. Champion (1990) concludes that they are inconsistent and are apt to vary, creating problems of consistency. Enos (1997) has commented about the issue of the problematic nature of psychoanalytic methods for professional work with ethnic minority persons, particularly offenders. Bowker (1982) cites two problems. First, the inability to generalize from one population of offenders to another with respect to geographic location; second, the lack of reliability and validity between groups of offenders at different points in time. The latter criticism suggests the significance of social conditions and historical conditions in determining outcomes. Actually, any type of testing instrument could be criticized on this basis.

However, juxtaposed to these potential weaknesses is a body of research which has been conducted concerning the use of probation risk scales in several cities and counties. Bowker (1982) discusses eight such scales. The research indicated that in each case the scales did differentiate between the success or failure of certain groups of probationers. These studies also supported the idea of generalizability across various regions of the country. In any case, it is important to note that these types of scales have a statistically higher level of predictive power with respect to success than do judges or probation officers. Unfortunately, these two groups often make such decisions without the benefits of risk assessment instruments. And, equally important is the finding that combining the clinical (subjective and experiential) evaluations of the probation personnel, with the use of risk assessment scale provides (such as the Level of Supervision Inventory), resulted in a higher degree of reliability in predicting success or failure than either method used alone (Van Voorhis, Braswell, & Lester, 1997). Probation risk assessment scales have been in use for a considerable period of time. On-going research efforts and improved statistical techniques, combined with advances in computer technology, facilitate the continued refinement and increased predictive robustness of risk assessment systems. Currently, most probation department have adopted various types of assessment instruments and have incorporated them into their departmental procedures.

THE EMERGENCE OF THE CONCEPT OF COMMUNITY CORRECTIONS

A very broad definition of community corrections is that it is a sub-field of corrections, consisting of correctional supervision and rehabilitation services operated outside institutional settings. In other words, it is non-custodial and non-institutional corrections. It can include a number of alternatives to incarceration such as: intensive probation supervision, restitution, fines, day reporting centers, forfeiture, boot camps, house arrest, electronic monitoring, and so forth. These alternative will be described in detail in Chapter 2. In Chapter 5, we will focus specifically on electronic monitoring, which is an enhanced type of house arrest or home confinement.

Community corrections may best be understood as an ideological or philosophical attitude concerning human nature and criminality which maintains that the correction of offenders is best accomplished in community settings, whereas institutionalized settings foster a prison culture that tends to breed more crime, thus exacerbating the problem of crime in society. However, it is also helpful to remember that most of what passes as innovations in the field of community corrections today is simply "old wine in new bottles." Or, as Yogi Berra (1998), the Baseball Hall of Fame former New York Yankees baseball player has often stated: "it was deja vu all over again" (p.30).

The ideological impetus for community corrections came about following the dissemination of a 1967 report by the President's Commission on Law Enforcement and Administration of Justice which championed the idea. Following this report, there was increased movement in the field of probation toward an approach to corrections which subsequently became labeled as the community model of correction or community corrections. The emergence of community corrections since 1967 represents one of the most significant developments in the field according to Cole and Smith (1996). The most recent versions of community corrections attempt to incorporate the traditional view of corrections (correction and reformation of behavior) with some innovative and different approaches toward reaching that objective. Because of the many variations and innovations in the field, one finds no common agreement about what the field of community corrections should encompass and, indeed, who should be administratively in charge of it: probation, parole, the judiciary, law enforcement, and so forth. However, when there is some general agreement, it tends to cluster on three features of this remedy:

1. That it ought to be an alternative that acts as a substitute for prison sentences.
2. That it should include non-custodial penal methods.
3. That it should include measures which reduce the length of incarceration by offering alternatives which result in early release (Vass, 1992).

However, with respect to the current state of community corrections, it seems clear that traditional probation approaches (supervision, surveillance, control and management of behavior), remain dominant rather than community correctional approaches which stress rehabilitation, resocialization, and reintegration of offenders into the community. Perhaps the reason for this is related to public attitudes that community correctional programs are soft on criminals. However, as Bohm and Haley (1996) note, many of the more recent community correctional programs emphasize punishment rather than rehabilitation.

PROBLEMS AND ISSUES IN PROBATION

One of the most problematic aspects of probation concerns the appropriate caseload size or the average number of probationers assigned to individual probation officers. Specifically, the concern has been about the optimal size of the caseloads. Exceedingly large caseloads are frequently cited as a significant problem with respect to accomplishing the goals and objectives of probation, and with the inefficient use of resources and the ineffective guidance of the offender. We are now at a point of a major crisis in the criminal justice system in this country as a result of the fact that the increase of the use of probation has been far more rapid than the training and employment of officers to supervise this process. If anything, this problem has increased in severity. It is difficult to discuss what constitutes an ideal caseload since there is no unanimity in the field concerning this issue. Caseloads vary greatly in size with an upward range of more than 160 probationers (U. S. Bureau of Justice Statistics, 1995). While various ideal sizes have been posited, little empirical evidence has been provided to support such claims. Caseloads of 33-50 are often described as being optimum size. The ideal of the 50 person caseload was established by the National Probation Association. A Presidential Commission in 1967 proposed a 35 person caseload. Arguments for caseload sizes have been predicated upon the belief that individual differences among probationers create differential demands upon a probation officer's time and energy. Cole reports that there are examples of caseloads of 150 to 300 offenders (Cole, 1992). In such situations, it is unlikely that the probation officer will be able to assist in providing many of the services needed by the offender. Yet, under these circumstances, supervision may be an impossible task as well. There appears to be no empirical support, either way, concerning the effectiveness of small caseloads compared to larger case loads. As a consequence, many probation service agencies are using a case management system, which is a case classification system based upon an assessment of offender risks and needs. They often use a model developed by the National Institute of Corrections (NIC). The NIC model matches the probationer risk and needs classification to the available correctional resources. What emerges in this system are types of offender caseloads ranging from maximum supervision to regular supervision to limited supervision. Many of the activities in the NIC model can be tracked by a computer and thus require very little personal contact with the probation officer (Enos & Southern, 1996).

Considering the other expectations associated with the role of the probation officer, it is realistic to believe that it may become almost impossible for he or she to provide proper assistance and supervision to probationers. A variety of pragmatic methods have subsequently been developed to respond to such situations. For example, situations exist in which the contact between the offender and the officer for supervision are primarily accomplished by telephone or by mail status reports. This procedure has been more prevalent in urban areas than in other geographic settings. Under such circumstances, it can be argued that the goals of criminal sanctions with respect to the judicial sentence cannot be accomplished.

At a minimum, the criminal justice system, and its limitations, should be more clearly and honestly represented to the public. Most practitioners and criminologists seem to agree that there is a point at which the caseload reaches a size beyond which any attempt to accomplish the expectations of probation are useless and sanctions have no effect. In the most extreme view, the inability to provide appropriate supervision may well have rendered the practice ineffective as a social control mechanism. Recent reforms, such as changes in classification approaches, reevaluation of offender service needs, analyses of the probation experience, more advanced training of officers, and the onrush of many new private and community probation alternatives have alleviated, to some degree, the crises that had existed with respect to size of the caseload.

A second, inter-related and equally important consideration which contributes to the problematic nature of probation, is the fact that with respect to recidivism, statistical analysis suggests that success rates are not significantly higher than those for incarceration, except for offenders on felony probation. An idealist might suggest that even though the differences between incarceration and probation with respect to the issue of recidivism are marginal, one might want to opt for probation because it is a more humane remedy. The fact is, all things being equal, the rise in the use of probation is more precisely attributable to its lower costs. And, as a consequence, we have seen the devastating impact when unsupervised felony probationers repeat their terrible atrocities.

The issues of recidivism and the size of probation officer caseloads are intricately related. This is particularly evident in the area of research on effective and efficient caseload size. As previously indicated, little research has been done in regard to the most ideal caseload size. The research which has been completed focuses on the effect of caseload size with respect to recidivism. The research methodology or model which has usually been used in an attempt to determine the effect of caseload size has focused on the extremes in caseload size. That is, either very large or very small caseloads. The former is designed to reflect the common caseload size while the latter reflects unique or unusual caseloads. Smaller caseloads are common in intensive probation supervision. In intensive probation supervision the underlying assumption is that the smaller the caseload, the more effective the supervision and, consequently, the less recidivism. In fact, however, the data suggests that caseload size is not a significant predictor of reduced recidivism for either adults or juveniles. Specifically, simply reducing caseload size is not highly correlated with successful reduction of recidivism (Robin, 1987). As is often the case with respect to human behavior, the limited research which has been done suggests that any reduction of recidivism is a result of multiple causes. In particular, some combination of the following factors seem to have some positive effect in reducing recidivism: smaller caseloads, differential treatment of each offender in the community according to the individual's specialized correctional needs, an appropriate treatment setting, and an appropriate matching of the offender's personality with that of the prospective probation officer (Robin, 1987).

Predicated upon the general societal views that probation may have become pointless, ineffective as a means of social control, and that the courts are consistently confronted with a lack of sufficient funding, plus an increasing need for additional probation personnel, has led many criminologists as well as probation personnel to argue that the role of the probation officer should be strictly limited to that of a supervisor of the offender. There are, however, still other experts who favor the service provider role. Such programs must also resolve the critical issues of the complex range of offender needs and the broad range of human and social services available. In other words, those who proffer the model of the probation officer as a "supervisor only" posit that individuals cannot and do not need to be fully knowledgeable or professionally trained in all or even one of the various human service fields in order to be an effective and successful probation supervisor for offenders. As a matter of fact, the real challenge of probation is the ability to provide assistance, guidance and perhaps even friendship within the political structures of the criminal justice system and in spite of limited resources (Cole, 1992). It seems evident that most probation officers who have training in the social service arena are most likely to adopt a rehabilitative or counseling perspective as opposed to supervision only. In the Chapters about case management with probationers and parolees on electronic monitoring which follows later in this book, the authors present a model for working with offenders which they believe helps to resolve the supervisor: counselor role dilemma of probation officers.

SUMMARY AND CONCLUSIONS

Probation is the remanding of an individual, as a result of criminal behaviors, to specified conditions of supervision within the community. This judgment permits the community to test the perception that this individual, in spite of his/her criminal behavior, can successfully avoid such behavior in the future. At the same time, it permits the offender to demonstrate or prove that this is, indeed, an accurate assessment of his or her situation. Probation is, thus, both a penalty within the justice system and a correctional practice within that system. In most instances, an individual who is placed on probation will not be incarcerated unless the conditions of probation are violated. This is in contrast with the practice of parole in which the individual is released to the community from a situation of incarceration.

There is some discussion among criminal justice professionals with respect to both who has the actual responsibility and authority over the probation system and who ought to have this responsibility and authority. On the one hand, arguments can be made that the practice is part of the judicial function and, as such, is commonly administered by the court system. On the other hand, it is a practice which occurs after the judicial process is completed and a penalty has been assessed by the court system. An important argument for administering it through the correctional system is that all of the other aspects of that system are then accessible to probation departments. It is contended that administration through the judiciary avoids the stigma for the offender that is a part of the correctional system. Additional arguments can be made for one system or the other.

Experts in the field of criminal justice do not agree on the origins of probation. However, its development is commonly attributed to the efforts of John Augustus of Boston, Massachusetts. The date which is assigned to the development of probation in the United States is 1841. It is important to recognize the roots of probation in English Common Law and concepts in Common Law such as benefit of clergy, judicial review and recognizance presage the practice of probation.

The earliest development of the practice of probation in the United States occurred as a result of the development of the juvenile court system. The establishment of the first juvenile court occurred in 1899. By 1925 all of the states were using probation for juveniles. However, it was not until 1956 that all of the states were using probation for adults. It is important to note that probation is the most frequently used form of punishment today in both juvenile and adult corrections.

The growth of probation has not been without criticism. Among the problems which critics note are caseload size and lack of supervision. Although research has not clarified what constitutes the ideal or most effective or efficient caseload, there is, without a doubt, a caseload size beyond which it is unrealistic to assume that a probation officer can even keep in contact with offenders, much less provide supervision or counseling. If some form of advocacy, therapy or life assistance is intended via probation, then the practical limits of time and interaction would require even smaller caseloads. A second criticism is that such programs are little more effective than incarceration. However, the telling element is that probation is less costly. Both of these criticisms also highlight the fact that there is limited data available by which to make judgments about the effectiveness of probation.

The controversy with respect to caseload size also underscores the various models of probation which have emerged in the practice of probation. The first model was that of the caseworker. Key to this approach is the holistic concern for and involvement with the probationer. This was the dominant model of probationary practice until the mid-1920's. Beginning the 1920's, the treatment model emerged as an addition to the practice model. The significance of this shift lies in the fact that the role of the probation officer began to become more limited and specific. In particular, the probation officer was expected to focus upon therapeutic models and practices. By the 1960's the treatment model had become the dominant approach in the practice of probation. During the 1960's a third variant of the role of the probation officer developed. This was the role of the advocate. This role, as the designation suggests, anticipates the role of the probation officer as an advocate for the probationer. In some respects this represents a return to the holistic concept. It may, again, be nothing more than "old wine in new bottles." With this model, the probation officer was expected to primarily play out roles in the community on behalf of his or her probationer such as, a broker of community services and a locator of community resources. The 1970's produced an increasing concern about the dangers that probated offenders represented in society. Probation officers became community police, supervisors and probation revocation judges. Finally, in the 1980's this model once again included a concern for the possibility that offenders might change socially and behaviorally to the extent that they could be a full and functioning part of society. The concern for risk was still an important function of the probation officer role. It was, however, balanced with a concern with returning or keeping the offender in his or her community. It also involved a genuine concern with attempting to assess the realistic possibility of the latter. More than a change in philosophies, the development of different models of probationary roles and services may reflect, instead, a practical political and economic response to the issues of increasing numbers of offenders assigned to probation, and concomitant limited economic resources available to provide sufficient probation officers, services and programs. These problems also led to several specific variations in the practice of probation itself which will be discussed in detail in the next Chapter.

REFERENCES

Allen, N. E., Carlson, E. W., & Parks, E. V. (1979). *Critical issues in adult probation.* Washington, DC: Law Enforcement Assistance Administration.

Baird, C., Prestine, R., & Klockziem, B. (1989). *Revalidation of the Wisconsin probation/parole classification system.* Madison, WI: Department of Health and Human Services, Division of Corrections.

Berra, Y. (1998). *The Yogi book: I really didn't say everything I said.* NY: Workman.

Bohm, R. M., & Haley, K. N. (1996). *Introduction to criminal justice.* Westerville, OH: Glencoe/McGraw-Hill.

Bowker, L. H. (1982). *Corrections: The science and the art.* NY: Macmillan.

Champion, D. J. (1990). *Probation and parole in the United States.* Columbus, OH: Merrill.

Clear, T. R. & Cole, G. F. (1997). *American corrections (4th ed.).* Pacific Grove, CA: Brooks/Cole.

Cole, G. F. (1992). *The American system of criminal justice (6th ed.).* Monterey, CA: Brooks/Cole.

Cole, G. F., & Smith, C. E. (1996). *Criminal justice in America.* Belmont, CA: Wadsworth.

Enos, R., & Southern (1996). *Correctional case management.* Cincinnati, OH: Anderson.

Enos, R. (1997). Social work practice with ethnic minority persons. In L. Naylor (Ed.), *Cultural diversity in the United States* (pp. 305-316). Westport, CT: Bergin & Garvey.

Glasser, W. (1965). *Reality therapy: A new approach to psychiatry.* NY: Harper & Row.

Holman, J. E., & Quinn, J. F. (1996). *Criminal justice: Principles and perspectives.* Minneapolis: West.

Kratcoski, P. C., & Kratcoski, L. D. (1979). *Juvenile delinquency.* Englewood Cliffs, NJ: Prentice-Hall.

Larson, C. J. (1984). *Crime, justice and society.* Bayside, NY: General Hall.

Mannle, H. W., & Hirschel, J. D. (1988). *Fundamentals of criminology.* Englewood Cliffs, NJ: Prentice-Hall.

McCarthy, B. R., & McCarthy, B. J., Jr. (1991). *Community based corrections.* Pacific Grove, CA: Brooks/Cole.

Reid, S. T. (1981). *The correctional system: An introduction.* NY: Holt, Rinehart & Winston.

Robin, G. D. (1987). *Introduction to the criminal justice system (3rd ed.).* NY: Harper and Row.

Siegel, L. J. (1998). *Criminology (6th ed.).* Belmont, CA: Wadsworth.

Stojkovic, S., & Lovell, R. (1992). *Corrections: An introduction.* Cincinnati, OH: Anderson.

Tewksbury, R. A. (1997). *Introduction to corrections (3rd ed.).* Westerville, OH: Glencoe/McGraw-Hill.

U. S. Bureau of Justice Statistics. (1995). *Sourcebook of criminal justice statistics.* Washington, DC: U. S. Department of Justice.

Van Vorhees, P., Braswell, M., & Lester, D. (1997). *Correctional counseling and rehabilitation (3rd ed.).* Cincinnati, OH: Anderson.

Vass, A. A. (1992). *Alternatives to prison: Punishment, custody and the community.* Newbury Park, CA: Sage.

RECENT DEVELOPMENTS AND EXPANSIONS IN PROBATION SERVICES

During the last few decades a number of expansions and developments in probation services have occurred. These have taken place under the rubric of "intermediate sanctions." Within the field of criminal justice, intermediate sanctions refer to types of sanctions or punishments for criminal behavior which array on a punishment to corrections continuum between prison and probation. These sanctions are administered by the courts, usually through probation services departments, and may operate both in the community (community corrections) settings or in jails or prisons (institutional settings). In a general sense, most of the types of intermediate sanctions which we will discuss in this Chapter function as alternatives to incarceration or as diversions from incarceration.

Although there is no precise definition or agreement regarding the term intermediate sanctions, a number of models are extant in the criminal justice literature and have been applied in various state criminal jurisdictions. In this Chapter we will describe many of the more viable developments and innovations in probation services including:

1. Intensive supervision probation.
2. Shock incarceration/probation.
3. Boot camps.
4. Restitution.
5. Fines.
6. Forfeiture.
7. Community service.
8. Day reporting centers.
9. Job banks.

10. Complex offender projects.
11. Community resource management teams.

Electronic monitoring is also one of the more recent developments. Electronic monitoring may be described as an enhancement of house arrest or home confinement by the addition of an electronic monitoring component to the house arrest sanction. Electronic monitoring will be described in more detail in Chapter 4.

These innovations and changes in probation services may be viewed as public responses to problems, crises and needs for change in the criminal justice system expressed by more hardened attitudes toward crime and criminals reflecting "just desserts" and "truth in sentencing" positions. These public concerns have often been used by politician as wedge issues when running for political office (Tonry & Hatlestad, 1997). Crime deterrence strategies, as exemplified by various "war on drugs" strategies dating back to the Nixon presidency, represent public concerns about crime that have been transformed into public policies through political action. Unfortunately, one of the effects of these kinds of policies has been prison overcrowding. Since expansion of prison facilities have not kept pace with the application of more stringent remedies, an increasing number of offenders are entering the probation or parole systems, causing attendant personnel, economic and administrative problems. For example, between 1982 and 1994, the adult probation population in the United States doubled to a whooping 2.9 million adults (Walker, 1998).

The effectiveness of the more recent developments and innovations in probation in dealing with the expansion of the probationary population have, up to this point, been problematic (Walker, 1998). Criminologists such as Gendreau, Cullen, and Bonta (1998) raise serious questions about the effectiveness of some of these innovations by questioning there impact upon criminogenic risk and needs. Others, such as Enos and Southern (1996), have joined the debate by presenting some ideas about the treatment conditions and rehabilitation structures that are necessary in order for correctional programs to be effective.

INTENSIVE SUPERVISION PROBATION

Intensive supervision probation (ISP) is characterized by the utilization of a more intensive application of the traditional concept and practice of probation supervision. This is accomplished by imposing stricter reporting standards by probationers and by allowing the probation officer to have a smaller caseload, generally in the range of ten to fifty probationers. Most ISP programs have four key components:

1. Weekly contacts with the probation officer.
2. Regular random drug testing.
3. More severe probation conditions imposed than those applied to traditional probationers.
4. Required participation in group, individual, or family therapy programs; vocational training; education; employment; or, community service programs.

Intensive supervision probation programs have been developed by various jurisdictions to supervise the small core of high-risk (risk principle) offenders who commit a disproportionate amount of crime. Intensive supervision probation programs have gained favor with criminal justice personnel, particularly with judges and probation administrators. Although ISP has experienced some problems, such as offenders choosing prison rather than ISP, and increasing complaints about its effectiveness, it appears to have revitalized probation (Cole & Smith, 1996).

SHOCK INCARCERATION/PROBATION

Shock incarceration/probation is a unique innovation in probation in that it combines incarceration with probation. Because of this feature, it is sometimes referred to as a split sentence or a combination sentence. Nationally, it is utilized with time in jail in approximately one fourth (26%) of all felony cases, with the usual jail sentence being seven months (Petersilia, 1997). According to Holman and Quinn (1996), shock probation is utilized in about twenty (20%) of probated sentences.

The split sentence concept is a means of utilizing both a community corrections approach and an incarceration approach. Usually, the offender is given a traditional prison sentence followed by shock probation. The intent is to shock the offender with respect to the seriousness of his or her behavior, and to bring into awareness the extreme consequences which have resulted from the behavior. That is, the offense that was committed has led to incarceration. It is anticipated that selected offenders, given a "sample" or a brief experience of those consequences will, if permitted, leave incarceration determined to pursue law abiding behavior. This technique is sometimes referred to as a "punishing smarter" strategy (Gendreau, Cullen, & Bonta, 1998). It utilizes an operant conditioning methodology to develop prosocial attitudes in offenders through experiential learning (Shoham & Seis, 1993). The key to the effective use of this strategy is for the actual incarceration to be brief (a few weeks or up to six months) and that the fact that an early release will occur is unknown to the offender. Thus, the offender is exposed to incarceration before imprisonization (prison cultural learning and socialization to a criminal life style) can fully occur.

Research regarding shock incarceration has produced mixed results. Some critics propose that it simply widens the criminal justice net (net widening). In other words, it results in a more severe sentence simply because it exists as a judicial remedy. Some contend that if it was not an option the offender would most likely receive traditional probation without any prison time (Tewksbury, 1997). Those who endorse shock probation point out that some evaluations have indicated that it is highly effective, i.e., in the 78 to 95 percent effective range. These proponents also emphasize that it reduces prison time and costs, more quickly reintegrates the offender back into the community, and allows for maintaining family ties and cohesiveness (Tewksbury, 1997).

BOOT CAMPS

Boot camps become extremely popular in the early 1990's. According to Mays and Winfree (1998), by 1993 an estimated 23 localities in this country were operating boot camps. We estimate that counting boot camps operated by state prison systems and local communities, by 1995 a total of seventy five such programs were operating nation wide. Although treated separately here, boot camps are viewed by many criminologists as another form of shock probation. Generally, boot camp programs are designed for young adult or juvenile first time nonviolent offenders. The rationale behind these programs is that a brief confinement of three to six months in a boot camp will have the effect of shocking the offenders into going straight (Siegel, 1998).

The major elements of boot camps include a military-style facility with rigid formalities and procedures, combined with physical training, and rigid rules and discipline. The correctional concept includes the notion of re-socializing offenders by breaking them down psychologically through physical and mental exhaustion. The thought is that through this process, their criminal attitudes and beliefs (criminogenic needs) will be replaced with a good citizen mentality (Tewksbury, 1997).

Many boot camps include rehabilitation-oriented components such as group therapy and substance abuse counseling programs. According to Walker (1998), a new generation of boot camps is developing which de-emphasizes military-style training and places more emphasis on traditional rehabilitation techniques such as education and job training.

Research evaluations of these types of programs have also yielded mixed findings (Austin, Jones, & Bolyard, 1993; MacKenzie & Piquero, 1994; MacKenzie, 1995). The authors of this book suggest that although boot camps are not the panacea that they were thought to be, they will continue to remain viable since prison overcrowding continues to be a serious problem and public attitudes support these kinds of humanistic responses to the criminal behavior of youthful offenders. This point is also supported by Roberts (1997).

RESTITUTION

During the 1980's and early 1990's, restitution became a common condition of probation. It has gained considerable support in a short period of time. Restitution is court-ordered offender repayment of his or her victim's financial or emotional losses or expenses. This may include payment of the victim's medical expenses or payment for replacement of damaged, destroyed or stolen property (Tewksbury, 1997). It can also involve repayment by working in a community service project. In essence, restitution represents an attempt to repay the victim for financial and material losses due to the crime. Unlike retribution, which focuses on punishment of the offender, restitution focuses on the victim (Holman & Quinn, 1996).

Restitution is part of what is now considered to be a new approach to offender rehabilitation: "restorative justice." Historically, the United States has considered the state as the victim of crime. Crimes are considered to be offenses against the public; therefore, the purpose of the criminal justice system is to deal with persons who committed public crimes. Simultaneously, our society developed a system to address private injury or torts with respect to the victim. Restorative justice represents a major paradigm shift in the field of criminal justice because it views the primary victim as the person who has been violated, while the state is the secondary victim (Walker, 1998). Restorative justice is founded on a social-psychological view of crime rather than a legal view. From this vantage point, crime is not seen as an abstract and somewhat impersonal legal violation against the state; rather it is seen as an injury to a person and to the community (Siegel, 1998). This is an important and vital distinction.

Historically, probation services have stressed the importance of work and gainful employment by offenders. The underlying ideology was that employment reduces recidivism and reoffense, while providing a sense of accomplishment and worth to the individual. This is now coupled with the notion that employment can serve as a means of offender restitution. As with other types of innovations in probation, the results of restitution programs have been mixed. Without this option, it seems clear that most offenders would have been placed into traditional probation programs anyway.

FINES

Fines, as the name implies, are court-imposed monetary payments that are made by the offender to the state or to the local judicial jurisdiction as a penalty for committing an offense. Fines are usually imposed for the commission of minor crimes, such as misdemeanors. Historically, the use of fines or "wergild" can be traced back to Medieval times when they were used in order to prevent blood feuds between the family or the victim and the family of the offender.

As Tonry and Hatlestadt (1997) have noted, this remedy is used in large measure in European countries and used very sparingly in the United States. The administrative and bureaucratic processes needed to collect fines and to enforce the order for the payment of fines make its usefulness very marginal. Objections also arise because much of the energy of collecting and administering a fine-system are consumed by its bureaucratic costs. In addition, the money often goes to the state or to the local judicial entity rather than to the victim. Of course, the use of fines will have little effect if the offender has no means with which to pay the fine. If employment is a condition of probation, then proceeds from a probationer's wages can be used for the payment of fines. From the standpoint of the writers, the use of fines and restitution are particularly important because they impose a moral lesson upon the offender to do penance for their transgressions.

A recent innovation in the use of fines is the so-called day fine. Some states and jurisdictions are experimenting with this iteration on the fine-theme. Day fines consist of imposing fines based upon the offender's daily income rather than a fixed amount of money (Siegel, 1998). This appears to be a more rational approach in the use of this sanction.

FOREFEITURE

Forfeiture may be defined as the seizure by the Federal state or local government of property or assets which have been derived from the commission of crimes. Again, like fines, forfeiture can trace its roots back to Medieval times when agents acting for the king were instructed to seize an individual's estate for the crown. Today, there are two major types of forfeiture: civil and criminal.

Civil forfeiture refers to legal action that is taken to seize property that was used in the commission of a crime. This remedy has long been available for use but it had seldom been used until the political notion of a "war on drugs" became a political priority beginning in the late 1970's. In terms of civil forfeiture, no finding of criminal guilt is required in the proceedings.

By contrast, criminal forfeiture is a special type of forfeiture and is directed primarily at property or assets that were used in an organized criminal conspiracy, especially with respect to drug trafficking. Criminal forfeiture laws began to emerge beginning in 1970 when a stream of Federal statutes began to appear designed to deal with organized criminal conspiracies. These pieces of legislation include: the Racketeer Influence and Corrupt Organizations Act (RICO), the Continuing Criminal Enterprise Act, the Comprehensive Drug Abuse Prevention and Control Act, the Comprehensive Crime Control Act, and the Money Laundering Act. Forfeiture is imposed at sentencing. Between 1985 and 1990, an estimated one billion dollars worth of criminal assets were taken from drug dealers (Cole & Smith, 1996). One can see the practical effect of these laws by noticing that some police departments have converted sports cars seized from drug traffickers to departmental use, for example, in school Drug Awareness Resistance Education programs (DARE). An interesting biographical description about the development of RICO and its use against major organized crime families can be found in an account by Bonavolonta and Duffy (1997).

Forfeiture has also faced criticism. Civil libertarians are often concerned about the application of this sanction without due process. Other concerns emerge from the issue of net widening because sometimes forfeiture is directed at the property not just of drug traffickers or organized crime figures, but also at innocent persons having no connection to the crime, such as the friends, spouses, or children of these kinds of criminals.

Because forfeiture is a concrete sanction, that is to say, has a readily observable effect, its is popular and may remain popular with the general public. Indeed, criminologists such as Abadinsky (1997), equate its use with the devastation of many organized crime families.

COMMUNITY SERVICE

Community service may be defined as a form of reparation for criminal behavior which requires the offender to provide voluntary and unpaid labor or services in order to compensate for his or her crimes. It is ordered by the courts and places the offender under the supervision of the probation department. It usually prescribes a number of voluntary hours of service or labor that an offender must give to a charitable or non-profit community agency over a specific period of time. Often the amount of time for community service roughly equates with the number of hours an offender would have been required to spend in jail for the same type of offense. For example, a drug abuser might be "sentenced" to do painting and carpentry work at a neighborhood alcohol treatment center for two hours a day for six months.

Community service is an alternative to incarceration which is often used with high media profile offenders such as professional athletes or television or film stars. This may be the case because a fine would have little effect upon their behavior due to their high income levels. However, notoriety and publicity about the offense might have a therapeutic effect. Community service seems to be the sanction of choice for first time substance abusers. High media profile offenders on community service are often sentenced to community service with the hope that they will bring a message to youth about the dangers of a particular criminal life style. A number of professional athletes, for example, who have abused drugs or alcohol, have been sentenced to spend time with gang members and other types of delinquent youth, describing to them the dangers of drug abuse or alcohol consumption. Although community service is usually imposed for non-violent, first time offenders, it may be combined with other sanctions such as restitution or fines.

The modern development of community service as an alternative sentence can be traced to the court system of Alameda County, California, beginning in the late 1960's (McShane & Krause, 1993). By the 1980's, it was commonly prescribed as a condition of probation. Today, there is no end of routinized and innovative methods by which the offender can serve his or her community service obligation. Service and labor forms of community service can include: cleaning a city park; painting county road guardrails; dispensing food at homeless shelters; cleaning up city swimming pools; working at a library, food bank, or animal shelter; or, picking up litter along roadways.

There are a number of issues regarding the use of community service. Often this sentencing option is used in order to have the offender come to grips with the reality of his or her behavior and the impact it may have had upon other people. In this way, it is often used as a means for developing empathy in the offender. In some cases it may be used with the thought that its application will force the offender to do some "reality testing" by seeing what happened to people who engaged in certain deviant behaviors. For example, by having a drug abuser perform his or her community service in a drug abuse treatment facility. However, rather than being a corrective experience, this exposure may, instead, cause the offender to have an adverse emotional reaction. This is sometimes the case with offenders who have been forced to do community service in agencies that serve drug abusers, alcoholics, sexual assault victims, and victims of other kinds of serious traumas. This raises the issue of legal liability with respect to the impact of community service on the offender. In addition, proper supervision of offenders placed in community service agencies is often inadequate, unprofessional, or simply lacking. In addition, there are other legal issues concerning injuries that offenders might sustain when volunteering their labor or services.

Supporters of community service point out that community service can be tailored to match the specific skills and talents of offenders with the needs and requirements of the community agency. Community service is a popular remedy because there is a great deal of symbolic and moral value inherent in the offender making reparation to the community for his or her offense. An opposing point of view is maintained by opponents of community service who claim that community service, like prison labor, removes opportunities for work for normal, law-abiding citizens. Others criticize it by maintaining that it is often used with upper socio-economic class offenders, or other types of social, or political elites, who would otherwise be placed into traditional probation programs or incarcerated. In any case, most courts and judges find it to be pragmatic way to deal with non-violent offenders because the notion of reparation, or giving back to the community, is pleasing to the public. We expect it to continually grow particularly because it satisfies politically liberal views about moral reconditioning and personal rehabilitation, and politically conservative views about cost effectiveness and "giving back" to the community.

DAY REPORTING CENTERS

Day reporting centers appear to been interesting innovation on the themes of halfway houses/groups homes, and day programs which operate out of comprehensive community mental health centers. Halfway houses are used as residential facilities in the community for offenders who have been recently released from the penitentiary. These types of offenders need more intensive supervision and help in reintegrating back into society. Halfway houses can also house many types of rehabilitation programs, such as alcohol, drug abuse, and sex offender counseling services. Day programs combine inpatient and outpatient community mental health services. Day programs allow mental health patients to reside in the facility at night while being up and about in the community during the day. It is designed for patients were demonstrate appropriate level of mental health functioning. Day programs provide a modicum of patient care and control with opportunities for the patient to pursue and maintain family, employment, education or other sorts of psychologically helpful contacts in the community. The major aim is reintegration into the community.

In the field of criminal justice, day reporting centers refer to facilities that probationers report to on a daily basis. These centers provide the offender with both structure and control of behavior, and opportunities for rehabilitation. Structure and control come about since probationers assigned to these centers are required to meet with case managers who plan with them in order to develop a detailed schedule of all of their activities for each day. These centers often have a rehabilitation focus as well because they may house various types of social service programs including job, education, life coping skills, and veterans benefit programs. In addition, they can also offer the traditional group therapy and support group programs such as Alcoholics Anonymous, Narcotics Anonymous, Sex Addicts Anonymous, and so forth.

Day reporting centers are a relatively new phenomenon in this country although they have been used in Europe, and principally in England, since the 1970's. Their beginnings in this country trace back to their use in several states such as Georgia, Massachusetts, and Minnesota, and in New York City, in the late 1980's. Their initial use was for the purpose of providing a mechanism for the early release for offenders in order to deal with prison overcrowding.

Currently, these centers are generally used for offenders who are about to be released from jail or from a penitentiary, or for probationers who have violated their probationary status. This is the case because these centers can provide more intensive, day-long supervision of the participants. However, day reporting centers are also prescribed for first-time probationers, especially when, in the judgment of the court, they appear to have the potential for committing more serious crimes.

McShane and Krause (1993), citing McDevitt (1988), report some promising results from one program. However, there does not currently appear to be any generally available research studies regarding the outcomes of these types of programs. Clear and Cole (1997) have suggested that what is needed in terms of day reporting centers are evaluation studies which can resolve two issues: ". . . How much do they improve probation's credibility as a sanction and . . . How well do they combat jail and prison overcrowding?" (p.223).

JOB BANKS

Job banks represent probationary approaches in which unique or special efforts are made to assist offenders in improving their job skills and employment prospects. Such programs generally emphasize "coping skills" training relevant to obtaining and sustaining employment. In some cases education and job training or retraining are essential aspects of the programs. Bowker cites research which suggests positive results from such an approach. In a comparison of probationer participants and nonparticipants in these kinds of programs, it was discovered that the most significant variable that correlated with success in the program was having a job. However, he also notes that critics have argued that the most significant variable was simply participation in the program (Bowker, 1982). The extent to which the results might be influenced by internal and external sources of experimentation bias are certainly at issue.

It is important to note that probation programs have stressed and attempted to include a focus upon job skills for a considerable number of years. The ideology underlying this approach in traditional probationary programs was the thought that employment reduces recidivism, and programs which foster employment also further the goal of reducing repeat offenses. Historically, the idea of work has permeated all Western-culture social welfare systems. Unemployment is a major problem for many offenders. Some, however, feel that it is unfair to provide employment services to offenders that are not available to the law-abiding.

COMPLEX OFFENDER PROJECTS

Complex offender projects envision the role of the probation officer as a counselor or therapist. Because of this, specially trained personnel are needed to implement these programs. Specifically, persons with appropriate training in counseling, psychology, social work, psychiatric nursing, and so forth, are required. Several additional personnel with less specific skills and training, e.g., mental health paraprofessionals, are also essential for assisting in these programs. This type of program could be said to harken back to the therapeutic emphasis of probation programs that existed from the 1920's through the early 1960's. This program requires that the offender be placed in intensive supervision probation.

The particular spin of complex offender projects is that these programs allow offenders to negotiate with their probation officer or with other correctional personnel regarding certain aspects of the treatment approach and/or the probation plan. It is a method for involving the offender in his or her treatment. In this manner, it makes the offender assume some responsibility for the outcomes of the treatment and the probation plan. To be successful, complex offender projects require probationary staff members who are knowledgeable about mental health approaches, well-trained and very professional. The similarity between complex offender projects and intensive probation supervision is suggested by the fact that contacts with individual clients are fairly frequent throughout the week and also are supplemented with numerous telephone contacts. Contact hours with various staff members may be as high as 20 hours a week in the event of a crisis (Bowker, 1982).

Of course, the intent of a program of this sort is to increase the ability of the individual to adapt to the local community and the larger society and to be able to function successfully in both of these environments. In addition, it introjects the medical (psychotherapeutic) model into the probation program. Some research indicates that when these kinds of programs are compared with traditional programs, the therapeutic gains are modest and the costs are high (Bowker, 1982). However, this is a criticism that is commonly made about all types of programs that have a psychotherapeutic focus.

COMMUNITY RESOURCE MANAGEMENT TEAMS

Community resource management teams promote the idea of providing the offender with direct assistance with problem solving while role modeling appropriate behaviors. This is in contrast to traditional probationary practices which focus mainly upon one-to-one counseling in office settings. Here, the idea is to use a team of resource persons as service providers on behalf of the offender. The role of the probation officer in this model is akin to that of a case manager of a team of resource persons. In other words, the probation officer does not attempt to meet all of the needs of the probationer, but instead, he or she plays a significant role in marshalling and managing the resources needed to resolve the problems and crises experienced by the offender. Such programs may result in shared caseloads by officers and in sharing and marshalling the expertise of their fellow officers in solving particular client needs. In order to accomplish its goals, the team may bring to bear all available public and private community resources, in addition to the resources of each individual team member (Robin, 1987).

SUMMARY AND CONCLUSIONS

Recent innovations in the field of probation include a number of specific variations in the practice of probation. In particular, these variations include:

1. Intensive supervision probation.
2. Shock incarceration/probation.
3. Boot camps.

4. Restitution.
6. Fines.
7. Forfeiture.
8. Community service.
9. Day reporting centers.
10. Job banks.
11. Complex offender projects.
12. Community resource management teams.

In summary, intensive supervision probation is a more controlling and ardent process than regular probation. It is usually accompanied by smaller case loads. Shock probation represents an attempt to shock the offender by varying a period of brief incarceration with a period of probation. It attempts to change behavior through an operant conditioning type of process which uses negative reinforcements for behavior. Shock probation also provides a secondary gain in that it also helps the offender avoid the stigma of incarceration and the possibility of socialization into a criminal lifestyles which often occurs via long term imprisonment. Boot camps are also a type of shock probation. Boot camps attempt to resocialize deviant youth toward a prosocial life style by blending a structured and disciplined military life style with physical conditioning, education, and counseling. It is particularly targeted at youthful offenders who are first time, non-violent offenders. Restitution requires that offenders provide money or services in order to help their victims make-up for the losses that they have experienced. Implicit in this approach is the notion of penance and moral relearning and imprinting. It also may help an offender learn to become more empathetic since they often have to encounter their victims in the course of making restitution. Fines are increasingly being used in this country, although their use is a more common practice in Europe. The use of fines, like restitution, contain the possibility of helping an offender change his or her behavior through moral relearning. Forfeiture of property or assets, as a criminal action procedure, is a common judicial sanction in use today in situations involving drug trafficking or organized criminal conspiracies. Forfeiture, as a civil action, was once a dormant judicial sanction in this country. Today, its use is rapidly increasing. Day reporting centers are generally used to house probationers who have violated their probation, although they continue to be used for recently released prisoners and, in some instances, for first time offenders who have the potential for committing serious crimes. Day reporting centers were originally conceived as a response to prison overcrowding. Day reporting centers provide intensive structure, control and supervision over the daily lives of their participants. Rehabilitation programs are also frequently available in the centers. Although there appear to be some promising results from these programs with respect to recidivism, more research is needed to examine their overall effectiveness. Job banks are special probationary programs which attempt to develop and hone the job skills of probationers in order to enhance their prospects of obtaining employment. Historically, with almost all types of social welfare target groups, having a job has been a singularly important variable with respect to achieving rehabilitation. Complex offender projects represent attempts by the correctional system to allow probationers more systematic participation in the probation process. Specifically, it allows offenders to negotiate with their probation officers, or with other types of treatment personnel, regarding certain aspects of the rehabilitation plan. It is based upon the premise that if offenders are allowed to actively participate in the rehabilitation efforts, then they will feel empowered to engage in self-help since they have a stake in the process of rehabilitation. These types of programs are generally more controversial because psychotherapeutic approaches are often held in ill-regard by correctional administrators who strongly believe in tradition probation practices. The final development in probation services that was described in this Chapter was the community resource management team. Community resource development teams are based on the idea that the offender can be provided with direct, one-to-one assistance in solving problems if a team of significant persons from the community could be organized to act as resource persons for the offender. In this type of arrangement, the probation officer acts as a case manager functioning in the organizing role. The individual citizens who comprise the team are often selected on the basis of the types of skills and resources that they may have. However, they often function as mentors, as significant others, or as collateral contacts for the probationers. In one variation of the team approach, the resource team might consist of a group of probation officers who share their case loads and resources and skills with each other on behalf of all of the probationers assigned to the department. Community resource management teams appear to be an innovation which has much to offer; unfortunately, like many of the other developments, expansions and innovations in probation, evaluation research is needed to measure their effectiveness.

REFERENCES

Abadinsky, H. (1997). *Organized crime (4th ed.)*. Chicago: Nelson Hall.

Austin, J., Jones, M., & Bolyard, M. (1993). The growing use of jail boot camps: The state of the art. Washington, DC: U.S. Government Printing Office.

Bonavolonta, J., & Duffy, B. (1996). *The good guys*. NY: Pocket Books.

Bowker, L. H. (1982). *Corrections: The science and the art.* NY: Macmillan.

Clear, T. R. & Cole, G. F. (1997). *American corrections (4th ed.)*. Belmont, CA: Wadsworth.

Cole, G. F., & Smith, C. E. (1996). *Criminal justice in America*. Belmont, CA: Wadsworth.

Enos, R., & Southern, S. (1996). *Correctional case management*. Cincinnati, OH: Anderson.

Gendreau, P., Cullen, F. T., & Bonta, J. (1998). Intensive rehabilitation supervision: The next generation in community corrections? In J. Petrersilia (Ed.), *Community corrections* (pp. 198-206). NY: Oxford.

Holman, J. E., & Quinn, J. F. (1996). *Criminal justice: Principles and perspectives*. Minneapolis: West.

Mays, G. L., & Winfree, L. T., Jr. (1998). Contemporary corrections. Belmont, CA: Wadsworth.

MacKenzie, D. L. (1995). Boot camp prisons and recidivism in eight states. *Criminology, 33 (3)* 327-358.

MacKenzie, D. L., & Piquero, A. (1994). The impact of shock incarceration programs on prison crowding. *Crime and Delinquency, 40 (2)* 222-249.

McDivitt, J. (1988). *Evaluation of the Hampton County day reporting center.* Boston: Crime and Justice Foundation.

McShane, M. D., & Krause, W. (1993). *Community corrections.* NY: Macmillan.

Petersilia, J. (1997). Probation in the United States. In M. Tonry (Ed.), *Crime and justice: A review of research: Vol. 22* (pp. 149-200). Chicago: The University of Chicago Press.

Roberts, J. V. (1997). American altitudes about punishment: Myth and reality. In M. Tonry & K. Hatlestad (Eds.), *Sentencing reform in overcrowded times* (pp. 250-255). NY: Oxford.

Robin, G. D. (1987). *Introduction to the criminal justice system (3rd ed.).* NY: Harper & Row.

Shoham, S. G., & Seis, M. (1993). *A primer in the psychology of crime.* Albany, NY: Harrow & Heston.

Siegel, L. J. (1998). *Criminology (6th ed.).* Belmont, CA: Wadsworth.

Tewksbury, R. A. (1997). *Introduction to corrections (3rd ed.).* Westerville, OH: Glencoe/McGraw-Hill.

Tonry, M., & Hatlestad, K. (1997).*Sentencing reform in overcrowded times.* NY: Oxford.

Walker, S. (1998). *Sense and nonsense about crime and drugs.* Belmont, CA: Wadsworth.

CORRECTIONAL PERSPECTIVES AND ISSUES AND ELECTRONIC MONITORING

The history of institutionalized punishment is often seen as progressing through several steps, generally beginning with severe physical punishment, including torture and death, usually performed in a public forum. Foucault's (1977) classic study describes the Medieval beginnings of the prison system as rather violent; the intention of punishment was to make the offender suffer physically as a way of paying for his or her "sin." The offender was subjected to numerous tortures often ending in a rather cruel and painful death. The idea was to make the offender suffer in proportion to the heinousness of the crime; so if the punishment for the crime was equal to one death, the prisoner would be tortured and killed fairly quickly, but if the crime called for greater penance, the prisoner would be brought to the point of death many times before being killed, hence the expression "to die a thousand deaths." Near the end of the Middle Ages, modes of punishment began to move from the public (community) realm to the private (prison) realm. In other words, punishment was inflicted within the walls of the penitentiary, away from the eyes of the general public. Many related changes occurred, including a reduction in physical cruelty, an increase in rehabilitation through religious or other instruction, and the use of criminals as laborers, sometimes with the intent of teaching a "work ethic." In addition, according to Foucault (1977) and others, prisoners became the subjects of Bentham's (1973) panoptic gaze, meaning that all behavior could now be scrutinized, recorded, and probably altered. Higher levels of surveillance and new techniques meant less privacy for the offender and a higher level of control and conformity for prisoners.

During the 1960's it became clear that incarceration was not working, as prisons were troubled by overcrowding, lack of funding, and other ills. A rash of prison riots led to changes in the system, such as the incorporation of educational programs, work release, home furloughs, and so forth. Prisoners' rights became a reality, and incarceration became increasingly expensive and complicated. Later, however, an increase in crime led to more stringent laws, which in turn caused an increase in the prison population. Currently, the corrections community is faced with a catch-22: the public is demanding that officials be tough on crime yet cut costs. Community-based corrections seems to be the best strategy for addressing both of these needs. As Tonry and Hatlestad (1997) put it:

> Caught between the rock of overcrowded prisons and the hard place of limited resources, states are considering the use of intermediate sanctions or alternatives to incarceration such as house arrest, community service, restitution, intensive supervision probation (ISP), boot camp, and day-reporting centers as a way to relieve prison overcrowding (p. 255).

Lilly and Ball (1990) agree, believing that the current stage in the history of punishment is the phase of alternatives to incarceration.

With the rise of the prison system as the main vehicle for punishing criminal offenders, many questions surfaced regarding whether or not imprisonment actually reduces crime. There are four basic theoretical perspectives which formed the concept of imprisonment as a means of punishing the offender:

1. The rehabilitation perspective. This is a perspective in which the goal of imprisonment is the rehabilitation of the offender so that he or she will not commit a crime again, after release. In this social-psychological approach, punishment is used sparingly and the focus is on improving the educational and psychological health of the offender. Acknowledgement of the sociopathy and psychopathy of offenders is necessary in this counseling-oriented approach.

2. The confinement perspective. The main purpose of imprisonment here is to prevent the offender from harming others by removing the offender from the general population. Removal from the population can range from a short period of time to permanent removal in the form of a life sentence or a death sentence. This is an older approach to dealing with criminal offenders.

3. Individual deterrence. The idea is that if an offender is punished after committing a crime, he or she will learn that the offending behavior caused personal discomfort or jeopardy. This is a behavioral approach which relies on cognitive learning on the part of the offender to deter crime.

4. General deterrence. In this view, punishment of an individual will create a generalized impression on others, dissuading them from committing crimes. General deterrence functions as a kind of social learning which operates through a vicarious process as potential offenders view what happens to others who offend. Thus, when the public sees an offender being punished, they realize that the same punishment awaits them if they behave criminally. Historically, this method of deterrence has been used when punishments and executions were made in public, as well as today, when notorious crimes are covered heavily by the media, and criminals become vilified in society.

The penal system has undergone many changes and has evolved since its inception, often integrating various forms of the four perspectives at different times. However, the most recent and innovative step in the evolution of correctional techniques during the last few decades has been in the area of community-based alternatives to incarceration, such as electronic monitoring of offenders. The purpose of this Chapter is to explore the theoretical basis for electronic monitoring, which mainly consists of various notions about criminal diversion and community-based alternatives to incarceration.

Alternatives to traditional incarceration have arisen due to recent evidence that for some offenders, imprisonment has the effect of increasing the individual's propensity to commit crimes after release. Sutherland's (1949) ideas about subcultural deviancy as expressed in his theory of "differential association" inure us to the fact that prisons are ultimately schools for crime. In addition, the growing number of prisons in the United States may indicate that imprisonment is not necessarily working as a crime deterrent. This growth has created a need to reduce correctional budgets and a desire to look to other solutions for dealing with offenders. In recent history, approaches to corrections have tended to run in cycles, alternating between rehabilitative and punishment-oriented methods, often depending upon the current political climate.

Community correction programs, such as electronic monitoring, emerged from the rehabilitative perspective of corrections as an alternative to incarceration. While the goals and methodologies of rehabilitative and punishment-oriented program strategies for coping with offenders are very different, their structures and effects on the offender are similar.

REHABILITATION OR PUNISHMENT?

Within the last few decades, a number of theorists in criminology have addressed the issue of community corrections. Ball and Lilly (1986), for example, proposed that a criminology that would consider the way in which people's perceptions of appropriate punishment change over time was needed. According to Ball and Lilly (1986), new alternative sentencing policies will most likely not be adopted unless the general population can understand and relate to the policies in a way that is realistic to the population at a given time or place. From this perspective, correctional programs must be compatible with the prevalent ethos, or norms, of the era in which they are to be employed. In other words, this means that to be successfully adopted, the public must consider the alternative sentences to be sufficiently harsh in meeting demands for deterrence, retribution and incapacitation, but flexible enough to be cost-effective. This last criterion implies that the sanctions must have a demonstrated effect on recidivism. Therefore, they also must succeed in altering certain aspects of offenders' behavior in order to deter crime. Tonry and Hatlestad (1997) indicate that there is support for rehabilitation programs, and that it is a common misconception that the general public favors punishment over other types of sentencing options. And, further, they cite data to support the fact that some politicians mislead the public about reforms by underestimating the amount of public support for alternatives to correction.

By providing general statements of the basic methods of rehabilitative and punishment approaches, a theoretical comparison can be made between them. Comparing the two approaches will reveal many commonalities between the methods used to rehabilitate offenders and those used to deter and incapacitate them in the community. Although there are differences in the socio-political justification for each method, community-correction sentences that stress rehabilitation, and approaches which emphasize control and punishment, have similar goals. Those goals are the prevention of reoffense and recidivism. Much of the literature on corrections appears to assume that deterrence and incapacitation are, at least to some extent, antithetical to rehabilitation. This assumption usually results from over-generalizations of research on the impact of total institutions. Review of recidivism rates and similar data on intermediate sentencing programs suggest that such a supposition is unjustified (Zedlewski, 1987).

According to Zedlewski (1987), deterrence and incapacitation are imperative elements if community corrections is to have a deterrent effect competitive with that of incarceration. That is, community corrections must be as effective as imprisonment in reducing the number of people who commit crimes. The two important concepts here are: deterrence effectiveness, and incapacitation effectiveness.

Deterrence effectiveness depends on how would-be offenders react to increased risks versus crime rewards, that is to say, whether potential new offenders will avoid crime under such conditions. Incapacitation effectiveness depends on the identification of the most frequent offenders and on the losses incurred by concentrating on frequent offenders. Existing data tentatively endorses the case for more incapacitation (Wilson & Herrnstein, 1985). Other writers have alleged that the dominance of the rehabilitative ideal in recent decades crippled the deterrence effectiveness sought by judges, legislators and the public (Bryne, 1988). While this may or may not have been true of past innovations in sentencing, the opposite is obviously false; that the goals of rehabilitation may be better served by cost-cutting programs that seek primarily to deter and control than by more humanistic approaches. The assertion is that the structured lifestyle imposed on offenders by alternative sentencing programs, though formulated to ease control, effectively serves the latent function of rehabilitation. An analysis of the basic similarities that exist between the rehabilitative correctional programs of the 1965-75 period and the control-oriented alternative programs that have emerged in the last decade is useful for several reasons. First, discussion of the manifest and latent functions of community-based correctional programs is essential to an understanding of program design and planning. Second, such discussion allows for an understanding of the internal conflict experienced by probation/parole officers and other criminal justice system workers in these programs. Their having to alternate between change and control agent roles often brings on this internal conflict. Currently, probation officers directed to be less concerned with the provision of rehabilitative services, such as counseling and employment assistance, and more concerned with such things as drug testing, curfew violations, employment verifications, arrest checks, surveillance, and revocation procedures is an example of this type of role conflict (Martinson, 1974).

Third, an explicit theoretical statement of the usefulness of community-based sentences, such as electronic monitoring, helps in understanding empirical evaluations of the rehabilitative and deterrent effects of both types of programs, as well as their selection methods. Finally, such a discussion is necessary in understanding the expansion of control-oriented alternative sentencing programs to include more serious categories of offenders. According to Petersilia, such expansion is necessary if these recent innovations in community corrections are to be truly useful in relieving correctional budgets and institutional crowding (Zedlewski, 1987).

SOCIAL, POLITICAL, AND ECONOMIC ISSUES

The introduction of indeterminate sentencing, offender risk assessment and classification systems, and a plethora of training and counseling programs were typical of early attempts to improve the correctional system. Theoretical effectiveness in rehabilitating criminal offenders largely justified these measures. Similar justifications were used to endorse the later changes in U.S. correctional policies, which focused on community-based treatment programs. The widespread acceptance of labeling theory and its implications in the 1965-75 period fueled attempts to divert offenders from the criminal justice system entirely. Many see this phase of correctional development as the high point of the rehabilitative ideal. Although well intentioned, this series of programs did not provide cost-effective remedies to crime and recidivism (Cullen, Clark, & Wozniak, 1985). With the political conservatism of the mid-1970's, control theory became the dominant approach to crime and corrections. A group of sentencing alternatives that are different from their predecessors in their philosophies and goals emerged from this philosophy. If only to a limited degree, this shift shows a more general rejection of the liberal rehabilitative ethos of earlier decades. Still, a total rejection of the rehabilitative ideal is not the case currently. According to public opinion polls, it appears that the public still acknowledges the need for rehabilitation and community corrections but seeks greater control over offenders than traditional probation and parole officers have generally exercised (Corbett & Fersch, 1985).

Due to the arrival of neo-conservative sentiments among the public beginning in the early 1980's, and the resulting emphasis on budget cutting and social control, the system's goals have changed from rehabilitation to retribution, deterrence, and incapacitation. In fact, because of public sentiment, these goals have come with a vengeance. One result has been prison overcrowding. Furthermore, the combination of conservative politics and prison overcrowding led to renewed interest in alternative sentences guided by a philosophy more attuned to punishment than to rehabilitation (Corbett & Fersch, 1985). Illustrating the problems facing the community correctional system are the facts that in 1985, 1.65% of males in the U.S. were under some form of correctional supervision, representing an increase of 600,000 offenders since 1983. By 1985, 64.4% of the 2,904,979 adult offenders under correctional supervision were on probation. Clear and Cole (1997), citing data from the Bureau of Justice Statistics, indicate that by 1992 almost three million persons were serving probation sentences. Petersilia (1998) states that in 1991 an estimated 435,000 probationers and 155,000 parolees who had been convicted of violent crimes were residing in local communities. And, what is especially disheartening are data compiled by Mauer (1997), which indicate that in 1990, one in four African American males aged twenty to twenty-nine were in jail or prison or on probation, and by 1995 one-third of African American males were under the control of the criminal justice system. This has resulted in prison overcrowding causing almost every state to adopt alternate methods of intensive community-based programs (Cullen, Clark, & Wozniak, 1985).

The new alternative sentencing programs are designed to reduce jail or prison populations and to improve the management of traditional probation caseloads, thus they are based and evaluated on criteria that reflect cost-effective deterrence or incapacitation. Additionally, these alternative sentencing programs have focused on the benefits gained by the offender and the community when the offender avoids incarceration (Kennard & Roberts, 1983). Typical of these innovations are shock probation, intensive supervision probation (ISP), house arrest, electronic monitoring, restitution, community service, and so forth. Sanctions such as these are usually designed for implementation by existing agencies, often without the addition of new staff positions. Counseling, education and other measures aimed at reforming the offender are strictly of secondary concern in the design of those programs that stress the surveillance and control of offenders. This often results in role-conflict for probation officers, who are trained in and oriented to rehabilitation, rather than social control (Zedlewski, 1987). At the same time, the long-term cost-effectiveness of sentences become very dubious if it is assumed that incapacitation, rather than behavior change, results from intermediate sentencing.

These alternatives to incarceration have been encouraged by scholars who have recognized the inherent contradictions between rehabilitation and imprisonment, as well as by the public, which has increasingly come to define traditional community correctional programs as a mere "slap on the wrist" for offenders. To assure public safety, as well as to satisfy the demands of judges, legislators and the voting public, intermediate sanctioning programs have tended to stress the punitive, deterrent and incapacitating potentials of community corrections over the rehabilitative potentials. Unlike the rehabilitative ideal, the new generation of alternative sentences lacks a singular motivating basis, and so is more diverse in the formats it uses than were earlier models of the correctional process. Also contributing to this diversity are the goals of various programs. Some seek to improve case management, while others are aimed at reducing jail or prison populations. As goals vary so also do selection criteria, staff attitudes toward clients, staff expectations of clients, methods of control and reform, and evaluation standards.

THE REHABILITATION IDEAL

Most of the innovations in twentieth-century correctional practices have been based on the rehabilitative ideal, stressing counseling, insight, vocational development and pre-trial diversion. Brickman, et al. (1982) have provided a useful model for distinguishing among various types of rehabilitation approaches which, in a general sense, involve therapy or counseling. The key distinction which Brickman and his colleagues make has to do with the attribution of responsibility for the problem, versus the attribution of responsibility for solving the problem. These two types of attributions comprise their typology which consists of four models of helping and coping:

1. The moral model, or people are responsible for their problems and solutions. The counseling effort directed at rehabilitation of the offender in this model consists of reminding offenders of the fact that they are responsible for their own fate and that it is very important that they help themselves. This is the so called "bootstrap" ideology, sometimes referred to as: "get over it."

2. The compensatory model, or people are not responsible for problems in their life but are responsible for solutions. In this model, people view themselves as having been victims or as having had to face irrational, prejudicial and discriminatory obstacles and barriers in life. These barriers or obstacles impact individuals or groups that have certain conditions which are often viewed pejoratively, such as: age, physical ability, gender, sexual orientation, social class, race, ethnicity and so forth. The rehabilitation goal is expressed by a counseling process directed at putting offenders in contact with various societal resources and opportunity systems, and encouraging them to act assertively to gain these resources and to take advantage of community opportunities for advancement.

3. The medical model, or people are not responsible for problems or solutions. In this model, the offender sees himself or herself as being ill or incapacitated. Similarly, society sees offenders as being ill or incapacitated. Offenders who are drug or alcohol abusers are often viewed this way. The rehabilitation effort consists of referring such persons to physicians or others who can apply medical and other types of technical remedies for the problems.

4. The enlightenment model, or people are not responsible for solutions but are responsible for problems. In this model, offenders must acknowledge responsibility for their problems but not responsibility for the solution of their problems. This particular perspective has been associated with the field of addictionology: the study and treatment of addictive behavior usually based upon the Twelve Steps Program of Alcoholics Anonymous (Alcoholics Anonymous, 1987). It assumes that since people are unable to solve their own problems, or do not have the ability to solve their own problems, they need to turn over responsibility for problem solving over to another person or

group or to a higher spiritual power. Various types of support groups fit the enlightenment model: Alcoholics Anonymous, Narcotics Anonymous, the Seventh Step Program, Sex Addicts Anonymous, and so forth. In this model, the counseling method used to promote rehabilitation consists of group processes and interactions used largely to stigmatize participants by having them admit that they have a problem and are helpless to do anything by themselves about it except though the support of the group and by following the processes and rituals of the program.

Currently, some criminologists are arguing for rehabilitation approaches that emphasize and target "the risk" principle. This means directing intensive services, behavioral in nature, to high risk offenders. They also are in favor of rehabilitation approaches that target the "criminogenic needs" principle, or the antisocial attitudes and antisocial associates of the offenders. Notable in this group are Andrews and Bonta (1994). The contention is that these approaches are more effective in changing behavior. Although the research evidence is not compelling, criminologists such as Gendreau, Cullen, and Bonta (1998) suggest that certain types of programs or approaches do not work. Their list includes:

1. Behavioral programs that target low risk offenders.

2. Programs that target offender need factors such as anxiety, depression, or self-esteem.

3. Traditional Freudian psychodynamic therapy or Rogerian client-centered therapy.

4. Pharmacological approaches, for example, testosterone suppressants.

5. Subcultural and labeling theory approaches; and,

6. Deterrence approaches, such as boot camps, electronic monitoring, shock incarceration, scared straight, and so forth.

In any case, the field of community corrections is very fluid. Many new and innovation approaches are being tried. Many of these innovations are merely reiterations of previous methods. Clearly, before we continue to promote correctional policies and programs which emphasize alternative sanctions, we will need to conduct more finely crafted empirical studies which focus on the rehabilitation effectiveness of these sanctions with respect to recidivism. Primarily, we need more micro-analytic studies in order to evaluate the effectiveness of intermediate sanctions as types of differential rehabilitation interventions. To be able to do this we must attempt, at a minimum, to control for the characteristics of the offenders participating in the programs (treatment amenability and matching of subjects); the nature and types of rehabilitation services (correctional counseling/treatment techniques); and, the training, education and experience of the staff administering the programs and services (qualifications of the therapists).

In the remainder of this Chapter, the writers will describe and discuss several types of rehabilitation programs that are common to the field of community corrections. These include therapeutic communities, the self-help approach, and the management and control of behavior approach.

THE THERAPEUTIC COMMUNITY

The therapeutic community is, in many ways, the epitome of efforts toward a rehabilitation-oriented correctional system. Therapeutic communities combine a broad range of rehabilitative techniques with a high degree of social structure and solidarity (Glasser, 1965). Therapeutic communities can, of course, be considered a form of intermediate sentence in themselves. While by definition they are residential facilities for persons with behavioral problems, they lack the extremes of bureaucratization, custodial security, and coercion that typify the total institution. Therapeutic communities accepting probated clients certainly involve an element of coercion, but no physical methods are used to prevent escapes (Glasser, 1965). Thus, they cannot offer the punitive and incapacitating impact sought by current innovations. For these reasons, along with the solidarity and quasi-democratic procedures that typify most therapeutic communities, this form of rehabilitation program is seen as the height of humanistic attempts to correct offender behavior.

Fundamentally, the therapeutic community represents a rehabilitative milieu in which a large number of more or less scientifically validated psychosocial behavior change strategies are employed jointly on a single population. The focus is commonly on individual or group therapy approaches. Prior research has shown that therapeutic communities can be extremely effective in bringing about permanent behavior change in a variety of populations (Kaufman & DeLeon, 1978). However, they are plagued by excessive costs and a high failure rate (Lester, 1981). Therefore, their popularity has faded rapidly as cost-efficiency and public safety have become the paramount goals of the sentencing process in the present neo-conservative era of the 1990s. Intermediate sentencing is currently designed to be cost-effective and to assure a high level of control. However, many of the structures it imposes on offenders are quite similar to those used by the therapeutic community.

THE SELF-HELP APPROACH

Scholars have for some time been aware of the fact that discipline can have therapeutic effects. Programs with a minimum of rules that are consistently enforced, with uniformly applied penalties at an accepted level of severity, will have maximum behavioral effect. They assert that program participants must be aware of the reasons for the rules, that the administrator of punishment should be a significant other, and that penalties for infractions should consist of constructive tasks or the natural consequences of the rule violation (Trice & Roman, 1970). These guidelines for therapeutic discipline form a substantial portion of the needed logistics (i.e., bureaucratic necessities) of many emergent sentencing alternatives. Coincidentally, they also form the basic structure or ground rules for establishing and maintaining a rehabilitative program in a therapeutic community based upon the notion of management and control of behavior with a secondary goal being parallel client insight-development with respect to behavior.

The self-help approach is the dominant method of many therapeutic communities. Based primarily on the philosophy and techniques of one particular support group, Alcoholics Anonymous (1978), the self-help model of behavior change stresses: first, the value of support from others with similar problems and experiences; and, second, the use of stigma to maintain and enhance changes in the desired direction. The use of stigma has been described as a "degradation ceremony" (Festinger, 1957). It is believed to motivate functional behavior by keeping the offender aware of his or her past and by using these past experiences to encourage the offender's rejection of problematic behaviors and perceptions. Solidarity among group members is stressed in order to offset the negative impact of stigmatization, to reinforce its positive uses, and to help the offender gain self-knowledge. This perspective is utilized in clinical group therapies involving current and former deviants with similar problems. Twelve-step groups such as Alcoholics Anonymous, Narcotics Anonymous, Sex Offenders Anonymous, and Gamblers Anonymous meet regularly to share problems unique to their members, to universalize about their behaviors, to develop better and more socially acceptable coping and adjustment skills, and to renew their commitment to following a conventional and functional lifestyle. The belief is that the only people who can be fully empathic in a way that is of practical and clinical utility are those who have experienced the same problems, and are therefore able to, for example, encourage insight into perceptual patterns and predict their outcomes. Because of this, self-help groups of this sort, although usually administratively supported by traditional social service and mental health agencies, are rarely led by "professional" counselors unless that person also has the same presenting problem.

Both therapeutic communities and probation agencies often require offenders' attendance of such meetings. Additionally, both kinds of programs force offenders into insight development by helping them remain aware of their stigma, their role in creating it, and its importance in their present and future decisions. Therapeutic communities and self-help programs do this through clinical groups, as well as through individual counseling sessions and routine interactions among members; hence, the idea of therapeutic communities and support groups as therapeutic milieux. The new generation of alternative sentences demonstrates very similar objectives by frequently demanding that electronic monitors be worn constantly as well as by the use of surveillance procedures, random drug testing and similar control procedures.

THE MANAGEMENT AND CONTROL OF BEHAVIOR APPROACH

While probationers and parolees officers are universally discouraged from contact with current offenders, contact is nonetheless inevitable as offender-clients queue up to pay fees, meet officials, and otherwise comply with the conditions of their release from custody. These interactions are not as thoroughly controlled as are those in therapeutic communities but, given the strict control-orientation of the new generation of alternative sentencing programs and their great readiness to revoke freedom, such interactions are likely to be far less criminogenic than in the past. Also, since offenders generally come from diverse backgrounds and value-orientations and are regularly subjected to the degradation of having to wait on and answer to legal officials, many goals of the self-help model are nonetheless accomplished by inadvertently reminding the offender of his or her stigma. That is, an offender will have much in common with certain other offenders but is likely to reject them in order to avoid further acts that would exacerbate contact with such undesirable individuals. This is a kind of "reality testing" that can also result in a secondary therapeutic gain.

Management and control of behavior approaches employ tactics that are often very overt in their demand that clients follow a course of action based on the "act-as-if" model (Lester, 1981). This model represents the clinical application of a synthesis of Festinger's cognitive dissonance theory and Bem's self-perception theory (Sandhu, 1981). Old "street" self-images are deliberately undermined, if not overtly violated, by individualized behavioral mandates that are symbolic of the direction of behavior change that is sought for the client. The new generation of alternative sentences is subtler in demanding particular behaviors, demeanor and associations. Offenders-clients are forced to maintain employment and clinical involvements, as well as to meet obligations to family, victims, and the community, while following strict curfews and permitting legal officials (or their appointees) to monitor other indicators of values and behavior. Programs stressing work, whether in the form of a regimented shock probation boot camp or the less formal labor required through community service, similarly act to pressure offenders into assuming a more acceptable self-concept and demeanor.

Various probation conditions can be used to influence an offender to behave in a manner to which he or she is not accustomed. Thus, these probation conditions can be said to contain the basic rudiments of the "act-as-if" model of behavior change. This imposed behavior is, to some extent, in contradiction with the offender's self-image or values. Because of rigorous enforcement of probation conditions, such self-violation can easily become defined as preferable to traditional incarceration and continued in spite of the fact that it may be unusual behavior for the offender. Seeking internal cohesion while attempting to avoid further formal sanctions, the offender must redefine the self. In so doing, he or she "gets" the basic objective of the correctional regimen. However, the desired results will only be obtained when probation conditions are complete enough to force offenders to structure their lives in a socially acceptable manner and when compliance is rigidly enforced. Thus the punitive attitude toward inappropriate behavior that is taken by these new sentencing programs can be defined as a therapeutic method which does not compromise the chief goal of enhancing public safety.

The management and control of behavior approach is reminiscent of the therapeutic community approach in that the client is forced to deal with reality in a functional way through deliberately structured confrontations with staff and peers as well as through individual and group counseling and didactic sessions (Kaufman & DeLeon, 1978). In addition, the conditions under which the offender may remain at liberty are, or should be, explained in a fashion congruent with social reality (Hirschi, 1969).

IMPLICATIONS

The implications of these new genre of innovations in sentencing (therapeutic communities; the self-help movement; and the management and control of behavior approach) represent a more tightly controlled version of traditional forms of sentencing. Therefore, for the public to understand the new forms of sentencing in a way that is congruent with social reality, greater explanation may be required due to the fact that more technological factors (e.g., electronic monitoring as an enhancement of the probationary sanction) are now involved. Also, technical revocations are more likely, and more detailed probation conditions are employed. The negotiation of probation conditions and their routine enforcement thus parallel the quasi-egalitarian counseling approach of the therapeutic community. The outcome of these therapies depends on successfully establishing planned and predictable routines and responsibilities in the offender's life. Therapeutic communities and similar facilities or programs designed to deal with offender populations allow their clients very little free time. Responsibility for enhancing one's social and vocational skills, maintaining the facility, providing for residents' daily needs, and getting treatment for individual problems occupy so much time that an occasional hour of leisure soon comes to be defined as a great luxury by residents.

The imposition of such structures on clients' time and activities has several beneficial consequences. First, limits of this nature tend to reduce the likelihood that clients will become bored and seek "adventure" or attempt to vent their frustrations in too wanton a manner. Since they are so occupied by various activities throughout the day, it is not likely that they will dwell on minor irritations and difficulties that could provide rationalizations for unwise or anti-social choices. Additionally, the continuous involvement of the client in activities that are at least minimally monitored by members of mainstream society reduces the likelihood that the client will rebel against rules imposed on him or her under the rationale of self-perception theory. Finally, by assuring the rarity of leisure, the subcultural values attached to free time are reduced and leisure becomes a reward, in itself, rather than a source of boredom that motivates deviance in the attempt to find new adventures or relieve discomforts. Many punitive (e.g., community service) and financial conditions of probation serve much the same purpose in the newer alternatives to incarceration. Similarly, the incapacitating effect of home confinement puts limits of its own on the recreational opportunities available to offenders.

SUMMARY AND CONCLUSIONS

In this Chapter the writers have reviewed the manner in which several distinct sets of alternatives to incarceration have been implemented in community correctional settings. The rehabilitative approach, as illustrated by the therapeutic community, sought to correct offending behavior by: (1) imposing functional routines and their inherent responsibilities on the offender, (2) reducing leisure time to an absolute minimum, (3) recognizing social realities, choice-making, and personal responsibility for choice outcomes by the offender, (4) altering self-image through the dissonance created by imposed behaviors and demeanor, (5) using stigma to motivate and maintain positive behavior changes; and, (6) using the insights of other offenders to identify and extinguish undesirable perceptual tendencies and behaviors.

It was noted in this Chapter that the fundamental attributes of the therapeutic approach to corrections could also be found in some of the newer, more punitive, programs. The imposition of structured routines on offender-clients is an inevitable logistical requirement of shock probation boot camps, house arrest, and intensively supervised probation. Such routines force the offender to lead a planned and predictable lifestyle and to discourage impulsive actions. Such structure fosters the development of foresight and should act to increase the offender's "time horizon" and thus reduce his or her proclivity to crime (Bryne, 1988). The new generation of alternative sentences is not designed to substantially reduce the offenders' leisure time, but shock probation boot camps keep this as a salient goal (Zedlewski, 1987). And, community service can easily be utilized by probation/parole officers to accomplish this goal.

The offender's awareness of his or her choice-making prerogatives is heightened by the imposition of structure on the offender's lifestyle. The strict enforcement of curfews, community service and other conditions of probation also force increased awareness of choice-making and perceptual tendencies, and result in change based on the offender's own insight or understanding of his or her psychological or emotional processes. The non-changing nature of social realities, such as the legal-bureaucratic system in which the offender is enmeshed, can be emphasized by the imposition of rigorously enforced probation itself. The same is true of individual responsibility for actions and their consequences.

These programs, through the imposition of demands on the offender, also surreptitiously invoke the "act-as-if" model of rehabilitation. Restitution, community service, and the demand that other routine financial and familial responsibilities be met can serve to encourage the development of foresight, empathy and accountability in offenders. They also consume the offender's time and form a bond of involvement with mainstream society (Hirschi, 1969).

The rigorous enforcement of employment requirements also tends to force offenders to maintain or enhance their ability to present themselves as socially acceptable persons. This demand is much less rigorously enforced in community-based programs than in residential ones for obvious reasons, but may still become an effective method for modifying the offender's self-image. This is especially true if employers, supervisors of community service work, and similarly placed individuals can be used as members of network teams to help probation officers monitor offender behaviors and self-presentation. Incorporating vocational placement programs into intensive supervision and similar programs also would facilitate this end. Under the auspices of the new generation of alternatives to incarceration, it is conceivable that inclusion in such programs could become an earned reward for appropriate behavior, rather than an expected service of community corrections. Perhaps this is the direction in which such programs are moving.

Stigmatization occurs through the processes of arrest, trial, conviction and assignment to correctional supervision. The use of electronic monitors increases awareness of stigma, as can the intensive surveillance of probationers in both its direct and indirect forms. Probation officers need to acquaint themselves better with the way that groups such as Alcoholics Anonymous use stigma to encourage and maintain positive behavior changes. The addition of this approach to their arsenal of rehabilitative techniques, while valuable in itself, will also help to alleviate the role conflict associated with rehabilitative use of the offender's stigma and related dissonance.

REFERENCES

Alcoholics Anonymous. (1987). *Twelve steps and twelve solutions.* NY: Alcoholics Anonymous World Services.

Andrews, D. A., & Bonta, J. (1994). *The psychology of criminal conduct.* Cincinnati, OH: Anderson.

Ball, R. A., & Lilly, J. R. (1986). A theoretical examination of home incarceration. *Federal Probation, L (1),* 17-24.

Bem, D. J. (1972). Self-perception theory. In L. Berkowitz (Ed.), *Advances in experimental social psychology* (Vol. 6, pp. 1-62).

Bentham, J. (1973). Punishment and utility. In J. G. Murphy (Ed.), *Punishment and utility* (pp. 68-77). Belmont, CA: Wordsworth.

Brickman, P., Rabinowitz. V. C., Jaruza, J., Jr., Coates, D., Cohn., E., & Kidder, L. (1982). Models of helping and coping. *American Psychologist, 37, (4),* (pp. 368-384).

Bryne, J. M. (1988). Probation. *Crime file study guide.* Washington, D.C.: National Institute of Justice, U.S. Department of Justice.

Clear, T. R., & Cole, G. F. (1997). *American corrections (4th ed.).* Belmont, CA: Wadsworth.

Corbett, R. P., Jr., & Fersch, E. A. (1985). Home as prison: The use of house arrest. *Federal Probation, XLIX, (1),* 13-17.

Cullen, F. T., Clark, G. A., & Wozniak, J. F. (1985). Explaining the get tough movement: Can the public be blamed? *Federal Probation, XLIX, (2),* 16-24.

Festinger, L. (1957). *A theory of cognitive dissonance.* Stanford, CA: Stanford University Press.

Foucault M. (1977). *Discipline and punish: The birth of the prison.* NY: Pantheon.

Gendreau, P., Cullen, F. T., & Bonta, J. (1998). Intensive rehabilitation supervision: The next generation in community corrections. In J. Petersilia (Ed.), *Community corrections* (pp. 198-206). NY: Oxford.

Glasser, W. (1965). *Reality therapy: A new approach to psychiatry.* NY: Harper & Row.

Hirschi, T. (1969). *Causes of delinquency.* Berkeley, CA: University of California Press.

Kaufman, E., & DeLeon, G. (1978). The therapeutic community: A treatment approach for drug abusers. In A. Schecter (Ed.), *Treatment aspects of drug dependence* (pp. 83-98). West Palm Beach, FL: C.R.C.

Kennard, D., & Roberts, J. (1983). *An introduction to therapeutic communities.* Boston, MA: Routlege & Kegan Paul.

Lester, D. (1981). The use of punishment in corrections and crime prevention. In S. Letman, L. French, H. Scott, & D. Weichman, (Eds.), *Contemporary issues in corrections* (pp. 1-6). NY: Pilgrimage.

Lilly, J. R., & Ball, R. A. (1990). The development of home confinement and electronic monitoring in the United States. In D. E. Duffee, & E. F. McGarrell (Eds.), *Community corrections: A community field approach* (pp. 73-91). Cincinnati, OH: Anderson.

Martinson, R. (1974). What works. *The Public Interest, 35,* 22-54.

Mauer, M. (1997). Young black men and the criminal justice system. In M. Tonry, & K. Hatlestad (Eds.), *Sentencing reform in overcrowded times* (pp. 219-220). NY: Oxford.

Petersilia, J. (1987). *Expanding options for criminal sentencing.* Santa Monica, CA: Rand Corp.

Petersilia, J. (1998). A crime control rationale for reinvesting in community corrections. In J. Petersilia (Ed.), *Community corrections* (pp. 20-28). NY: Oxford.

Sandhu, H. S. (1981). *Community corrections.* Springfield, IL: Charles C. Thomas.

Sutherland, E. H. (1949). *White collar crime.* NY: Holt, Rinehart, Winston.

Tonry, M., & Hatlestad, K. (Eds.). (1997). *Sentencing reform in overcrowded times.* NY: Oxford.

Trice, H. M., & Roman, P. M. (1970). Delabeling, relabeling, and Alcoholics Anonymous. *Social Problems, 17, (4),* 538-546.

Wilson, J. Q., & Herrnstein, R. (1985) *Crime and human nature.* NY: Simon and Schuster.

Zedlewski, E. (1987). Making confinement decisions. *Research in brief.* Washington, D.C.: National Institute of Justice, U. S. Department of Justice.

ELECTRONIC MONITORING
AS AN ALTERNATIVE SENTENCE

Historically, correctional policies have reflected the values and concerns of society. Over time, the crucial central value expressed in all correctional policies was the idea that society was established in order to develop and maintain certain rights for individuals. This charged society with a mandate to exercise certain responsibilities toward the members of its collectivity. Explicitly, this meant extending protection to individuals from law breakers through the formation of certain criminal justice policies, and by the development of a criminal justice system to carry out these policies. Hence, social order and the preservation of health, safety and public order became key responsibilities of the criminal justice system.

However, these policies have not been unitary. Some scholars maintain that it is even problematic as to whether or not such policies exist. This may be particularly true in the criminal justice field for a number of reasons. First, instead of a unitary set of policies, what we seem to have is a an array of on-going decisions, retrospective analyses, implicit and explicit sets of principles, currents of case law and legalistic decision making, procedures and con-straints, and an array of programs and services disguised as policy formula-tions. In total, a kind of schizophrenic array. In a second instance, it may be the case that the term criminal justice policies may be an oxymoron because of the overlapping and confounding nature of the policies that we do have. For example, at any one time we have a number of policies coexisting; some of which are fully developed, or are evolving and are (or are not) being implemented at various Federal, state, and locals levels. And, finally, what we may think of as policies may be nothing more than the exercise of various kinds of discretionary actions at certain political and administrative levels by an assortment of political and administrative personalities who may be capriciously chasing one or more of any number of value orientations.

However, the general trends in policy-making which are clearly identifiable have been of two types. The first type are policies of a reformist-moralist nature. In these kinds of policies the explicit purpose seems to be tied-into the notion of upholding the morals and values of society. Some of these morals and values are enduring while others are in fashion at any one time or another. The emphasis with these policies, however, is on punishment and retribution. Second, one can also find in the criminal justice arena policies which are usually referred to as social welfare types of policies. These policies emphasize the ideal of rehabilitation of offenders and sees punishment as having only a minor impact on criminal behavior.

If we examine general correctional policy objectives in more recent history, beginning with the onset of the 1960's, we can see some distinctive patterns being played out. For example, the decade of the 1960's was marked with rehabilitation efforts. Rehabilitative efforts intensified beginning with the passage of the Economic Opportunity Act of 1964 and other sorts of related social welfare legislation that followed. However, in the 1970's, and particularly as the Vietnam War began to wind down, the emphasis shifted toward concerns about managing the risk of criminal behavior with respect to public safety. Although today incarceration is the preferred response, dissatisfaction with incarceration as the principal method of sanctioning criminal offenders has grown over the last two decades for a variety of reasons. First, the costs of incarceration and prison construction are staggering. To house, guard and provide for a single inmate, the estimated costs are between $10,000 - $30,000 per year, depending on the state (Doble, 1997; Petersilia & Turner, 1998). To put this cost structure into perspective, the upper end of this scale would pay for room, board and tuition for one year at most of the Ivy League colleges and universities in this country. Furthermore, each new bed space added to the prison system costs approximately $50,000 (Petersilia, 1988). Exacerbating the direct costs of imprisonment are indirect costs such as public and child welfare for the inmate's family and loss of taxes that would have been paid by the offender had he/she remained in the community. Second, the efficacy of institutional (and other) rehabilitative efforts have been brought into serious question in the last decade. Simultaneously, public opinion has shifted from concern with individual rights and welfare to the enhancement of public safety through improved control procedures.

Finally, the tremendous growth in the number of incarcerated felons has resulted in prison overcrowding. In tracing the prison population of the United States during the last two decades, one notes that the United States General Accounting Office (1984) reported in 1983 that the number of state and Federal prisoners grew by 24,000 to total 438,830 inmates at year's end. This Office estimated that by 1990 there would be a total of 438,830 inmates at year's end, and estimated that by 1990 there would be a total of 528,193 inmates within the prison and jail systems of the United States. This would occur at a time when the total prison capacity was estimated to be 419,869. The U.S. Bureau of Justice Statistics (1985) reported that 26,618 prisoners were added to prison rolls in 1984 alone. This brought the total growth to more than 134,000 inmates since 1980. This was a 40% increase over a four-year period. Current data from the Bureau of Justice Statistics (1997) are even more startling. The data in the following Table paints the picture.

TABLE 4.1
CURRENT U. S. PRISON POPULATIONS:
BY TOTAL, FEDERAL, AND STATE CATEGORIES

1. In 1997 the total U. S. prison population was estimated at 1,244,544. Of this number, 112,973 were Federal prisoners while 1,131,581 were state prisoners.

2. In 1996 the total U. S. prison population was estimated at 1,183,368. Of this number, 105,544 were Federal prisoners while 1,077,824 were state prisoners

3. Between 1996 and 1997, the U. S. total increased by 5.2 percent.

4. Between 1997 and 1996, the Federal total increased by 7.0 percent.

5. Between 1997 and 1996, the state total increased by 5.0 percent.

6. The mid-year (June 1998) estimate of the total U.S. prison populations, including jail populations, is 1,725,842.

The results, of course, are prison overcrowding, the development of various programs for diversion from prison, early release orders, and the implementation of numerous alternatives to incarceration. The net effect has been to thwart the incapacitation and deterrent functions of penal sanctions. It has also caused many states, counties, and cities to rapidly expand their jail or prison bed spaces or to board-out their felons to other states where more space is available. Indeed, some counties which have excess jail space, are now in the business of renting out such space. This necessity is causing extreme fiscal problems for many cities and counties, especially for those that are less urban.

As Petersilia (1988) has remarked, the nexus of two particular concerns: the costs of incarceration; and, the faith that increased public safety will obtain through incapacitation, has resulted in the rapid growth of sentences which are more stringer than traditional probation or parole methods, but are less costly than imprisonment. These alternatives to incarceration are designed to expedite the management and control, rather than the rehabilitation, of offenders. Most of these types of alternatives to incarceration are discussed in Chapter 2. Concerning EM, two trends are associated with its utilization and development as a form of alternative sentencing currently: first, there is an increase in the number of prisoners held in the local city or county jails; and, second, there is a rapid increase in correctional costs.

ALTERNATIVE SENTENCING

Overcrowded prisons, the apparent failure of the rehabilitative ideal, fiscal pressures, an ever-increasing crime rate and similar exigencies set the socio-political stage for a new generation of sanctions intermediate between incarceration and the cursory supervision of traditional community corrections. These alternatives to incarceration are currently used as a control-oriented approach to penal sanctions that are less costly but more incapacitating than traditional methods of community supervision.

In Texas, the Texas Board of Pardons and Paroles (1987) disseminated five cogent explanations for the use of alternative sentences. These reasons have served to provide a basis for both EM program design and evaluation in the state:

1. If the offender is held accountable for his crimes in the community where they were committed, then restitution can be provided if appropriate.

2. Use of a genuine deterrent by punishing the offender in the community may be successful because more can be done with existing resources while simultaneously reducing the costs per offender.

3. Rehabilitation is more successful when the community plays a part in the outcome and the offenders' ties to family and employers remain intact.

4. Non-violent offenders can avoid the criminogenic learning and socialization/acculturation influences of the prison subculture.

5. Finally, it is not possible to bestow a prison sentence upon every offender and expect to have enough prison space. Overcrowding can and has resulted in the premature release of serious offenders so as to free-up space for other, often less dangerous, convicts.

Friel, Vaughn, & Del Carmen (1987) have described some of the potential uses and misuses of electronic monitoring as an alternative to incarceration. These uses are: for pretrial diversion; as weekend sentences; for work release participation; for use with juveniles; and, for use when offenders have certain health and allied health problems such as pregnancy, AIDS, or other mental, physical, or emotional difficulties. There are, however, many possibilities for misuse of the technology. For example, sometimes it is prescribed for use with unsuitable types of offenders, especially those who have a history of violent criminal re-offense or flight. In some instances, it is used for extremely long periods of time. In this case, it become a kind of incarceration vehicle in itself, figuratively, like an albatross around the neck of the probationer or parolee. Other examples abound: using it for offenders when the chances are good that they would, in any case, have been sentenced to community supervision; using it as an expediency to relieve prison over overcrowding; using it in lieu of hiring additional probation and parole officers; and, using it because of a variety of other economic considerations.

Wahl (1988), while citing additional sources, has summed up the difficulties with the use of electronic monitoring as a supervisory tool by stating that:

> First, many agencies are not clear why they are using electronic monitoring. . . From what I have observed, I would say that some agencies are 'widening the net of social control'. . . Second, every agency has fit its electronic monitoring program into the structure of their agency and as such criteria, policy and operation differ. . . Third, each agency defines 'option' differently. Some define option as an alternative. Several agencies. . . do not use it in this way. Consequently, it would take an examination of each program that is being used throughout the United Sates to confirm that electronic monitoring is an option rather than widening the social control net. (pp. E22-E24)

HOME CONFINEMENT

In the criminal justice literature, there seem to be general agreement about what constitutes home confinement (HC). Schmidt's (1989) description of it in terms of levels of sanction harshness is instructive. For example, there are at least three levels of home confinement. The first, which is the lest severe, is the curfew. This is a type of HC which requires the client to stay in his or her residence during a limited period of time, usually at night. The second type of HC is home detention. With this method, the offender is required to remain in his or her residence at all times, except for employment, education, medical or mental health treatment reasons, or other types of necessary and authorized leave. The third type is the most severe. It is incarceration at home or, in reality, house arrest. In this instance, the client must remain in the home at all times with few exceptions made except for medical treatment for serious illnesses or, in some cases, for participation in religious services.

Tonry (1998), in reviewing the distinctions between house arrest or home confinement and electronic monitoring, traces its historical development. Home confinement has its origins in the use of curfew as a probationary measure. Today, HC can be imposed as a criminal sanction of its own, and is typically imposed as a condition of intensive supervision probation. Most offenders who are sentenced to HC are not required to stay at their homes throughout the day and night. Instead, they are often granted permission to leave to go to work, or to school, or to attend group or individual therapy sessions. Home confinement can be monitored in a number of ways. For example, the probation department may make a telephone call to the home of the offender, or a probation officer may make a random home visit. Home confinement may have, as an enhanced sanction, electronic monitoring. This, however, is not always necessary if traditional means are available for monitoring the offender.

ELECTRONICALLY MONITORED HOME CONFINEMENT

Electronically monitored home confinement (EM) is a supervisory method used as an alternative to jail or prison. It is implemented as a condition or sanction of probation or parole. Although EM uses modern technology to assure that an offender complies with the temporal restrictions of his/her release from custody, the concept of electronic monitoring was developed as early as 1919 (Friel, Vaughn, & Del Carmen, 1987).

Since its beginnings in the mid 1980's, EM programs have expanded rapidly across this country. The initial programs were small, having only 30 to 50 offenders enrolled, and confined primarily to DWI and minor property offenders By 1986, seven states had EM programs, and by 1990, all 50 states had such programs. In 1987 there were 821 offenders in 21 states being monitored electronically. In 1988 the number of offenders being electronically monitored increased to 2,300 in 33 states. In both 1987 and 1988 men were primarily monitored. For example, only 10.2% of monitored offenders in 1987 were females. Similarly, in 1988 12.7% of the offenders being monitored were females. In 1987 the majority of the offenses committed by offenders being electronically monitored were DWI's and other major traffic offenses (Schmidt, 1989; Tonry, 1998).

Since 1988, EM has increasingly been used to monitor the perpetrators of more serious offenses including theft, burglary, criminal conspiracy, and drug trafficking, and is expanding to include offenders at even higher risk levels, for example persons awaiting trial for homicide. The same reasons that are giving impetus for the use of EM with this group of offenders gave impetus for the use of electronic monitoring in the first place: monetary costs and prison over-crowding. The implications of the use of EM with higher risk offenders are very problematic and some examples of the tragic consequences of its use with these types of offenders are just now being reported in the media.

Electronic monitoring systems are divided into two broad categories: Those that operate with a telephone and those that do not require a telephone. In the first category, operating with telephones, there is a continuous signaling system which constantly monitors the offender. A sub-type also requires a telephone. With this system the telephone is a programmed-contact system that randomly calls the offender and verifies his or her presence at the time of the call. The second category does not require telecommunications; rather, it relies on radio signals. The monitor, usually a court or law enforcement officer, uses a car with a monitoring receiver to oversee compliance instead of a computer. The transmitter is attached to the offender, and when the officer drives by the residence being monitored he/she is able to detect if the person being monitored is inside the residence or not. There is also another type of radio signal system that operates similarly to continuous telephone signaling, but uses radio transmitters (Friel, Vaughn, & Del Carmen, 1987). Although there are numerous types of continuous and random electronic monitoring devices in operation today, the most widely used one is the continuous type. With this type, a monitoring transmitter is attached to the offenders' ankle, and a monitoring receiver attached to the telephone, so that a break in the signal between the monitoring transmitter and receiver alerts the monitoring office of curfew violations. Random electronic monitoring, as the name implies, does not involve continual monitoring of the offender, instead it verifies that the offender is at home through either random contact by telephone or telephone contact at pre-specified times during the day. Random electronic monitoring devices generally utilize some type of voice, picture, or transmitter verification.

Persons placed on home confinement are usually non-violent or first offenders who are generally not considered a threat to society, but are still in need of supervision. Courts and parole boards or departments are placing these offenders on EM as a condition or sanction of their probation or parole. The usual amount of time a probationer or parolee must serve on EM is 30 to 90 days.

When an offender reports to his or her probation or parole officer, he or she must obtain a weekly schedule which specifies what times during the day the offender may be away from his or her residence for work, treatment (psychological, alcohol, drug), medical, or religious reasons. If the person is not at their residence according to the time schedule, a violation is reported and the probation or parole officer is notified. If a serious violation occurs or a number of minor violations occur, the offender's probation or parole can be revoked and the offender sent to prison in the case of probation, or returned to prison in the case of parole.

It appears to be legally difficult to challenge the use of electronic monitoring. It seems to meet the Constitutional test because the offender is, after all, just that: a convicted criminal who has lost many Constitutional rights. In addition, offenders generally must give informed consent for the use of the device and, its use is entirely voluntary. Offenders who opt not to choose electronic monitoring are usually placed on traditional probation or parole.

The curfew restrictions and other conditions of probation, parole, and other diversionary programs are considered valid as long as they are reasonably related to rehabilitation of the individual and/or to the protection of society. When an offender volunteers, he or she denotes consent and this provides a valid wavier of rights. Electronic monitoring does not violate the Fourth Amendment Constitutional right against unreasonable search and seizures because the device is used to determine that the offender is confined to his or her residence, not to determine what he or she is doing in the home. There is no violation of the Fifth Amendment right against self-incrimination because the incrimination is physical and not testimonial. It is a humane alternative to incarceration, therefore it is not cruel and unusual punishment. Electronic monitoring does not intercept any verbal or oral communication so it does not violate Federal Law (e.g. Title III of the Omnibus Crime Control and Safe Streets Act of 1968). Each state must determine if there are existing statutes authorizing, limiting or prohibiting electronic monitoring (Friel, Vaughn, & Del Carmen, 1987).

Due to the problems associated with offenders housed in county jails while awaiting transfer to penitentiaries, brief mention should be made of the fact that many of the arguments used in favor of increased use of EM in lieu of prison also apply to the increased use of EM in lieu of jail. For example, the costs of jailing offenders are considerably higher than those of EM. The average daily cost of housing an offender in jail is estimated to be between $40 and $56 per day, depending upon the agency and the type of facility in question. Electronic monitoring, on the other hand, has an average daily costs of $7 to $14 per offender per day, depending upon whether the electronic monitoring equipment is purchased or leased, or the service is contracted (Petersilia, 1988).

If used selectively, EM as well as other alternatives to incarceration such as Client Specific Planning, advocated by the National Center on Institutions and Alternatives, have the potential to have a leveling effect on prison and/or jail populations, that is, to maintain them at their current levels. There is also some possibility of actually reducing them over time. As already noted, EM along with other alternative sentencing sanctions, have the potential for reducing the rate of prison expansion in the future, the need for new construction, and the size of the existing imprisoned population. They can also serve to improve the efficacy of rehabilitation under community supervision.

Electronic monitoring can be responsive to the needs of the criminal justice system and the needs of individual offenders because of its flexibility. Individual offenders can be placed on EM at any time (e.g., in lieu of jail, after a short-term jail, in lieu of prison, after a prison term, or as a condition of probation or parole). It can also be used for different types of offenders, accommodate various schedules for work and clinical activity, and special cases; e.g., offenders who are mentally retarded, terminally ill, elderly, or stricken with AIDS. Electronic monitoring programs are relatively easy to implement and the EM conditions and sanctions imposed on the offenders are easily understood by them. Electronic monitoring does not require any new facilities or personnel (when technical services are provided by contractors) and can be used at minimal expense relative to prison costs. In addition, should the offender violate his/her conditions of EM, they can be removed quickly from the community (Petersilia, 1988).

Electronic monitoring should not be viewed and/or used as a substitute for traditional probation or parole supervision. Computers and transmitters should not replace the human contact needed for proper supervision. It appears to be the case that electronic monitoring can serve as a punishment. But, it is problematic as to whether or not it contributes to the rehabilitation of offenders. However, Moran and Linder (1987) may be correct in their statement that the high-technology revolution currently under way, which includes EM, will reshape the nature of probation services by expanding its use as a law enforcement tool, rather than as a means for rehabilitation. In later Chapters, the authors present a description and the results of a study directed at the question of the effectiveness of the use of EM with parolees and probationers on house arrest. In the judgment of the writers, in certain significant areas, the use of EM makes a difference. Examine, for example, the data in Chapters 8 and 9.

To date, we know of no scientific evidence demonstrating that criminal activity is reduced while electronic monitoring is being utilized or after the use of the technology with offenders. Currently, the research, derived from relatively small samples of offender populations, suggests that when properly utilized, EM provides another alternative to incarceration, but nothing else. Electronic monitoring has been used with both probationers and parolees. Preliminary data indicate it to be relatively successful in reducing revocations for new crimes, but its impact on the psychological welfare of offenders and members of their households have not been scientifically explored. For example, Schmidt (1989) found that for the most part, EM programs reported a variety of problems associated with EM, such as the need for proper training, family adjustment difficulties, equipment malfunctions, and poor telephone lines or wires.

In a different aspect, Friel, Vaughn, and del Carmen (1987), examined the use of electronic monitoring by ten programs. Their information was gathered by interviews and questionnaires, and also included interviews of 55 offenders exiting from EM programs concerning behavioral effects. They found that a majority of the agencies in their study started to use EM because of overcrowding of jails and prisons. The agencies had learned of the technology by attending professional meetings, through visits by vendors, or by word of mouth. Generally, state and local governments bought the equipment for these agencies, and the offenders placed on EM were charged a daily fee, usually of $7.00. They also reported that the average number of offenders in the ten programs they studied ranged from 4 to 20 per month, with an average duration between 1 and 2 months. The primary problem that they noted in their study was with the equipment itself. The benefits reported were that electronic monitoring was a humane yet restrictive alternative to jail or prison, in that offenders in the EM programs had to work and, therefore, paid fines and restitution, supported their families, paid taxes, and lived a relatively normal life. Most of the offenders did not mind being monitored, but found curfew to be difficult. They also reported that their peer group relations changed mainly because of the curfew. They became more dependent on their family and friends because they were home-bound. They also became more domestic. The majority reported that the device they had to wear was not socially embarrassing and some even used it as an excuse for not doing something or going somewhere. They reported being healthier and wealthier and the experience was generally defined as rewarding.

Goss (1989) also found the programs to be useful in easing the transition from the institution to the community. He further found that agencies utilizing EM found relief from the population increase while still punishing and controlling offenders. He also reported that most programs require the offender to be employed, thereby allowing for the offender to be able to pay part of the cost. Lilly, Ball, Currey, & McMullen's (1993) research suggests that with DWI offenders, EM is cost-effective and had an almost 100 percent success rate.

They also reported that there was no net widening effect as a result of using EM, nor were their any serious discriminatory selection bias in its application.

ADULT PROBATION AND ELECTRONIC MONITORING

Grinter (1989) noted that probation is normally seen as a form of community supervision in which the offender contractually surrenders certain freedoms and submits to various conditions in exchange for being permitted to remain at liberty in the community by the court. Probation is well-suited to the needs of and risks posed by non-violent offenders who do not yet have an extensive criminal history. It allows the convicted offender to live normally within the community, pay taxes, support dependents and make restitution for his/her crime, instead of being imprisoned. The offender is assigned to a probation officer and must comply with the rules and conditions imposed by the court. The sentencing court may also impose probation fees, court costs, fines, court-appointed attorney fees, and restitution fees.

By examining the use of probation in one state jurisdiction, perhaps some valid generalizations may be made about its use in other jurisdictions. In order to do this, the writers observed the probation services offered through by Denton County, Texas, Court Services (1987). In Texas, probation departments are partially funded by the state, but administrative control remains firmly grounded at the local level. Probation departments are under the direct control of the local judiciary which allows them great flexibility in customizing the conditions of release to the needs of both the community and the particular offender. This presents an opportunity for the use of EM.

In Denton County, probation officers classify offenders based on risk scores (risk scales) according to the level of supervision they require - minimal, normal, and intensive, as well as by the probationers' clinical and vocational needs. Thus a continuum of incapacitation, and implicitly punishment, is established within each probation department's caseload. Electronic monitoring is generally considered to be intermediate between intensive supervision in the community and incarceration. After the offender has gone through the probation department's intake process and has been assigned to an officer, he/she fills out a number of forms for informational purposes. This information is used to assess the offender's needs as well as the nature and severity of the risks that the offender may pose to others and to the community-at-large. Specific conditions, which are applied to each offender, can be modified during the course of a probated sentence. Failure to submit to any of these conditions can result in the placement of sanctions (additional conditions of probation) or revocation of probation. The offender would, in the case of sanctions, remain in the community and have to adhere to the original conditions of probation plus the additional conditions imposed as sanctions, or in the case of revocation serve the remainder of his/her sentence in prison.

Currently, one of the best administrative or programmatic locations for the use of electronic monitoring lies in "intensive supervision probation" programs (ISP). These types of programs are in vogue in most probationary departments. The primary purpose of intensive service programs is to act as a diversion from incarceration. The program is designed to provide a higher level of supervision than usual so as to produce positive changes in high risk probationers while more effectively insuring public safety. In Denton County, offenders are placed on intensive supervision as a method of diversion from incarceration. This decision is made at the initial stage when the decision to incarcerate is first presented in court or can be imposed as a sanction. Within intensive supervision programs per se, it is also possible to structure levels of intensive supervision by using various types of rating systems or risk scales, i.e., a kind of case classification system. The intensive supervision approach allows probation officers to focus their rehabilitative efforts in a more selective and non-random way. If employed as a sanction it is generally imposed on probationers on regular probation who have violated their condition(s) of probation. Offenders who do well under ISP are then placed on regular probation. Offenders who are unable to comply with ISP conditions then become candidates for electronic monitoring so long as they pose no apparent threat to the community. Offenders who are eligible for ISP include persons that have:

1. Been considered for shock probation.

2. A current felony probationary status and have been charged with a violation of probation.

3. A prior commitment to jail or prison.

4. Chronic unemployment problems.

5. Prior felony convictions.

6. Documented substance abuse problems.

7. Documented limited mental capacity, mental retardation, or learning disabilities.

8. Been charged with serious offenses.

Intensive supervision probation is usually imposed for a period of one year. Offenders on ISP must report twice a month during the first and third weeks on specified days as compared to once a month on for those offenders who are on regular probation. After the one year period, probation is reassessed and the offender is placed on regular probation if he or she has successfully completed ISP. Intensive supervision can, however, be extended for an additional year should any problems remain unresolved. The vast majority of offenders who have been placed on EM are probationers who have been placed originally on ISP and who have violated their conditions of release.

SUMMARY AND CONCLUSIONS

In summary, even though correctional policies seem to be somewhat problematic in our society, correctional policies have tended to reflect, at one time or another, the ebb and flow of popular and political opinions and concerns about incarceration. These concerns and opinions have centered about incarceration as an opportunity for punishment and/or retribution or incarceration as an opportunity for rehabilitation. These value sets are now over-shadowed because of more pragmatic concerns about the economics of imprisonment. It does appear that, regardless of one's value orientation about the issue of incarceration, we cannot simply build more prisons and furnish more prisons beds. The problems stemming from incarceration and the advantages of EM for non-violent offenders jointly provide an opportunity for improving community corrections. Prison is expensive, decreases chances of reintegration into society, reinforces criminal acculturation and socialization, provides opportunities for learning more sophisticated criminal techniques, creates racial divisions, and promotes gang violence and sexual assaults. In short, it is not a realistic response to all forms of crime (Arrigona & Fabelo, 1989). In the opinion of the authors, these arguments appear to provide strong social-psychological and political rationalizations for the use of EM.

Some of the advantages of the use of EM are that it is cost effective in that it saves states yearly prison housing costs. These cost now average between $10,000 - $15,000 per year. It also reduces the pressure to build new prisons. New prison construction now averages approximately $50,000 per bed (Petersilia, 1988). The estimated daily cost per EM unit per day for purchase ranges from $1.29 to $9.04; from $0.95 to $7.00 per day for a lease-purchase agreement; and, from $1.19 to $7.00 per day to lease (Friel, Vaughn, & Del Carmen, 1987). From the perspective of the writers, these data seem to argue well in terms of economic and business rationalizations for the use of this technology.

However, administrators must consider the opportunity costs when using alternatives such as electronic monitoring. That is to say, a consideration must be given to the trade-offs that society must be willing to consider in adopting the technology. These trade-offs have to do with issues of freedom and authority in the humanistic sense. For example, the issue of Constitutional rights have not be entirely explored and considered. The use of electronic monitoring is in its judicial infancy with respect to this issue. Another humanistic issue concerns the use of all forms of behavioral management approaches per se. Electronic monitoring and the technology its spawns for purposes of intruding into the life space of offenders carries implications for the possibility of intrusion into the life spaces of all of us. It is far too early to determine the actual cost efficiency of the technology relative to other sorts of programs currently available in probationary departments. There are trade-offs in cost benefit terms, but it seems to be neither humanistically nor economically beneficial to hold people in jail or prison who need not be there. This last point is perhaps the most telling argument in favor of EM.

REFERENCES

Arrigona, N. & Fabelo, T. (1989). *Probation and prison populations in Texas: Potential diversions and hardening of prison population.* Austin, TX: Criminal Justice Policy Council Interim Report to the 71st Texas House of Representatives.

Denton County (Texas) Court Services. (1987). *Intensive supervision probationer's guide.* Denton, TX: Denton County Court Services, Adult and Juvenile Probation Department.

Doble, J. (1997). Survey shows Alabamians support alternatives. In M. Tonry, & K. Hatlestad (Eds.), *Sentencing reform in overcrowded times* (pp. 255-259). NY: Oxford.

Friel, C. M., Vaughn, J. B., & Del Carmen, R. (1987). *Electronic monitoring and correctional policy: The technology and its application, research report.* Washington, DC: National Institute of Justice, U.S. Department of Justice.

Goss, M. (1989). Electronic monitoring: The missing link for successful house arrest. *Corrections Today, 51,* 106-110.

Grinter, R. C. (1989). Electronic monitoring of serious offenders in Texas. *Journal of Offender Monitoring, 2,* 1-14.

Lilly, J. R. (1993). Electronic monitoring in the U. S.: An update. *Overcrowded Times, 2,* 4, 15.

Lilly, J. R., Ball, R. A., Currey, G. D., & McMullen, J. (1993). Electronic monitoring of the drunk driver: A seven year study of the home confinement alternative. *Crime and Delinquency, 39,* 462-484.

Moran, T. K., & Linder, C. (1987). Probation and the Hi-Technology revolution: Is reconceptualization of the traditional probation officer role model inevitable? *Criminal Justice Review, 3,* 25-32.

Petersilia, J. (1988). *House arrest: Crime file study guide.* Washington, DC: National Institute of Justice, U.S. Department of Justice.

Petersilia, J., & Turner, S. (1998). Prison versus probation in California: Implications for crime and offender recidivism. In J. Petersilia (Ed.), *Community corrections* (pp. 61-67). NY: Oxford.

Schmidt, A. K. (1989). *Electronic monitoring of offenders increases.* Washington, DC: National Institute of Justice, Office of Justice Programs, U.S. Department of Justice, No. 212.

Tonry, M. (1998). Evaluating intermediate sanction programs. In J. Petersilia (Ed.), *Community corrections.* NY: Oxford.

Texas Board of Pardons and Parole. (1987). *Annual statistical report.* Austin, TX.

U. S. General Accounting Office (1984). Washington, DC.

U.S. Bureau of Justice Statistics (1985; 1997). *Sourcebook of criminal justice statistics.* Washington, DC: U. S. Department of Justice.

Wahl, R. (1988). Electronic home monitoring: Is it a working viable option? In American Correctional Association (Ed.), *Correctional issues: Probation and parole/electronic surveillance* (pp.E21-E29). College Park, MD: American Correctional Association.

BASIS FOR CORRECTIONAL CASE MANAGEMENT

As previously noted, electronic monitoring of offenders may be described as an enhancement of home confinement or house arrest by the addition of an electronic monitoring component to the house arrest judicial sanction. More precisely, electronic monitoring is a type of intermediate sanction that may be used as an alternative to incarceration for certain types of offenders, especially non-violent offenders who are not presumed to be a risk for re-offense or elopement. Electronic monitoring has often been idealized as being socially useful with respect to dealing with the problems of prison overcrowding, and, especially, the problem of the disproportionate incarceration of ethnic minority offenders. In this sense, electronic monitoring is often thought of as an alternative to imprisonment for certain types of offenders since it can save jail and prison space, reserve such space for more serious offenders, and help address perceived social and political injustices in the criminal justice system. In a more humanistic sense, it has been viewed as a more socially useful way to treat certain classes of offenders, such as: misdemeanants, youthful offenders, persons not at risk for flight or elopement, and others who might be physically damaged, psychologically traumatized, or at-risk of becoming acculturated and socialized by certain prison subcultures, such as prison gangs, through "doing time." With respect to the latter group, electronic monitoring, when applied after careful risk assessment, social and psychological differential evaluation and diagnosis, and case classification, may help fulfill a social mandate to deal with certain kinds of offenders more humanistically.

Jails and prisons have been primarily used for isolation, retribution and punishment of criminal offenders. They are necessary in order to provide, at least for a time, a modicum of safety and security of the larger community and society. They can usually provide opportunities for rehabilitation in only a very marginal way. As a consequence, imprisonment often results in the degradation and stigmatization of offenders. This appears to be counterproductive to their resocialization and reintegration into society, as can be noted by high rates of re-offense.

The authors subscribe to the ideological position that electronic monitoring, when used appropriately, is socially useful in a humanistic sense. However, the fact of being on electronic monitoring is, in itself, a punishment or sanction. It is not necessarily a form of rehabilitation. It represents a kind of external force which provides a physically controlling and structuring advantage and hold, through the process of monitoring, that correctional personnel have over the offender. In other words, we have their attention because it gives the correctional officer technical, coercive and authoritative power over the offender.

In our opinion, in order to maximize its social usefulness, offenders on electronic monitoring ideally need to become engaged with professional personnel, such as probation officers, correctional case managers, counselors, psychologists, social workers, or other types of therapeutic personnel, in a process of correctional counseling, through which the counselor and the offender become engaged in an interpersonal interaction characterized by the use of certain communication, empathetic, persuasive, and directive skills and techniques in order to help the offender:

1. Avoid relapse or reoffense.

2. Become resocialized.

3. Reintegrate into their community.

We believe that electronic monitoring may, by itself, condition an offender in the direction of rehabilitation by its surveillance and monitoring features. These features may be instrumental in operationally conditioning the offender since violation of the rules of behavior, as expressed in the judicial order controlling the conditions of eligibility for home confinement, can result in a consequence, such as removal of the status of home confinement and subsequent placement in an institutional correctional setting. Rehabilitation may come about if the offender learns the rules for behavior through external conditioning.

However, the use of electronic monitoring as a means for externalizing the rules for behavior is often not sufficient in terms of maximizing the goal of rehabilitation. This may not be enough for rehabilitation since some of the empirical research in criminal justice about the psychology of the offender points to the importance of the criminogenic need principle in terms of effective prevention and treatment of offenders. Andrews and Bonta (1994), from their research concerning factors in successful prevention and rehabilitation outcomes of offenders, indicated that promising intermediate targets for prevention and rehabilitation include social and psychological traits such as antisocial attitudes and antisocial feelings (pp. 232-233). Of course, we have been aware of these factors in criminality since the Glueck and Glueck studies of the 1950's. In our opinion, correctional case management complements and helps to balance the externalizing and coercive power of electronic monitoring by helping the offender, through a process of social and psychological learning, to internalize prosocial rules of behavior.

The purpose of this Chapter is to present a foundation for correctional case management. The next Chapter presents a specific application of correctional case management for work with offenders through correctional counseling derived from a case management basis.

THEORETICAL SUPPORT FOR CORRECTIONAL CASE MANAGEMENT

We believe that cognitive behavioral theory provides a theoretical paradigm which provides substantive support for correctional case management. Cognitive behavioral theory differs from behavioral theories, such as classical conditioning or operant conditioning, in that its focus is upon both the external aspects of the individual's environmental situation, and upon the internal operations or psyche of the individual. That is to say, it is concerned or with how one thinks about the self and about other people, and how reacts based upon that thinking process. Cognitive behavioral theory encompasses several conceptual notions.

INDIVIDUALS CHOOSE PROSOCIAL OR ANTISOCIAL BEHAVIOR

The first premise of this theory is that men and women have free will. Assuming that they are not severely psychosocially, organically, or developmentally impaired, individuals can choose prosocial or antisocial behaviors. Frankl (1969) calls this "the will to meaning." He defines it this way:

Man is never driven to moral behavior; in each instance he decides to behave morally. Man does not do so in order to satisfy a moral drive and to have a good conscience; he does so for the sake of a cause to which he commits himself, or for a person whom he loves, or for the sake of his God. (p. 158)

CRIMINAL BEHAVIOR IS A FUNCTION OF AN OFFENDER'S PERSON: ENVIRONMENT INTERACTION

The second idea encompassed by this theory is that criminal behavior is shaped by the process of interaction between the offender and the environment. Bandura (1977) referred to this notion as the concept of "reciprocal determinism." For Bandura, the human personality was constructed through the interplay of three dynamic factors: one's external behavior, cognition, and the environment. In depicting Bandura's paradigm (Bernstein, Roy, Srull, and Wickens (1988), state that:

. . . the way we think, how we behave, and the nature of our environment are all determined by one another. Thus, for example, hostile thinking can lead to hostile behavior . . . which in turn can intensify hostile thoughts . . . At the same time, all that hostility is likely to offend others and create an environment of anger. . . which calls forth even more negative thoughts and actions. . . These negative thoughts then alter perceptions, making the environment more threatening. . . (p. 529)

The concept of reciprocal determinism emphasizes the importance of (internal) personal and individual variables in cognitive social learning. In contrast to radical behaviorists, it attaches lesser importance to the role of the environment and external factors in cognitive social learning.

AN OFFENDER'S THINKING PROCESS IS ORIENTED TO REALITY

Choosing to "do" crime is a rational choice. The thinking process is oriented to reality and is, therefore, done consciously. Bandura (1977) notes that learning takes place through a vicarious process of observing others and by imitating their actions. This kind of social learning is based upon the individual's perception of future outcomes or consequences which follow from one's modeling and imitation of the behavior of others. From Bandura's point of view, cognition leads to behavior which subsequently influences how an individual interacts in a particular environment. For Rotter (1954), the thinking process relates to the expected reinforcement. For Wilson and Herrnstein (1985), the expected reinforcement to do crime will come about if the offender perceives that the net rewards for doing crime exceeds the net punishments.

OFFENDER BEHAVIOR REPRESENTS IRRATIONAL AND ILLOGICAL THINKING

Irrational and illogical thinking results in criminal behaviors manifested by antisocial acts which are damaging and detrimental toward others, toward the self, toward the family, and toward the community or society in general. Historically, in psychoanalytic literature, thinking errors referred to certain kinds of ego defense mechanisms (Freud, 1965), which were used compulsively and in a routinized and stereotypical manner by certain types of personality disorders (psychopaths, sociopaths, and neurotics) in order to neutralize their behavior. Offenders typically make attributions about their behavior by using ego defense mechanisms such as denial, rationalization, minimizing, projection, displacement, compartmentalizing, and so forth, in order to avoid responsibility for their behavior. For example, In the case of the antisocial personality, such as a "con man" who swindles an elderly woman out of her life savings, a neutralization such as rationalization, allows the offender to enjoy his criminality guilt free (Redl & Wineman, 1965). In the case of a neurotic personality such as a sex offender (who is anxious, fearful and feels guilty about his behavior) a neutralization expressed in the form of a statement such as "I was only teaching her about sex" allows him to rationalize his behavior by viewing it as fulfilling some higher purpose.

Descriptions of irrational and illogical descriptions of thinking disorders of criminals abound in the sociological, psychological and criminology literature. These range from descriptions by Burgess and Shaw (Toch, 1986), of "Stanley, the self-defender" to Yochelson's and Samenow's (1976) "thinking errors" of offenders to Prendergast's (1991) characteristics of sex offenders.

THE NATURE OF THE CASE MANAGER: OFFENDER RELATIONSHIP

Unless the case manager is able to establish a therapeutic relationship with the parolee or probationer probably very little will be accomplished in relation to moving in a positive direction in reference to the resocialization, reintegration and rehabilitation goals that had been established for the offender. The validity of this point has been well established in psychological and counseling literature across a variety of disciplinary fields and client types (Truax & Mitchell, 1971). Terms such as therapeutic relationship, supportive and sustaining relationships, rapport, and so forth, refer to a set of interpersonal values which are an essential part of the personal dynamics of successful counselors. Across the literature, this set of interpersonal values have been most clearly identified with the work of Rogers (1951; 1957), a phenomenological and humanistic psychologist. Over time, they have been referred to as the "core conditions" of positive outcomes in counseling (1951).

The writers prefer to refer to counselors who have some good measure of these kinds of characteristics as "empathetic counselors." Empathetic counselors manifest their acceptance, respect and positive regard for clients through the mechanism of their counseling service delivery. That is to say, their interpersonal values are behaviorally manifested in their interpersonal counseling encounters with the client. In short, empathetic counselors translate acceptance, affirmation and respect in the interpersonal counseling relationship with the clients into counseling or treatment techniques.

CORE CONDITIONS OF EMPATHETIC CASE MANAGERS

Although Rogers (1951;1957) identified a number of core conditions that he believed to be associated with positive therapeutic outcomes in therapy, in our opinion four, in particular, are most useful for case managers who work with parolees and probationers on electronic monitoring. These conditions are: genuineness, congruence, unconditional positive regard, and empathetic understanding. These four conditions comprise Rogers' "self-actualization" theory.

Self-actualizing theory holds that all human beings have an innate tendency toward maximizing the healthy aspects of their personality. It refers to a kind of psychological wisdom of the body which is inclined to move the personality toward healthy psychological functioning. There are many theoretical antecedent of self-actualization. For example, for Frankl (1969), it is embodied in kind of "psychiatry rehumanized" in which the therapist must understand that: "A human being is not one thing among others; *things* determine each other, but *man* is ultimately self-determining. What he becomes - within limits of endowment and environment - he has made of himself" (p. 203). In Adler's (1963) "individual psychology" one notes his idea that all human beings are unique and have unified personalities. Furthermore, that all human beings strive for superiority which is "A universal, innate drive to achieve a satisfactory level of adaptation and become superior to one's environment. Healthy strivings are guided by social interest, whereas pathological strivings ignore the welfare of others" (Ewen, 1998, p. 132). Finally, Jung described one's true identity by the use of the term "individuation" which refers to "The unfolding of one's inherent and unique personality, aided by the transcendent function and leading to the formation of the self. A lifelong task that is rarely if ever completed" (Ewen, 1998, p. 105).

Obviously, the use of these core conditions to facilitate self-actualization may be compromised or limited by the structure of the criminal justice system, the controlling judicial administration, and the particular agency. These are some of the realities that one must respect when working as a counselor in community correctional systems since the clientele are usually non-voluntary and are criminal offenders.

GENUINENESS

Genuineness has two components. The first has to do with the counselor's ability to share and self-disclose meaningful information about his or her history and experiences which may be helpful in promoting positive psychological growth in the client. Through self-disclosure, the client comes into contact with the humanness of the counselor. Self-disclosure, according to Rogers (1957), is one of the necessary and sufficient conditions to facilitate personality change.

Genuineness has a second component. It refers to the ability of the counselor to be open, honest and candid with the client. Andrews and Bonta (1994) maintain that one of the five dimensions of effective correctional supervision are relationship factors, which they define as: "relating in open, enthusiastic, caring ways" (p. 234). We believe that this is especially true with respect to the counselor's expression of feelings, attitudes, beliefs and values. Correctional counselors represent just that: "correctional" figures in the life of the offender. As such, the writers maintain that they need to demonstrate and project a positive imagery and model appropriate behaviors for their clientele. In keeping with Rogers' (1957) notion of therapeutically facilitating conditions, open communication with an offender demonstrates to the offender how to recognize one's feelings, express the feelings and, subsequently, move toward healthy psychological growth and self-actualization. Hepworth and Larsen (1986), while defining it as authenticity, describe it in this fashion: "Authenticity involves the practitioner's sharing of self by relating in a natural, sincere, spontaneous, open, and genuine manner. Being authentic, or genuine, involves relating personally so that expressions are spontaneous rather than contrived" (p. 424).

CONGRUENCE

Congruence refers to the degree of interface or match between the counselor's thoughts, feelings, expressions, affect and body language and his or her verbal and non-verbal (physical) communications to the client. The successful case manager must send a straight forward, non-ambiguous, clear verbal and physical message to the parolee or probationer. His or her verbalizations to the offender should not be confused or negated by non-verbal messages (such as body language or facial expressions) which implicitly convey a contrary message. In addition, the verbalizations and other forms of communication to the offender must not be paradoxical, contain hidden messages or meta-messages, or represent an attempt to "con the con." As Englander-Golden and Satir (1990) have stated in their book, which contains numerous therapeutic examples of open communication, we need to "say it straight." Keefe and Maypole (1983), drawing inferences from their research concerning relationship factors which promote positive outcomes in therapy, state that:

> Several nonverbal behaviors of communicating empathy are related to a positive outcome of the helping relationship when they are congruent with corresponding verbal responses - that is, when practitioner's feelings and thoughts are in harmony with their words, tone of voice, facial expression, movements, and gestures. (p. 71)

UNCONDITIONAL POSITIVE REGARD

Unconditional positive regard is an additional virtue of successful case managers. For Meador (1974), interpreting Rogers, unconditional positive regard meant:

> . . . a non-possessive caring or an acceptance of his individuality . . . This attitude comes in part from the therapist's trust in the inner wisdom of the actualizing processes in the client, and in his belief that the client will discover for himself the resources and directions his growth will take. (p. 127)

Unconditional positive regard means acceptance of the personality and humanness of the offender. This promotes in the other person feelings of self-regard and self-worth. However, unconditional positive regard does not mean acceptance of the behavior, particularly if the behavior is deviant. As Ewen (1998) (commenting about Rogers) notes, it is conditional: "Conditional positive regard (means). . . Liking and accepting another person only if that individuals's feelings and self-concept meet one's own standards. The typical way in which parents behave toward the child." (p. 393).

Specifically, in terms of the case manager in criminal justice settings, perhaps Biestek's (1957) definition of the term "acceptance" comes closest to being a realistic charge for successful correctional case management.

Acceptance is a principle of action wherein the caseworker perceives and deals with the client as he really is, including his strengths and weaknesses, his congenial and uncongenial qualities, his positive and negative feelings, his constructive and destructive attitudes and behavior, maintaining all the while a sense of the client's innate dignity and personal worth. Acceptance does not mean approval of deviant attitudes or behavior. The objective of acceptance is not 'the good' but 'the real'. . . (p. 72)

EMPATHETIC FUNCTIONING

This concept refers to the ability of the counselor to achieve an empathetic understanding of the client's personal frame of reference. Rogers (1957) sums it up this way:

The fifth condition is that the therapist is experiencing an accurate, empathic understanding of the client's awareness of his own experience. To sense the client's private world as if it were your own, but without ever losing the 'as if' quality - this is empathy, and this seems essential to therapy. To sense the client's anger, fear, or confusion as if it were your own, yet without your own anger, fear, or confusion getting bound up in it. . . (p. 99)

To be successful, the correctional case manager needs to develop both a sense of awareness of the problems that offenders bring to them, and an ability to focus on their problems in a sensitive and caring manner, while at the same time, not trampling on the meanings for the clients that are contained within their problems and in their expressions of feelings about their problems. For Enos and Southern (1996), empathetic functioning means that the case manager must respond in an appropriate professional manner by not "playing into" or getting "caught up" in the problems of the client. It also means that the correctional case manager must become aware of his or her own "psychological softspots," i.e., his or her needs, wishes, desires, and insecurities, because offenders often play "con games" in order to exploit these softspots in an attempt to manipulate or control the case manager. In short, it means that the case manager tries to understand what it must be like to "walk in the shoes of the probationer or parolee" but, at the same time, he or she must be able to establish appropriate professional, social and psychological distance or space between these clients and their problems and the case manager's own needs, wishes, desires, and insecurities.

A FRAMEWORK FOR CORRECTIONAL CASE MANAGE-MENT

In addition to establishing a therapeutic relationship with his or her parolees or probationers, correctional case managers need to develop a structure or plan relevant to how they will proceed to engage the individual offenders in their case loads in planned change. The structure or plan for case management consists of several important steps that provide a logical framework to facilitate the process of engaging offenders in correctional case management activities, particularly correctional counseling. These steps form the basis from which an identification of the problems in social and psychological functioning derive, and suggests avenues for treatment or intervention in order to move parolees and probationers toward personal rehabilitation and societal reintegration goals. Specifically, the steps that will be described include several skills in that are needed for problem-solving.

SKILLS FOR PROBLEM-SOLVING: DATA COLLECTION

Skills for problem-solving involve three sets of activities. The first set of activities includes data collection, assembly, and organization. Obtaining comprehensive available data about the offender is a prerequisite for effective correctional case management.

Data collection begins with data that correctional case managers can obtain through their own efforts. The first type of data are "available data." Available data are data about the offender that are available in the agency, or can usually be obtained from other sources. These data provide general empirical information about criminal background and history, educational achievement, health and physical ability, employment, financial status, medical treatment, hospitalization, and so forth. In addition, data may also be obtained by the correctional case manager from three other sources: through in-office interviewing of the offender; by making home visits; and, by obtaining information by interviewing the offenders' significant others, such as family members and spouses, or by collateral contacts with other individuals such as employers, ministers, teachers, coaches, and others who impact upon the life of the offender. These sources of data are generally more subjective and impressionistic in nature.

It is also very important to obtain data concerning the offender's psychological status before proceeding with the correctional case management plan. These data are usually obtained from external sources such as clinical social workers, clinical psychologists, counselors, and, sometimes, from psychiatrists. There are three usual types of psychological data: the psychosocial history, psychological evaluations, and psychiatric examinations.

Psychosocial histories include systematic data about the developmental history and progress of the offender. These data are usually both empirical and impressionistic. The psychosocial history may include data about physical development; socio-cultural, ethnic, and social-economic class background; religious and spiritual values; circle of friends and acquaintances; family roles, status, structure and cohesiveness; educational and vocational attainment; veteran's status; employment history; sexual development and orientation; health and mental health disposition and characteristics; substance use or misuse, and a number of other factors which paint a picture of an offender's developmental history and his or her current life style.

Psychological evaluations comprise performance tests, objective tests, and projective tests. These data are both experiential and impressionistic. Performance tests generally refer to testing devices which measure intelligence, educational achievement, or vocational ability. I.Q. tests, vocational aptitude tests, and the Scholastic Aptitude Test (SAT) are in this category. Objective tests, by contrast, attempt to measure a psychological variable or trait. Examples include the Beck Depression Inventory (Beck, 1978), which is discussed in length in Chapter 9 of this book and, very commonly used in criminal justice and in mental health fields: the Minnesota Multiphasic Personality Inventory or MMPI (Graham, 1987).

Projective tests refer to testing devices which are employed in order to characterize an individuals' psychological personality. The types of offender personality profiles that can be generalized from projective tests range from neuroticism through psychoticism, and may include an assessment of competency to stand trial or status with respect to forensic definitions of insanity. Projective test employ a series of ambiguous written, verbal, or pictorial vignettes. The offender responds by drawing inferences in terms of how he or she perceives the meanings in the example. A diagnosis is then developed, in part, from their reactions. The Rorschach or inkblot test (Exner, 1974), and the Thematic Apperception Test (Murray, 1971), are common projective tests.

Psychiatric examinations are rarely uses in traditional criminal justice settings. They are more likely to be employed in forensic settings. Forensic settings include mental hospitals, diagnostic units in inpatient or outpatient mental health clinics, or dedicated areas in prisons, jails or detention facilities for diagnostic evaluations. Psychiatric examinations come into play when the issues of competency to stand trial or insanity are of concern. Traditionally, the psychiatric examination included a number of tests of mental competency and status. These tests involve in-depth interviews and testing protocols in order to evaluate an offenders psychological characteristics with respect to sense of logic, rationality, and the nature of his or her ideations. Examination instruments include, among others, the Competency Screening Test (Lipsitt, Lelos, & McGarry, 1971), and the Interdisciplinary Fitness Interview (Golding, Roesch, & Schreiber, 1984). Increasingly, during the psychiatric examination phase, attention is being directed at examining biological and physiological factors in offender behavior.

The data obtained from these sources can be used to construct a case classification profile of the offender, or may be used to inform other types of case classification systems. Major classification systems used in the criminal justice field include the DSM-IV classification (APA, 1994). The DSM-IV includes five axes which provide descriptive data concerning various clinical syndromes. Of particular importance to correctional case managers is Axis II, "antisocial personality disorder":

There is a pervasive pattern of disregard for and violation of the rights of others occurring since age 15 years, as indicated by three (or more) of the following:

1. Failure to conform to social norms with respect to lawful behaviors as indicated by repeatedly performing acts that are grounds for arrest.

2. Deceitfulness, as indicated by repeated lying, use of aliases, or conning others for personal profit or pleasure.

3. Impulsivity or failure to plan ahead.

4. Irritability and aggressiveness, as indicated by repeated physical fights or assaults.

5. Reckless disregard for safety of self or others.

6. Consistent irresponsibility, as indicated by repeated failure to sustain consistent work behavior or honor financial obligations.

7. Lack of remorse, as indicated by being indifferent to or rationalizing having hurt, mistreated, or stolen from another. (pp. 279-280)

There are a number of other types of classification systems used in criminal justice. The MMPI (Graham, 1987) classification system includes a variety of scales which include profiles of various types of psychological dispositions. Of special interest to correctional case managers is "Scale 4, psychopathic deviate." This scale describes the characteristics of recidivist and career criminals. There are numerous classification systems. Megargee and Bohn (1979) developed a system for classifying various types of offenders derived from the MMPI. The Interpersonal Maturity (I-Level) Classification System (Jesness, 1988), is used to classify adolescents with respect to their level of cognitive ability, psychological integration, and interpersonal maturity. The AIMS system or Behavioral Classification System for Adult Offenders (Quay, 1983), is very useful for correctional case managers. Although this classification system is primarily used in institutional settings, it can be applied to other types of setting, such as community correctional settings. The AIMS model groups offenders into five types. Each type reflects a judgment concerning degrees of supervision needed when working with the offender. The five personality types from Quay and Parsons (1971) are:

1. Aggressive psychopath.

2. Manipulative.

3. Situational.

4. Inadequate dependent.

5. Neurotic anxious.

All of the personality types in the above list, except those in group one, are amenable to counseling efforts in community settings. Group three type offenders are particularly good targets for correctional case management interventions.

Another classification system, which is of singular importance to correctional case managers, is the Level of Supervision Inventory or LSI (Andrews, 1982). The LSI was designed to address the issues of risk for recidivism and reoffense. A series of studies provides support for its predictive validity (Andrews & Bonta, 1994). A number of similar risk assessment systems are available. Van Voorhis, Braswell, and Lester discuss them in detail (1997).

Harris's (1988) work concerning predictors of community treatment, i.e., probation and parole, represents a type of classification and prediction system that correctional case managers will also find very useful. Predictions for community supervision are based upon an analysis of these salient factors:

1. Seriousness of the offense.

2. Attributions of the offender.

3. History of criminal activity.

4. History of drug and alcohol use.

5. History of violence.

6. Past behavior in institutions.

7. Age of offender.

8. History of employment.

9. Status of marriage and family life.

10. Contact with criminal associates.

11. Length of sentence.

SKILLS FOR PROBLEM-SOLVING: THE COUNSELING PLAN

The second set of activities encompasses an identification of the problems and services needed by the offender, prioritizing the problems and needs, setting the goals, planning, and contracting concerning the nature of the counseling activities and the responsibilities of each party. The second set of activities is based upon the data obtained from the data collection phase. Enos and Hisanaga (1979) have described what should occur during this activity:

First, the correctional case manager and the offender identify, describe, and clarify the particular problems that need to be addressed. These problems are then specified as goals.

Second, both parties examine and survey the available services and resources that may be available to address these goals, and a decision is made with respect to which services and resources will be utilized.

Third, the offender and the counselor agree upon and delineate the actions and behaviors that the offender would have to demonstrate in order to accomplish the goals. A realistic time frame for the completion of the goals is also established. In addition, each goal is prioritized with respect to its urgency and importance. The agreements reached at this point may be formalized by developing a contract.

Fourth, the attainment of each of these goals is described in behavioral terms. Behavioral descriptions are used in order to avoid making evaluations concerning the outcomes of offender activities based upon impressionalistic measures, such as the case manager's subjective judgments, or by relying upon an offender's self statement.

SKILLS FOR PROBLEM-SOLVING: EVALUATION OF THE OUTCOMES

The third set of activities has to do with evaluation of the outcomes of the counseling services. Since behavioral descriptions concerning the performances required by the offender have been used, the correctional case manager is now in a position to be able to determine, in a sensory or empirical manner, if the offender has achieved the goals. Therefore, the correctional counselor follows-up and evaluates the outcomes in relation to the degree of progress toward goal attainment vis-a-vis the criteria established during the second set of activities. There are a number of case recording formats, many of which are on computer software, that can be used for more precise evaluations of the outcomes of human services. The prototype for recording outcomes of client services is traceable to the work of Weed (1971). His "problem oriented record" begins with a listing of all of the problems that the client has, and the dates at which the problems were first noted. This is followed by a summary recording procedure consisting of four steps, which are commonly referred to as "SOAP." These steps are:

S: The client's subjective views about the problems.

O: Objective data about the problem derived from available data, various records, testing results, observations, collateral contacts, and so forth.

A: The counselor's professional judgment about the problem.

P: A plan for remediation of the problems stated in a precise way through the use of behavioral descriptions, and including a time line for completion of the problem-solving activities.

SUMMARY AND CONCLUSIONS

The purpose of this Chapter has been to provide a foundation for correctional case management by providing theoretical support for the use of case management, by describing the particular interpersonal variables that are necessary in order to develop and sustain a positive correctional counselor and offender relationship, and by providing a framework which can direct and inform correctional case management methods and roles. The presentation of these points paves the way for an understanding and application of correctional case management generalist and counseling methods and roles which are described in the next Chapter.

REFERENCES

Adler, A. (1963). *The practice and theory of individual psychology.* Patterson, NJ: Littlefield Adams.

American Psychiatric Association (1994). *Desk reference to the diagnostic criteria from the DSM-IV.* Washington, DC: American Psychiatric Association.

Andrews, D. A. (1982). *The level of supervision inventory (LSI): The first follow-up.* Toronto: Ontario Ministry of Correctional Services.

Andrews, D.A., & Bonta, J. (1994). *The psychology of criminal conduct.* Cincinnati, OH: Anderson.

Bandura, A. (1977). *Social learning theory.* Englewood Cliffs, NJ: Prentice-Hall.

Beck, A. T. (1978). *Beck depression inventory.* NY: The Psychological Corporation.

Bernstein, D. A., Roy, E. J., Srull, T. K., & Wickens, C.D. (1988). *Psychology.* Boston: Houghton Mifflin.

Biestek, F. (1957). *The casework relationship.* Chicago: Loyola University Press.

Englander-Golden P., & Satir, V. (1990). *Say it straight.* Palo Alto, CA: Science & Behavior Books.

Enos, R., & Hisanaga, M. (1979). Goal setting with pregnant teenagers. *Child Welfare, 58,* pp. 541-552.

Enos, R., & Southern, S. (1996). *Correctional case management.* Cincinnati, OH: Anderson.

Ewen, R. B. (1998). *An introduction to theories of personality (5th ed.).* Mahwah, NJ: Lawrence Erlbaum Associates.

Exner, J. E. (1974). *The Rorschach: A comprehensive system.* NY: Wiley.

Frankl, V. (1969). *Man's search for meaning: An introduction to logotherapy.* NY: Washington Square Press.

Freud, A. (1965). *Normality and pathology in childhood.* NY: International Universities Press.

Glueck, S., & Glueck, E. (1952). *Delinquents in the making: Paths to prevention.* NY: Harper and Row.

Golding, S. L., Roesch, R., & Schreiber, J. (1984). Assessment and conceptualization of competency to stand trial: Preliminary data on the Interdisciplinary Fitness Interview. *Law and Human Behavior, 3,* 321-324.

Graham, J. R. (1987). *The MMPI: A practical guide (2nd ed.).* NY: Oxford.

Harris, P. W. (1988). The interpersonal maturity level classification system. *Criminal Justice and Behavior 15,* 58-77.

Hepworth, D. H., & Larsen, J. (1986). *Direct social work practice (2nd ed.)* Chicago: Dorsey.

Jesness, C. F. (1988). *The Jesness inventory (rev. ed.).* Palo Alto, CA: Consulting Psychologists Press.

Keefe, T., & Maypole, D. E. (1983). *Relationships in social service practice.* Monterey, CA: Brooks/Cole.

Lipsitt, P. D., Lelos, D., & McGarry,, A. L. (1971). Competency for trial. *American Journal of Psychiatry, 128,* 105-109.

Meador, B. D., & Rogers, C. R. (1974). Client-centered therapy. In R. Corsini (Ed.), *Current psychotherapies* (pp. 119-165). Itasca, IL: F.E. Peacock.

Megargee, E. I., & Bohn, M. J. , Jr. (1979). *Classifying criminal offenders: A new system based on the MMPI.* Beverly Hills, CA: Sage.

Murray, H. A. (1971). *Thematic apperception test.* Cambridge, MA: Harvard University Press.

Prendergast, W. (1991). *Treating sex offenders in correctional institutions and outpatient clinics.* NY: Springer.

Quay, H. C., & Parsons, L. B. (1971). *The differential behavioral classification of the juvenile offender.* Washington, DC: U. S. Bureau of Prisons.

Quay, H. C. (1983). *Technical manual for the behavioral classification system of adult offenders.* Washington, DC: U. S. Department of Justice.

Redl, F., & Wineman, D. (1965). *Children who hate.* NY: Free Press.

Rogers, C. R. (1951). *Client-centered therapy.* Boston: Houghton Mifflin.

Rogers, C. R. (1957). The necessary and sufficient conditions of therapeutic personality change. *Journal of Consulting Psychology, 21,* 95-103.

Rotter, J. B. (1954). *Social learning and clinical psychology.* Englewood Cliffs, NJ: Prentice-Hall.

Toch, H. (Ed.). (1986). *Psychology of crime and criminal justice.* Prospect Heights. IL: Waveland Press.

Truax, C. B., & Mitchell, K. M. (1971). Research on certain therapist interpersonal skills in relation to process and outcome. In A.A. Bergin & S.L. Garfield, (Eds.), *Handbook of psychotherapy and behavior change: An empirical analysis* (pp. 299-344). NY: Wiley.

Van Voorhis, P., Braswell, M., & Lester, D. (1997). *Correctional counseling and rehabilitation (3rd. ed.).* Cincinnati, OH: Anderson.

Weed, L. L. (1971). *Medical records, medical education and patient care.* Cleveland, OH: Western Reserve University Press.

Wilson, J. W. , & Herrnstein, R. J. (1985). *Crime and human nature.* NY: Simon & Schuster.

Yochelson, S., & Samenow, S. E. (1976). *The criminal personality: Volumes I & II.* NY: Jason Aronson.

CORRECTIONAL CASE MANAGEMENT
COUNSELING WITH OFFENDERS

Case management refers to a process for providing tangible resources and social and psychological services to individuals and to families that have a multiplicity of social and psychological problems. The approach emphasizes the targeting of resources and services to meet these social and psychological needs by the use of a structured delivery system which tries to match the types of services provided with the specific needs of the client. The needs of the client, in this case an offender placed in a community correctional setting while being electronically monitored, are ideally derived from a comprehensive assessment, diagnosis, classification and treatment planning and referral process derived from interviews, home visits, contact with significant others, as well as psychosocial, psychological, and psychiatric evaluations. In case management, the service delivery system always requires a method for monitoring the use and outcomes of the service delivery system.

Case management is a relatively recent approach with respect to the general notion of how social and psychological services ought to be delivered. Its roots go back to the latter part of the 1950's when it began to become apparent that traditional mental health approaches which emphasized psychoanalytical treatment of clients in institutional settings, especially in mental health settings, were only marginally effective (Stanton & Schwartz, 1954; Ullmann & Krasner, 1975). About the same time, behavioral and, especially, operant conditioning treatment approaches, as well as a new emphasis upon group approaches, such as milieu therapy, began to appear in institutional settings. Increasing, the efficacy of institutionalized treatment was called into question. By the early 1960's a movement toward community psychiatry had begun (Cumming & Cumming, 1962). The original focus was upon the mental health field but, ultimately, other kinds of institutions became impacted as well: gerontology, developmental disabilities, substance abuse, and criminal justice.

There has always been a great deal support of the notion that certain types of social and psychological problems are best treated within the context of the family, the neighborhood, the community, and the larger society (Jones, 1953). In terms of the development of the case management approach, what seems to have happened, in retrospect, beginning in the early 1960's, was a melding of an historic humanistic and practical imperative for treatment in the community, with changing economic and political priorities, such as those exemplified by the War on Poverty. In the opinion of the authors, this resulted in macro-level political policy changes which resulted in increased Federal support for community based social and psychological service programs. This policy and ideological direction, with some backsliding, continues today. In any case, the Federal government began, increasingly, to move in the direction of placing its imprimatur upon deinstitutionalized services through the passage of various legislative acts which tended to set the policy directions and even prescribe the treatment methods for various types of individuals with social and psychological problems, including criminal offenders. In actuality, even the term "case management" appears to be a creation of the Federal government (Family Support Act of 1988).

With respect to the issue of the use of case management as a method for correctional counseling offenders on electronic monitoring, the term case management, as used in this Chapter, will refer to two distinctive methods of correctional counseling: the case manager generalist method, and the case manager counselor method.

THE CASE MANAGER GENERALIST METHOD

The correctional case manager as a generalist focuses his or her correctional counseling activities upon the social environment of the offender on electronic monitoring. It is a process that is directed at the services and resources in the environment which may impact and influence the ability and opportunity for an offender to engage in problem solving activities which might promote an offender's resocialization into society in general, reintegration into a particular family, neighborhood, or community, and rehabilitation with respect to criminogenic risks and needs.

In the generalist method, the case management correctional counseling activity is directed at marshalling concrete or tangible resources and services, such as: public welfare programs, vocational training, housing assistance, medical care, education, food stamps, social security or supplemental security income programs, unemployment insurance, and workmen's compensation programs. It can also include referral for mental health and social services programs, such as: individual and group psychotherapy, substance abuse counseling, sex offender counseling, marriage and family counseling, social skills training, anger management training, money management skills training, and AIDS services and counseling. It may also take the form of support group, peer counseling, or Twelve Step type programs such as: Alcoholic Anonymous, Narcotics Anonymous, Al-Anon, the Seventh Step Program, and so forth.

It is a process that begins with an assessment and identification of the individual problems of the offender, and of his or her problems, in terms of family relationships and interactions with other social systems in the community. This is followed by structured and focused efforts to intervene and interact with all of these systems in order to achieve the offender's reintegration, resocialization and rehabilitation goals.

CORRECTIONAL CASE MANAGER GENERALIST ROLES

There are a number of case manager roles that the correctional counselor can utilize with respect to his or her professional interactions and supervision of the offender on electronic monitoring in terms of operating within the social environment. The following roles will be discussed and pertinent examples will be presented:

1. The epidemiologist.

2. The broker.

3. The organizer.

4. The monitor.

5. The enabler.

6. The advocate.

THE EPIDEMIOLOGIST ROLE

This role addresses the substance of prevention rather than the control and management of social problems. It is proactive rather than reactive in nature. It was derived from the field of public health with its emphasis upon prevention of health problems and maintenance of wellness through early case finding, identification, and treatment of health and medical problems. An example of this would be an early childhood immunization program, while another more controversial approach would be clean needle programs for heroin addicts.

In terms of correctional case management, it refers to the role of identifying potential factors and situations in an offender's physical and social environment which may cause future problems, or which may detract from the correctional goals. Having identified such factors, the correctional case manager must take action to interdict and control for these potential problems. Epidemiological roles can be directed at potential problems which can arise from an environment in which a number of organized and consensual criminal activities are taking place. For example, these activities can include illicit drug trafficking and usage, gang activities, prostitution, and substance use and abuse of various sorts.

The epidemiological role represents the point at which correctional case management should start. The problem areas identified by this kind of case finding approach can be impacted by referral to appropriate criminal jurisdictions or perhaps remediated through the use of one of more of the additional correctional case management generalist roles which we will now proceed to describe.

THE BROKER ROLE

We are more familiar with the activities encompassed in this role if we think of the roles played out by certain types of business professionals. Hoffmann and Sallee (1994) describe it this way:

> The familiar stock broker and real estate agent broker roles shed light on the social broker role. Real estate agents find out the buyers' needs, wants, and financial resources, and then they scout for an available house that seems right for the buyer. Stock brokers attempt to help buyers find the investments that fit their pocketbooks as well as their plans for the market. (p.77)

With respect to correctional case management, the case manager as generalist is the broker and the offender is the client. This type of role is sometimes described in the counseling literature as "networking" or as the "linkage" role. It involves linking the offender with services and entitlements that are necessary for his or her rehabilitation and that are available in the community. In order to be successful in this role, the case manager must have very good knowledge of the social services and resources in the community. In addition, he or she must develop a relationship with various professional persons in community agencies in order to enhance the opportunity for the offender to take advantage of these resources and services.

The role of the case manager as a social broker is usually accomplished through the use of information and referral. Many communities, especially the larger and more urban ones, maintain lists of their social services and programs. Often these are available as pamphlets or as booklets. Sometimes these lists are computerized and can be readily accessed. In addition, many cities and counties have community development or community services and referral offices which can quite helpful to the correctional officer. The following case example illustrates the use of the social brokering role on behalf of an offender on electronic monitoring.

CASE EXAMPLE 6.1
BROKER ROLE

A probation officer in an urban area was asked to speak at a Rotary Club breakfast about the nature of his work. In the course of the presentation, he mentioned that several of the offenders in his intensive supervision case load had problems with anger management and had battered their spouses or girlfriends. Following the presentation, a member of the club thanked the correctional officer for his presentation. In the course of the discussion which followed, he mentioned that he was a member of the board of directors of the local battered women and children's center. He then proceeded to describe one of the newer services at the center, a group therapy program for male abusers conducted by a local psychologist. Although the correctional counselor was aware of the services that the shelter provided to women and children, he was not aware that it had recently received a state grant to provide anger management training for batterers. With this information in hand, and through this newly developed contact, the counselor was able to refer several of the offenders in his case load to this service.

THE ORGANIZER ROLE

In this role, the case manager works to ensure that all of the elements of the service plan for the offender are synchronized. This role is especially incumbent upon correctional personnel since the offender is their primary client. This is often a difficult task because many service providers are often working with the offender and/or with his or her family. Some of these agencies might typically include: public welfare and child protective services departments, employment services, health and mental health services, labor and job training offices, the public schools, and so forth. This role encompasses two major activities.

The first activity requires that the case manager exercise some leadership in order to implement the service plan for the offender. Weil, Karls, and

Associates (1985) describe it as the process of putting all of the pieces of the service plan together and in sequence and then making sure that the plan is carried out in a logical manner. The goal is to make sure that the services of the various agencies are not mutually exclusive but are, instead, integrated and complimentary. In this role, the case manager must often do a great deal of follow-up work, trouble-shooting, and consensus-building among the personnel in the various agencies. Much of this work can be facilitated by case conferences, luncheon meetings, telephone conference calls, or by networking over computer link-ups.

The second activity involves case coordination. In this role, the case manager tries to make sure that all of the service providers that are working with the offender are working together in an harmonious, agreeable, and complimentary fashion. Again, the reason for this activity is to ensure that the service plan is carried out in a logical and coordinated manner. The major activity for the case manager in this role is conflict management. Often, personnel in different agencies are at odds about the purpose of the service, the amount of resources needed, or have various philosophical differences about the issue of individual offender rehabilitation. When such conflicts become apparent, a number of important conflict management skills need to be exercised by the case manager. Hoffman and Sallee (1994) have presented a description of the kinds of conflict management skills that are relevant for successful professional work by many types of human services personnel. These skills include:

1. Listening to each point of view. Listening to how each person in the dispute frames each issue and the importance they attach to these issues.

2. Clarifying each point. The case manager responds in an empathetic manner in order to enable each person in the dispute to clarify their point of view.

3. Defining the problem. The case manager defines the problem or problems that are causing the disputes.

4. Recognizing clues of conflict. The case manager recognizes that sometimes people only give superficial agreement to resolving a

conflict while still holding on to deep-seated disagreements. It is often important to not gloss over difficulties.

5. Avoiding win-lose outcomes. Conflict resolution should never become a zero sum game. Each participant in the dispute should have something to gain and something to give up in the process of conflict resolution. Otherwise, the seeds of future conflict are sowed.

6. Encouraging cooperation. The case manager needs to be a cheerleader for cooperation. He or she must continue to be optimistic, encouraging, and supportive following the resolution of the conflict. (pp. 92-94)

THE MONITOR ROLE

The major activity of the correctional case manager in this role is to continuously assess and monitor: first, the participation of the offender in the services, and, second, the nature and substance of the services being delivered to the parolee or probationer. This requires ongoing contacts with agency personnel; intensive supervision of the offender; and, follow-up with significant others, such as family members, employers, teachers, and others. The primary purpose of monitoring is to make sure that the offender is participating in the service, that the service is appropriate, and that the service is being delivered in a continuous and effective way. The monitoring role is differentiated from the organizer role in that it primarily has to do with quality control.

Much of the monitoring functioning is routinely facilitated since the offender usually reports to the correctional officer on a regular basis though office visits and by telephone calls. Home visits and visits to significant others and collateral sources can amplify the process. The fact that the offender is on electronic monitoring tends to make the process of monitoring more efficient and effective.

Miller (1983) gets at the heart of monitoring in noting that monitoring assure that the clients are receiving the proper, matching, and on-going services that they require. Monitoring is intrinsically related to service implementation and coordination since it is the vehicle through which the service plan can be implemented and conflicts about service delivery resolved. A case example will now be presented to illustrate the concept of case management monitoring. The example that follows is not intended to indicate successful monitoring, instead it is intended to be an example of what not to do. It illustrates how problems and breakdowns can occur in the correctional supervisory system when case organization, implementation, and coordination are absent, and when monitoring is used ineffectively.

CASE EXAMPLE 6.2
BREAKDOWN IN THE MONITORING ROLE

Robert, a convicted sex offender (pedophile), was granted parole after serving five years of his ten year felony sentence. One of the terms of his parole order was that he participate in an outpatient sex offender counseling program acceptable to the district parole office. Another term of his parole order was that he not have contact with pre-adolescent or adolescent boys. Robert participated in the program on a weekly basis with Dr. E., a clinical psychologist. Dr. E. had been nationally recognized for his work with pedophiles. His clinical treatment involved the use of adversive behavioral conditioning techniques to enable a sex offender to learn to respond only to age appropriate sex partners. Much of this work involved the display of age appropriate and non-age appropriate sexual partners. Adversive reinforcement was applied whenever Robert responded to inappropriate sexual images, while adversive reinforcements were withheld when Robert responded to age appropriate sexual images. During one of his weekly visits with his parole officer, and upon her urging, Robert described the course of his treatment with Dr. E. The parole officer, Ms. J., was incensed. She felt that Robert had violated his probation order because the treatment brought him into contact with provocative pictures of boys. The upshot was that Robert's parole order was revocated because he was found to have violated a condition of parole and he was subsequently returned to prison.

It should be clear from this example that had the parole officer followed proper case management procedures, the condition of parole requiring Robert to enter out-patient sex offender treatment would have been implemented properly and the service would have been coordinated with the district parole office. Proper monitoring would have turned an ambiguous condition of parole into a viable treatment goal.

THE ENABLER ROLE

In the enabler role the case manager helps the client maximize the use of appropriate programs and services in the community. Many types of enabling activities are contained within this role. For example, a basic stance is one of describing and discussing information about various programs or services and the array of associated options, contingencies and opportunity costs associated with each program or service with the offender. This is followed by encouraging the offender to act on the information. Another stance might involve the expression of a professional opinion concerning the importance or the need for the offender to use a certain program or service. This kind of enabling is important for clients who may have certain psychological or developmental deficiencies which make it difficult for them to make responsible or rational choices. Sometimes they need to "float" upon the ego of the case manager.

The classic enabling activity involves the use of support. This can take the form of verbal reassurances as well as non-verbal supportive clues, such as body language. These activities may be used to convey the message that there may be some hope; that something can be accomplished; that there may be some "light at the end of the tunnel." The use of imagery techniques, for example, could be used at this junction. At the far end of the enabling scale, perhaps a kind of "friendly persuasion" may be in order. This activity may be operationalized via a candid discussion with these individuals concerning the social and personal costs and benefits in relation to using or not using the programs or services.

There are some important considerations in the enabling process that need to be considered. The enabling process must first be tempered with an understanding by the case manager that the program or service that he or she is promoting is appropriate for the client and that the client should have a reasonable chance of success in the program. Second, the case manager cannot enable clients to act on a goal unless they are willing or motivated to take action. We cannot create motivation. We can, however, promote people toward motivation by support, reassurance, encouragement and, when appropriate, by persuasion. With regard to persuasion, sometimes the process of discussion, when directed at the client and his or problematic life situation, may stimulate a measure of anxiety, or perhaps create a crisis mentality which may cause them to become motivated to make use of a service. We must not use force or coercion. Similarly, we cannot want or wish for them to accomplish something out of our own needs for self-reassurance, ego-gratification or self-aggrandizement. Conversely, the case manager generalist must respect their right to self determination in terms of acting on service options, even if that self-determination is ultimately exercised in a self-defeating way. Oftentimes success derives from failure.

THE ADVOCATE ROLE

It becomes important for the correctional case manager to play out the social advocate role when it becomes apparent that in the community certain types of social services or programs, which could be of significant benefit to offenders, are either not available, incomplete, or fragmented and disorganized. Correctional counselors have a certain status in the community. In addition, they are often perceived as having a certain degree of expertise and technical skills with respect to criminal justice issues. Their clients, on the other hand, generally do not have these dynamics. The case manager as social advocate basically uses his or her status and role as leverage in order to help a community either develop a needed service, or coordinate and more efficiently manage incomplete or fragmented services. The primary way in which this role is played out is through persuasion and the presentation of technical or pragmatic arguments with respect to the needed service. This can be accomplished in a number of ways:

1. By testifying at a city council or county commissioners meeting.

2. By speaking before social, philanthropic, or fraternal organizations such as, the Kiwanis Club, the Junior League, or the United Way.

3. By speaking before business and professional groups, for example, the Chamber of Commerce, the League of Women Voters, the board of directors of the local hospital or mental health agency.

4. By making a presentation to groups which have political and/or ideological goals including, the National Association for the Advancement of Colored People (NAACP), the League of United Latin American Citizens (LULAC), the Urban League, or the local Republican or Democratic party organizational boards.

The following case example illustrates the process of social advocacy. In this example, although the direct beneficiary of the advocacy appears to be the probation agency, the immediate impact upon the offenders was also very significant.

EXAMPLE 6.3
ADVOCACY ROLE

Ms. A. is an adult probation officer in a small rural county. The county that she works in encompasses a geographic area of approximately 200 square miles. Because of large case loads and the geographical size of the county, as well as the increasing burden of paperwork, she and the other correctional personnel have had to primarily rely upon telephone contacts and in-office visits in order to manage the supervision of their clients. Personal, face-to-face contacts have been limited to the more problematic probationers. Ms. A., in collaboration with the other staff and professional members of her department, decided that they needed to approach the agency director about automating the office. At the present time the automation was limited to word processing software and some intra-office networking. The director was accepting of the proposal but was concerned about finances. A technical expert was then brought in to discuss the issue and to present make some cost : benefit analyses utilizing various scenarios. It appeared that after an initial cost run-up, computerization would ultimately lead to a more efficient operation of the department and some budgetary savings. It's chief virtue, however, would lie in providing the agency with more technically advanced systems in order to facilitate its mission. Following this, the agency director made a presentation to the judges of the court systems served by the agency. They were supportive of the proposal. Their support, plus support from other significant individuals and groups in the community, especially the editorial support of the local newspaper, led the elected county officials, after a series of public hearings, to approve the new system. Now the department is able to more efficiently and accurately manage and organize its data bases about the probationers with respect to their course of probation. In addition, the agency's data bases are linked with the data bases of other criminal justice agencies in the county and in the state. As a secondary gain, the correctional officers now have more time to direct their supervisory and counseling energies toward more personal contact with larger numbers of probationers who need more intensively supervised encounters.

Sometimes, however, advocacy may spill-over into social activism. Generally speaking, social activism consist of more aggressive and assertive actions for change directed at political systems and individual politicians. Activism roles may include testifying before the state legislature, campaigning for particular political party candidates, boycotting products or services, political demonstrations, forming social action coalitions, and various types of coalition-building including unionizing activities, work stoppages, and work slowdowns or strikes.

Most of these types of activities are prohibited by state and federal legislation, especially if the individual involved is a member of a civil service system. Therefore, with few exceptions (such as by virtue of membership in a professional organization or union), activist roles are usually unavailable to correctional counselors.

THE CASE MANAGER COUNSELOR METHOD

The case manager counselor method may be described as a reality therapy. It focuses on the here and now of the offender's behavior. It is used when the case management generalist method efforts toward the resocialization, reintegration and rehabilitation of offenders on electronic monitoring are not achieving the counseling goals. This may be the case due to certain embedded characteristics of some types of offenders. These characteristics include distorted and irrational thinking processes, incorporation of antisocial beliefs and values, and the use of antisocial neutralizations to support or defuse social stigma attached to their antisocial values, behaviors and activities. With the case manager counselor method, the professional counseling energies of the case manager are directed toward the internal psychological world of the parolee or probationer on electronic monitoring. The case management counselor roles utilize a series of techniques that direct verbal communications at the thinking, feeling, and behavioral realms of the persona of the offender. The goal is help offenders achieve insight concerning the history and development of the problem, their circumstances and roles in developing and maintaining the problem, and the impact of the problem in terms of their present social and psychological functioning.

One of the difficulties about psychotherapeutic methods which aim for client insight attainment is the confusion which exists about the nature of psychotherapy. The aim of such methods is not principally to "cure" a client. The ideal outcome of the treatment is to bring the client to the level of understanding the genesis of his or her problems, while at he same time challenging them, in a directive and forthright way, to act on the insight by changing or modifying their behavior. Mangrum (1975), in discussing correctional treatment, clarifies this issue, especially for professional practitioners in probation:

> Rather than to think of correctional treatment in terms of a *cure,* we should consider it in terms of problem resolution which results in progress toward the goal of improved social adjustment. There are two levels toward which such treatment efforts can be directed. The first is to bring about sufficient problem resolution and understanding of himself and his situation that the client is able in daily living to

avoid confrontation and conflict between himself and others and between himself and the expectations of the community. The second level is to bring about sufficient self-awareness to enable the client to develop personally, realize personal goals and reach self-fulfillment. (p. 188)

CASE MANAGEMENT COUNSELOR ROLES

The case manager as counselor role with probationers or parolees on electronic monitoring is based upon three assumptions derived from cognitive behavioral theory. These assumptions correlate with the viewpoint of the phenomenological nature of mankind (Enos & Black, 1982).

1. The first assumption is that the individual can create his or her own social reality and, further, that this occurs through conscious processes.

2. The second assumption is that an individual can create his or her psychological reality via conscious processes.

3. The third assumption rests on the point of view that society is a human product. In short, it is the aggregate or the sum of individual creations of social and psychological realities.

In holding to these assumptions, the case manager as counselor becomes, ipso facto, a reality-level therapist. The counseling focus is upon "today and now." When working with the parolee or probationer this means that unconscious processes, for example: repressed and suppressed feelings, are not addressed unless they have become problems of social and psychological living in the "here and now." Similarly, a traumatic developmental history which may have been characterized by abuse and neglect, is only addressed if these traumata can be observed and directly linked to current problems in social or psychological functioning. In practice, the case manager focuses his or her counseling efforts upon the cognitive, affective, and behavioral aspects of the personality structure of the parolee or probationer by utilizing some or most of the roles described in the next section.

MODELING BEHAVIOR ROLE

In this role, the case manager as counselor projects or models for the probationer or parolee stereotypes of normative, i.e., socially and psychologically acceptable attitudes, values, and behaviors, and overtly models appropriate ways of dealing with life and its problems and contingencies in keeping with normative attitudes, values, and behaviors. It is a kind of social and cultural mentoring. And, it also consists of an educational or teaching role. Pullias and Young (1969) describe the kinds of life problems and experiences that the successful counselor as teacher ought to project to his or her clients:

> The teacher who meets the class has also lived life to this point and bears in his personality the wounds and scars of that experience. He comes to the teaching responsibility as a personality who also has developed a style of life, a way of dealing with his needs and the demands of the environment. It is hoped that special study and training, growth in self-understanding and perhaps in wisdom will have healed some of the worst wounds and produced a style of life better than that of the less experienced students. (p. 94)

If the process has been effective the client will have incorporated some of the norms and will model or play them out in his or her own life style. It is not always possible to measure in any clinical way how the process of incorporation takes place because it is an unconscious process. However, it can often be noted by certain verbal or physical clues that the client puts forth, such as similar dress or appearance, a commonality of ideas and attitudes with the case manager, or imitative career, social, and cultural choices.

DISCUSSANT ROLE

In this role, the case manager as counselor becomes involved in a more direct way in a process of logical discussion through which the offender is forced to contemplate and appraise:

1. His or her present behaviors, thinking processes, attitudes, and values. The intention is to make the offender consider his or her role in the problem.

2. The consequences of these behaviors, thinking processes, attitudes, and values upon himself or herself; his or her family, friends, and significant others. Consideration is also given to these factors with respect to involvement with the criminal justice system and the subsequent consequences.

3. His or her exercise of free will in terms of making choices which bring criminal sanctions. A discussion at this point would involve an examination of choices and the net rewards or punishments inherent in various choices. The contingencies and opportunity costs involved in making criminal versus non-criminal choices would be appraised, and alternative, more socially acceptable choices would be emphasized.

Offenders often engage in verbal guerilla-war tactics with correctional personnel. These verbalizations are aimed at neutralizing the extent and impact of their criminality. Some of the more common types of neutralizations, which have historically been referred to in the psychological and psychoanalytical literature as ego defense mechanisms, include: rationalization (defending or excusing) the behavior, projection and displacement of guilt and blame upon others, denial of the behavior, diminishing or demonizing the victim, trivializing the behavior, and various other kinds of anti-social and asocial ideations and manipulations. Through logical discussion the counselor challenges, confronts and makes professional judgments about the behavior, attitudes, values and, especially, the thinking processes of the offender. He or she repudiates and rejects the anti-social behavior and illogical and deviate thinking processes.

THERAPIST ROLE

In the therapist role, the case manager as counselor directs his or her counseling energies toward an exploration of the dynamics of the developmental history of the offender. The counseling intention is to explore, with the offender, his or her developmental experiences, especially episodes of abuse, neglect, and faulty parental role modeling. The purpose is to bring the offender to an understanding (insight) with respect to the influence of these experiences on the affective component or feelings of the offender, and on his or her thinking processes, and how these may be linked to current problems and offender behavior. The case manager engages the offender in a verbal process directed at uncovering and interpreting subjective material from his or her developmental history. The offender is encouraged to recount his or her developmental history and to ventilate his or her feelings about that history. The role of the counselor is enhanced by the development of a positive transference relationship which allows the offender to feel comfortable in making an honest and authentic revelation of his or her developmental history, and in expressing and ventilating feelings, especially negative feelings. The counselor responds in a neutral, objective, and benign manner to the client.

CASE EXAMPLE

The case example which follows illustrate how case management generalist roles and case management counselor roles with probationers or parolees on electronic monitoring might be applied.

CASE EXAMPLE 6.1
DAVID, AN ANTI SOCIAL PERSONALITY

David, age 23, a white male, was placed on intensive supervision probation in May of 1997. The term of his probation was two years. David has a history of petty thefts since he was an adolescent. In the most recent instance, David stole a blank check from his former employer, forged his name on it, and cashed it at the local drive-in liquor store. The store owner discovered the canceled check and filed charges against David. The amount of the check was $179.69.

Currently David is unemployed. He explained that he stole the check because he needed money. He stated that he had promised his step son that he would enroll him in a summer basketball camp. David explained that he did not have the money but that he did not want to let his step son down, especially since he had promised the child the camp experience.

David was an adopted child. His mother was 16 years old when he was born. She was a chronic alcoholic and heroin user. He was placed in foster family care until he was adopted at age three by an older couple. They already had two children of their own and felt that they needed a "little brother" for their biological children. David's adoptive father worked for the city as a maintenance worker. His adoptive mother worked in the laundry department of the city hospital. Both parents are now deceased. David was a hyperactive and aggressive youngster. His intelligence was at the normal level but medical screening indicated that he had a learning disability. In addition, there was a note in his medical history that he may have been a fetal alcohol syndrome baby. He was disruptive at school and was placed in special education. By age six, he had developed a pattern of stealing small items from other children and from convenience stores. He did not finish high school, having been expelled in the eleventh grade for behavioral problems. His parents often compared him in an unfavorable manner with his brother and sister. His father often punished him severely. His mother often told him that he acted like a devil. David did not find out that he was adopted until he was 12. When he was 15, he was able to find his natural mother. She was living in the same neighborhood. Although he attempted to establish a relationship with her, she was not interested; especially since she had married the owner of a local food store, and now had four children of her own. Last year, David married Nora, 24, a single mother with a eight year old son, Evan. She works as a cashier in a supermarket.

David has a long criminal record beginning at age 15. The record includes petty theft, car theft, possession of a dangerous weapon, attempted rape, and drug trafficking. David spent 9 months in a juvenile facility at age 12, and two years in the state psychiatric hospital beginning at age 18. For the last two years, he had apparently been "clean" until the check forging incident.

When confronted with his behavior, David customarily states that he stole because he needed the money, or that he was arrested because the police were retaliating against him, or that his employer was treating him unfairly, or that he was "set up" by others who had a grudge against him.

CASE MANAGEMENT GENERALIST ROLES WITH DAVID

EPIDEMIOLOGIST ROLE

- Take preventive measures concerning the possibility of reoffense by encouraging David and his family to move out of their current neighborhood and into a new low income housing project, currently under construction, which is located closer to his wife's job, and which is in a school district which has a higher performing elementary school.

BROKER ROLE

- Refer David to the Mrs. S., the director of the high school's adult education department, for enrollment in its G.E.D. program.

- Refer David to the local Narcotics Anonymous support group so that he can learn some skills in drug avoidance and relapse prevention.

- Take steps to identify and clarify the status of David's medical condition. Previous available information indicated possible organic impairment and mental health problems. Refer David to the local county mental health agency, university teaching hospital facility, or state mental hospital for diagnostic medical and psychiatric procedures.

ORGANIZER ROLE

- Nora, David's wife, was previously on public welfare: Aid to Families with Dependent Children. She received monthly payments because she had been abandoned by the biological father of her child, Evan. Currently, she receives, on an irregular basis, child support payments from the father of the child through the county court. In addition, Evan has been experiencing problems at school. Specifically, he has been diagnosed as being learning disabled and has been placed in special education. Furthermore, he is hyperactive and aggressive and takes Ritalin (a tranquilizing drug) to control this behavior.

To ensure that David makes good progress during his probationary status, the case manager must coordinate the various service elements and professional personnel described above who significantly impact the psychosocial functioning of David's wife and son, in order to maximize effective family functioning.

MONITOR ROLE

- Follow up and assess David's participation in the G.E. D. program. Is he enrolled? Does he attend regularly? Is he motivated? Is he making progress? Does he have a constructive relationship with the staff members in the program?

- Follow up concerning David's participation in the Narcotics Anonymous program. Is he attending regularly? Does he follow the steps in recovery? Can he verbalize the "triggers for relapse and the slogans in recovery"? (Enos & Southern, 1996).

- Follow up with Evan's special education teacher concerning his participation and progress in that program.

- Check with the medical clinic concerning the conditions concerning Evan's use of Ritalin.

- Contact the clerk of the county court to ensure prompt child support payments by Nora's ex husband. Be prepared to discuss with Nora the possibility of a referral to the county district attorney for collection of non support.

- Check with the local public housing department to see where the family stands in terms of availability of public housing.

ENABLER ROLE

- You provide David with information about a new program that has been developed by the local college in conjunction with an aerospace company to train individuals for electronic systems assembly. You and David meet with the director of the program at the college. He describes the program in detail. David seems very interested. You explain the options, contingencies, and expectations associated with enrolling in the program to David. You encourage him to enroll in the program.

- David has always been concerned about his lack of social skills. You provide him with information about a social skills development course that will soon be available at the neighborhood community service center. In addition, you encourage David and his wife to enroll in a country and western dance class that is being offered as a non-credit mini course at the college.

ADVOCATE ROLE

- On the basis of your position as a member of the board of directors of the local county mental health clinic, you try to influence the other members of the board to support the application by the executive director of agency for a grant from the state to expand the family preservation program.

- You approach the director of community services for the city. The city receives funds each year from the state for "public service" activities. In the past, most of these funds have gone toward neighborhood beautification and downtown historic preservation projects. You discover that the scope of public service projects is ill-defined. An opinion from the state attorney general is secured which states that these kinds of funds may be used to fund various type of community service programs. You, and other interested citizens, develop and present a proposal to the mayor and city council members for the funding of a community resource management team. The team, consisting of a number of important resource persons in the city, agrees to provide probationers and parolees with direct assistance in obtaining education, training, and employment in the community.

CASE MANAGEMENT COUNSELOR ROLES WITH DAVID

MODELING BEHAVIOR ROLE

- Discuss with David his lack of progress and motivation in the G. E. D. program. You ask him about the types of jobs that he has had in the past. He describes a series of menial and labor-intensive jobs. You share with David certain aspects of your life history and experiences. You note that your parents were divorced when you were 12, and that your mother had to take a full-time job to meet the economic needs of the family. You describe to him the nature of the various types of part time jobs that you had during high school and college in order to have enough resources to complete your education. You describe how education has made a difference in your life. You ask David to describe to you how you he is dealing with his problem of a lack of education and ask him to compare and contrast his behavior with how you dealt with this issue in your life.

- David's attendance at Narcotics Anonymous has been irregular. You discuss this behavior with him. You make arrangements so that you and David can visit the local inpatient drug treatment center. During the visit, David has an opportunity to meet and speak with several of the patients. He makes a positive contact with Ralph, a former heroin user, who is now a peer counselor at the facility. With Ralph's urging, David decides to do some volunteer work at the facility. Later, you ask him to discuss with you his feelings about what he saw at the center and his plans for volunteer work.

• You and David have a discussion about social skills. You ask him to do some homework each week. The homework consists of a number of questions that you give him each week. He has to spend time at the library doing research to arrive at the answers. He discusses his answers each week with you during his probationary conferences.

• You make a home visit for the purpose of demonstrating what you call "family quality home time." You model, through your communications and behavior, appropriate ways a husband and father should relate to his wife and child. This is followed, during subsequent visits, by role playing exercises in which David, Nora, and Evan, with you as the group leader, verbally act-out various family dramas. These dramas focus upon topics such as how to communicate needs, wishes, and feelings; appropriate child management, discipline, and parenting skills; how to share roles and responsibilities in marriage, and so forth. You ask David, Nora, and Evan to describe to the family group what they had learned from the experiences.

• It has been some time since David filed his application for public housing. He has become frustrated with the process. He feels that they are ignoring him and may dislike him. You have David make an appointment to see the director of the public housing bureau. You discuss with David certain personal issues before making the visit, especially his dress, appearance and grooming. You and David meet with Mr. Jones, the director. David observes your physical and verbal interactions as you discuss the status of David's application Mr. Jones. You take care to be personable, professional and courteous with Mr. Jones. Mr. Jones states that they are having come construction problems with the last phase of the housing development. However, he assures you and David that the project will probably be completed on time. Mr. Jones gives David a date when he can telephone in order to get a more precise answer about the availability of his unit. Following this meeting, you ask David to describe to you what he has learned from this encounter.

DISCUSSANT ROLE

- David tells you that he stole from his last employer in order to have some money to send Evan to summer basketball camp. He loves Evan very much and, in a way, sees him as a mirror of himself. His statements about his criminal behavior in the past had a similar theme: the theft was necessary in order to provide for something that he needed or for something that someone whom he was closes to and loved needed. You verbally confront and reject his illogical thinking. You interpret for him how this kind of thinking serves as a rationalization for his irresponsible and criminal behavior. You connect it to his problems with the criminal justice system. You want to help him reframe his thinking. To do this you pose a series of reflective questions to him. The intent of these kinds of questions is to help David reflect upon his deviant behavior and think through and then verbalize better behavioral alternatives. For example, you engage him in a process of logical discussion in which you ask him to consider how he could have come up with the money without committing forgery and theft. What about taking a second job? Couldn't he have described the problem to his wife and Evan and dealt with their disappointment? Could he have asked his employer for an advance on his salary? Could he have worked more overtime?

- Engage David in some futurism exercises. In this process you describe two possible futures for him: in the first scenario he continues to use heroin and alcohol. He eventually becomes addicted and has to be institutionalized. Later, after leaving the treatment facility, he relapses, takes an overdose and dies. In second futurism scenario, he actively participates in Narcotics Anonymous. Whenever he feels under stress he recites the "steps" from the manifesto of the program. He continues to participate in the drug treatment program at the local clinic. Eventually, he becomes "clean." He completes the G.E.D. program and is able to secure a job at a nearby electronics company. He enrolls in the local community college applied electronics science program. Following this presentation, have David identify what types of thinking patterns, attitudes, behaviors and activities would result in the outcomes depicted in the first scenario. Subsequently, have him describe what thinking patterns, attitudes, behaviors and activities might lead to the second scenario.

- David tells you that the charge of attempted rape was not correct. He said that the charge came about as the result of a drug deal that had gone bad, and that the woman he was dealing drugs to reported to the police that he had tried to rape her as retaliation for the bad drug deal. You point out to David that even if the story is true, he was still involved in an illegal activity. Her allegations about his sexual behavior do not neutralize the criminal activity. You point out that his description of the activity shows his need to project blame for the problem onto her in order to avoid a full acknowledgement of the fact that he had a major role in the problem. You discuss with him that fact that on several occasions he has also blamed his treatment as a child by his adoptive parents for his turning to crime. You challenge him to "own" his problems of criminality.

THERAPIST ROLE

- David has discussed with you the fact that he hated his adoptive father and mother and siblings. He tells you that his father physically abused him and that his mother often told him that he was a devil and that God would punish him for his sins. You respond to this statement by David in a benign and supportive manner. You ask him to elaborate and discuss this history in more detail. You ask him to consider that they did adopt him and provide him with a home, albeit one that appeared to be dysfunctional. You ask him to speculate about what would have become of him had he been adopted by more caring parents or, alternatively, if had never been adopted and had to grow up in a series of foster homes and group homes. Here, you are trying to get David to understand that sometimes life is like a lottery, and that we often have no control about what happens to us. We can, however, make choices about how we choose to respond to life's circumstances. We tell him that he can choose to fixate upon the negatives of his developmental history and see himself as a victim having little control over his fortunes in life, or he can choose to be a survivor who overcomes and rises above and succeeds in spite of his developmental history. With someone like David, it is important to not let him portray himself as a victim of childhood traumas, although those traumas may have been very deleterious, because victim status would provide neutralizations for his criminal behavior. We conclude our discussion by loaning David a copy of Viktor Frankl's (1984) book: *Man's Search for Meaning.* We ask him to read the book and to describe what he has learned about personal and psychological survival based upon Frankl's descriptions of his experiences in a concentration camp during World War II. We ask him to describe how he might implement some of the strategies that Frankl presented.

- David describes his contact with his natural mother and her rebuff of his attempts to establish a relationship with him. He believes that she didn't love him or else she would not have put him up for adoption. You ask him to reflect upon the circumstances of his mother at the time of his birth: a young, soon-to-be single parent, addicted to drugs and alcohol. You ask him to consider the choices that were available to her under those circumstances. Wasn't she faced with a terrible dilemma?   What choices would he have made under the same circumstances? Could he understand that it was necessary for her to spend psychological energy walling off the guilt associated with that part of her past, and that it was now difficult for her to reopen that chapter of her life. You state that he try to get some closure of this issue through ventilation of feelings. You suggest that he write a letter to her in which he expresses his feelings about her and about the circumstance of his being placed for adoption. He is given the option of sharing the contents of the letter with you. You recommend that at a later point, after he has had some time for reflection, he should decide whether or not he should mail the letter to her.

- You ask him to describe why he chose to marry Nora and to adopt her child, Evan. You ask him if he sees any parallels between their life circumstances and his life history. You focus on the fact that the marriage presents him with an opportunity to make a healthy sublimation through which he can convert his repressed yearnings for the family life that was denied to him by taking positive action now to be a proper father and husband. You encourage him in this role and suggest that avoidance of the criminal path is the best way to achieve that ideal.

Obviously, many examples could be presented which would serve to illustrate both the generalist and counselor case management counseling roles. The types of roles and activities that are encompassed by the generalist method, since they involve concrete and externally-oriented planned change activities with respect to changing the social environment of the offender, are somewhat universal and easily generalizable for work with most types of offenders in community correctional settings. The implementation of most of these activities are merely limited by the time, energy, creativity and resourcefulness of the correctional case manager. The use of the counseling roles are more problematic for typical correctional personnel.

Effective case management counseling is built upon a broad theoretical knowledge base concerning social, cultural, and psychological behavior; a deep knowledge about the intrinsic and extrinsic variables which comprise the dynamics of individual personality; an understand of family dynamics and family therapy; positive personal and professional characteristics and relationship skills; supervised experiential learning encounters; and an acquaintance with social science research methods and analytical procedures, and so forth. Many correctional counselors possess these characteristics. Others can obtain them though in service training, workshops, or through graduate education in corrections, or in one of the helping professions. Prominent counselors, such as Rogers (1965), and Carkhuff and Anthony (1979), have indicated that persons from a variety of backgrounds can be prepared to be effective therapists. Rogers' (1965) comment in this regard is most cogent:

> In our own courses we have had students from the fields of education, theology, industrial relations, nursing, and students with interdisciplinary training. It has been quite impossible to see any significant differences in the rate at which such students become therapists. It would seem that the orientation to personal relationships with which they enter a training program is more important than specific course work they have had or the scientific knowledge they possess. (pp. 435-436)

The writers agree with Rogers' point of view and would add that the burgeoning criminal justice populations entering community correctional settings because of the deinstitutionalization of traditional correctional facilities, and prison overcrowding, make the issue of who can do correctional counseling academic.

SUMMARY AND CONCLUSIONS

In this Chapter the process of correctional case management counseling was discussed, and specific descriptions were presented concerning the case management generalist and the case management counselor methods, including a description of these roles and a presentation of some pertinent case examples. Increasingly, clinical outcome research with clients in mental health settings seem to suggest that cognitive behavioral approaches hold the promise of being effective treatment strategies. There is some data to suggest that it may be a useful method for working with several types of offenders in criminal justice settings (Kennedy, 1984; Hains & Hains, 1988; Andrews et al., 1990; Brame, MacKenzie, Waggoner, & Robinson 1996). By extension, the authors conclude that this may also be true of other special populations within the criminal justice system such as probationers and parolees on electronic monitoring. In the future, this assertion will be tested given the explosive growth of electronic monitoring programs now in evidence in this country across city, county, state and federal criminal justice jurisdictions. The authors believe that such a test may well demonstrate the effectiveness of this approach.

REFERENCES

Andrews, D. A., Zinger, I., Hoge, R. D., Bonta, J., Gendreau, P., & Cullen, F. T. (1990). Does correctional treatment work? A psychologically informed meta-analysis. *Criminology, 28,* 369-404.

Brame, R., MacKenzie, D. L., Waggoner, A. R., & Robinson, K. D. (1996). Moral reconation therapy and problem behavior in the Oklahoma Department of Corrections. *Journal of the Oklahoma Criminal Justice Research Consortium, 3,* pp. 63-84.

Carkhuff, R. R., & Anthony, W. A. (1979). *The skills of helping: An introduction to counseling skills.* Amherst, MA: Human Resource Development Press.

Cumming, J., & Cumming, E. (1962). *Ego and milieu.* NY: Atherton.

Enos, R., & Black, C. M. (1982). A social construction of reality model for clinical social work practice. *The Journal of Applied Social Sciences, 7,* 83-97.

Enos, R., & Southern, S. (1996). *Correctional case management.* Cincinnati, OH: Anderson.

Frankl, V. (1984) *Man's search for meaning.* NY: Simon & Schuster.

Family Support Act of 1988, Pub. L. 100-485.

Hains, A. A., & Hains, A. H. (1988). Conitive-behavioral training of problem-solving and impulse control with delinquent adolescents. *Journal of Offender Services and Rehabilitation, 12,* 95-113.

Hoffman, K. S., & Sallee, A. L. (1994). *Social work practice: Bridges to change.* Needham Heights, MA: Allyn and Bacon.

Jones, M. (1953) *The therapeutic community.* NY: Basic Books.

Kennedy, R. E. (1984). Cognitive behavior interventions with delinquents. In A. Meyers & W. E. Craighead (Eds.), *Cognitive behavior therapy with children* (pp. 351-376). NY: Plenum.

Mangrum, C. T. (1975). *The professional practitioner in probation.* Springfield, IL: Charles C. Thomas.

Miller, G. (1983) Case management: The essential services. In C.J. Sanborn (Ed.), *Case management in mental health service* (pp. 3-16). NY: Haworth.

Pullias, E. V., & Young, J. D. (1969). *A teacher is many things.* Bloomington, IN: Indiana University Press.

Rogers, C. R. (1965). *Client-centered therapy.* Cambridge, MA: The Riverside Press.

Stanton, A. H., & Schwartz, M. (1954). *The mental hospital: A study of institutional participation in psychiatric illness and treatment.* NY: Basic Books.

Ullmann, L., & Krasner, L. (1975). *A psychological approach to abnormal behavior (2nd ed.).* Englewood Cliffs, NJ: Prentice-Hall.

Weil, M., Karls, J.M., & Associates (1985). *Case management in human service practice.* San Francisco: Jossey-Bass.

DESCRIPTIONS OF THE USE OF ELECTRONIC MONITORING IN THREE SELECTED PROBATION AND PAROLE DEPARTMENTS

The purpose of this Chapter is to provide the reader with detailed descriptions about some of the electronic monitoring (EM) programs in current use. Toward this end, data were obtained from three large metropolitan probation and parole departments: The Dallas County (Texas) Adult Probation Department (Dallas County Adult Probation Department, 1989); the Harris County (Houston, Texas) Adult Probation Department (Harris County Adult Probation Department, 1989); and, the Harris County (Houston, Texas) Board of Pardons and Paroles (Harris County Board of Pardons and Paroles, 1989). These departments were chosen because of their size, the diversity of their client caseloads, and because of their use of "state-of-the-art" electronic monitoring technologies. In addition, this Chapter contains the results of a survey research study directed at discerning the attitudes and levels of satisfaction of the criminal justice staff members in these three departments with respect to the use of EM in their departments.

DALLAS COUNTY ADULT PROBATION DEPARTMENT

At the time of this study, Dallas County had a population of 1,833,100. The city of Dallas is the largest city contained within the county. The total population in the county included 419,852 males over 25 years of age. Of these, 72.6% had a high school diploma and 61,351 held college degrees. The county was 71.4% white, 17.6% African American, 9.5% Hispanic, 1.1% Asian and 0.4% American Indian. Only 16.3% of Dallas County's population was classified as rural by the U.S. Bureau of the Census (U.S. Department of Commerce, 1983). The county had a 5.7% unemployment rate. In 1985, 183,712 serious crimes were reported to police and 17,322 (9.4%) of these crimes involved violence (U.S. Department of Commerce, 1988).

The Dallas County Adult Probation Department exercises a control-strategy probationary method. This approach emphasizes supervision and restitution rather than personal adjustment and rehabilitation. The department deals with clientele in a major urban center and many of its probationers reside in the inner city. Client socioeconomic statuses range from lower-class to middle class. The majority of the clients served by this department are Hispanic or African American, work at relatively low-paying jobs or were unemployed at the time of this study (Dallas County Adult Probation Department, 1989).

The Dallas County Adult Probation Department offers both group and individual counseling, in addition to referring clients to Alcoholics Anonymous, Narcotics Anonymous, Al-Anon, and so forth. The department encourages the use of community resources which include: substance abuse and chemical dependency programs; elder assistance programs; child care programs; educational programs; emergency assistance programs; employment assistance programs; halfway houses/emergency services; health needs; immigration services; legal aid services; mental health/mental retardation agencies; mental health practitioners; veteran's services; vocational and physical rehabilitation services; and, women's concerns programs. The Dallas Department also makes use of the Community Control Program (CCP) which was developed to provide the courts with a sentencing option (Dallas County Adult Probation Department, 1987). This program has two goals: (1) to decrease the growth of the prison population and associated costs and (2) to satisfy, at least in part, the demand that criminals be punished. This program provides increased surveillance and services to probationers who have failed to comply with traditional probation programs. This program uses electronic monitoring to assist the surveillance effort.

The purpose of the CCP is to provide an alternative to prison while continuing to protect the community through surveillance and control of the offenders by utilizing appropriate resources. The offender is confined to his/her residence where strict non-institutional sanctions are imposed. To facilitate this, the CCP provides a constant, around-the-clock surveillance through electronic monitoring. This program uses a team approach and restricts their caseload to 25 cases per team.

An offender is eligible for CCP if the courts order it, if the offender is subject to a hearing on a "motion-to-revoke" or if the offender is a "shock probationer." The offender must also meet the following criteria:

1. The probationer should request CCP.

2. The probationer should have "something to lose" if he or she absconds.

3. Probationers must have a telephone in their home and have a RJ11X connecting jack.

4. The probationer must have been convicted of a felony.

Two CCP officers are assigned to a caseload of 25 probationers. One officer acts as the surveillance officer and the other officer is a casework officer. The surveillance officer's primary responsibility is to provide surveillance services, such as: home and job visits, drug and alcohol screening, and to maintain regular contacts with the EM agency. The casework officer assists the surveillance officer and provides casework services, including: job placement, planning activities in conjunction with other court ordered programs, and also maintains each case file. The casework officer must also write a "supervision summary report" at the end of the first 45 days in the program and after three months in the program in relation to each probationer's progress. This report focuses on areas such as personal, legal, home, and employment problems, as well as attitude and adjustment issues.

The CCP Team is responsible for the following at the initial visit of the probationer:

1. Issue and review the CCP Handbook (which describes the program) with the probationer.

2. Explain any "special conditions" with the probationer.

3. Explain CCP's expectations of the probationer.

4. Notify the EM agency and arrange for the hook-up.

5. Briefly explain the EM system to the probationer.

6. Prepare a "daily activity log" with the probationers schedule.

7. Discuss the consequences of violations.

8. Review the monthly report.

9. Have the probationer report immediately to his or her home for the EM hook-up.

10. Go to the probationer's home with the monitoring representative to hook-up the system.

The CCP officers must complete training in "Computerized Cases Classification," "Strategies for Case Supervision" (SCS), and "Case Planning/Documentation." The reasons for placement in CCP must be submitted and justified for each CCP probationer accepted into the program. An intake form must also be completed so that it is easy to identify a probationer. The purpose of SCS is to provide a more efficient and effective case management system. An assessment is made to aid the officer in making decisions on the risks and needs of the offender. Information is gathered from the pre-sentence investigation report, by reviewing relevant reports, by interviewing the family of the probationer, by interviewing the victims, and by interviewing the probationer. A supervision plan is then completed about each CCP probationer in order to assure close attention to the problems and needs of the offender. The same information gathered at intake is also gathered at the discharge level in order to evaluate the effectiveness of the program.

Each probationer will have a minimum of three face-to-face contacts with the officer per week. There will be at least two face-to-face field contacts each week and at least four face-to- face contacts on the weekends during the month. The probationer must report weekly to the casework officer. Those who are unemployed must report daily, Monday through Friday. The CCP team will make at least two contacts with collaterals, including: employers, family members, and others who are in a position to facilitate the supervision objectives.

If a probationer is placed on CCP, he/she must adhere to certain special conditions of probation. Some of these conditions are as follows:

1. The probationer must reside at a specified address.

2. The probationer must observe approved hours of absences.

3. The probationer is responsible for the financial costs of EM services.

While a probationer is on CCP status, he/she is under house arrest. The offender is restricted to the residence with the only exceptions being employment, court-ordered activities, and life-threatening emergencies. All CCP probationers will be expected to maintain employment and work schedules are submitted to the officer weekly. The probationer must provide CCP officers with proof of employment. Those who are unemployed will be allowed time to search for work, but these search efforts must be carefully documented and given to the officer weekly. The court-ordered programs must be approved in advance and noted on the "Daily Activity Log" weekly. In the event of a life-threatening situation, the offender must try to contact the officer first, if he/she is unable to reach the officer then he/she must provide the officer with written verification within 24 hours.

Two types of EM devices are used in Dallas County. One is a continuous signaling device that consists of a transmitter attached to the probationer's ankle with a receiver installed in the home. The probationer is to remain within a 150 foot radius of the receiver or the host computer will indicate an absence. The system operates 24 hours a day, seven days a week. This system is used to indicate whether or not the offender is at home. The other type of system is the Luma Video Phone System. In this system, the Luma Video phone is placed in the probationer's home. The EM agency makes random calls to the home and asks the probationer to send a photo through the Luma system to verify his/her presence in the home. With both systems, the agency will notify the probationer's surveillance or casework officer in the event of a violation of house arrest.

There are two categories of violations, minor and major. Minor violations are discrepancies (absences) of 30 minutes or less. In these cases, the officer is not immediately notified. Major violations are discrepancies of 30 minutes or more. In these instances the officer is notified immediately; i.e., no later than the following business day. When the officer is notified, he/she will try to confirm the violation. If there is a violation the CCP Staff will contact the court of jurisdiction. After the EM probationer successfully completes the CCP, he/she will be transferred to an Intensive Service (ISP) caseload or to a Specialized Supervision Caseload (SSC). This transfer must be ordered by the court. Any changes in the duration of EM must be agreed upon and ordered by the court.

Many benefits seem to be inherent in the CCP. For instance, it costs less than jail or prison; the offender remains in the community with a job, thus supporting him/herself and, paying taxes. Many probationers pay part, if not all, of their own monitoring fees. In addition, the CCP helps to reduce the overcrowding of jails and prisons. Those offenders with communicable diseases will have reduced the cost of isolation and medical care that a jail or prison is required to pay. Furthermore, the CCP will also help avoid the damaging experience of a young offender going to jail or prison.

As of August 18, 1989, 75 probationers on CCP were being monitored. This number changes daily because probationers will either complete the program, abscond, be revoked, or commit a new offense and be in jail. The department has the capacity to handle 120 EM clients. In the month of December 1989, 23 offenders were hooked-up to the system. In January 1989 approximately 44 were hooked- up. In February, approximately 63 were hooked-up. And, in March, approximately 77 were hooked-up.

In interviews with Dallas County Adult Probation Department staff, several staff members indicated that the main problem with EM was that the equipment sometimes registered false violations. Specifically, because of technical problems with the equipment, the devices were recording violations of offenders leaving their residences when, in fact, they had not left. The also mentioned other minor problems, such as the clients complaining about "cabin fever," being "watched" 24 hours a day, and being awakened at odd hours of the night as a result of random phone verifications (Dallas County Adult Probation Department, 1989).

HARRIS COUNTY ADULT PROBATION DEPARTMENT

During the time of this study, Harris County had a population of 2,604,882. This figure included 661,038 males over 25 years of age; and, 72.0% of those had a high school diploma while 98,302 held college degrees. Houston is the largest city within Harris County. The county was 65.6% white, 18.1% African American, 14.1% Hispanic, 1.9% Asian and 0.3% American Indian. Only 13.4% of Harris County's population is classified as rural by the U.S. Bureau of the Census (U.S. Department of Commerce, 1983). The County had a 10.3% unemployment rate. In 1985, 213,322 serious crimes were reported to police and, 20,462 (9.6%) of these crimes involved violence (U.S. Department of Commerce, 1988). Like Dallas County, the majority of the Harris County probationary clients were from lower and middle socioeconomic classes. Occupations ranged from managerial types of employment to the chronically unemployed. The Harris County Adult Probation Department, just as the Dallas County Probation Department, utilizes EM through a contractual arrangement with a private vendor, Program Monitor, Inc. (PMI). The capacity of their EM program is 90 with an average caseload of 25-30 clients per officer (Harris County Adult Probation Department, 1989).

The Harris County Adult Probation Department utilizes EM to monitor regular and ISP offenders in their special programs division. Electronic monitoring is employed as a diversion from incarceration in jail in order to help reduce jail overcrowding. Their program has four criterion for placing offenders on EM:

1. The offender must have committed a felony offense.

2. The offender must be in custody at the time of placement.

3. The offender must have a telephone at time of placement.

4. The offender must remain on EM for 90 days.

In addition to the criteria described above, clients' eligibility for the program are conditioned upon:

1. A demonstration by the probationer of a lack of stability and self-discipline.

2. Evidence that the probationer has a social history containing unplanned and spontaneous acts with negative results.

3. Indications that probationers who are chemical abusers are being monitored thus restricting further opportunities for repeated chemical abuse.

4. Data that probationers who are convicted of sex offenses will need intensified supervision of their movement in the community.

3. Evidence that probationers with a history of violent or assaultive behavior are being monitored for the safety of the community.

Clients on EM are required to turn-in a schedule each week indicating the times when they were out of their residences. Legitimate client absences from a residence include: work, church, medical treatment, shopping, and court appointments. All other client out-of-residence activities must be presented in writing and approved by the probation officer. Clients must report to the probation office twice monthly and allow visits to their home once a month. Any reported violation is investigated the same day. Clients must follow all of the other stipulations of probation imposed, as well as those imposed as a result of being placed on EM (Patton, 1988).

HARRIS COUNTY BOARD OF PARDONS AND PAROLES

A control-strategy is also utilized by the Harris County Board of Pardons and Paroles. Control-strategy emphasizes supervision and restitution. The board also utilizes other ancillary programs, such as: Alcoholics Anonymous, Narcotics Anonymous, and Project Rio (an offender re-integration program), to help facilitate its efforts of supervision and restitution (Harris County Board of Pardons and Paroles, 1989).

The Harris County Board of Pardons and Paroles parole officer caseloads are specialized along several dimensions. Clients on EM constitute one such group of specialized caseloads. Six parole officers and one supervisor routinely supervise these offenders. Supervisors in the Harris County Board of Pardons and Paroles assign only parole officers who have experience and have expressed interest in EM to a specialized EM caseload.

Other specialized caseloads located in the board (e.g. sex offenders, drug offenders) occasionally employ electronic monitoring with some of their more problematic clients. The services in the specialized caseloads for sex offenders emphasizes rehabilitation over supervision. The sex offenders in this caseload are closely monitored and are required to have psychiatric treatment and/or mental health services, counseling, and various types of individual and group testing.

The Harris County Board of Pardons and Paroles has established the following parole releasee eligibility criteria for placement on EM:

1. The releasee must chronically fail to adjust to the requirements of the specialized caseload to which they are assigned.

2. The releasee must fit the following set of circumstances-
   a. The releasee was convicted of DWI where there was evidence of continuous alcohol abuse.
   b. The releasee was convicted of non-assaultive crimes and was unemployed for thirty days after completing Project Rio (an offender reintegration program).
   c. The releasee missed more than two consecutive appointments with their caseload officer.
   d. Be a releasee who has pending charges and has been released on bond or had current warrants against them withdrawn.
   e. A releasee who refuses to submit to urinalysis, or who submits two positive samples.
   f. A releasee who was placed on EM in lieu of a summons.
   g. A releasee who refuses needed treatment.

The Harris County Board of Pardons and Paroles requires a minimum of four face-to-face (offender-parole officer) contacts per month. Releasee are placed on one of two levels for the purpose of EM feedback from EM contractors. On level one, the officer is required to visit the offender if the reason for a EM signal interruption is not resolved by telephone. At level two, violations are reported the following day. Releasees are moved from level two to level one if there are two EM interruptions in the signal during one month. The releasee's progress in the program essentially determines the level at which he/she is dealt with during his/her time in the program.

Electronic monitored offender case conferences are held with a supervisor if a releasee fails to attend two scheduled counseling sessions in one month, fails to return home at a scheduled time, or leaves home at unapproved times on three or more occasions for more than thirty minutes. If the offender is continuously violating the conditions, an officer can request that additional special conditions be imposed, such as: letters of reprimand and case conferences with the supervisor; referral to specialized treatment; a summons hearing; referral to Bexar (San Antonio, Texas) County Parole Violator Facility; or a pre-revocation warrant request. A releasee is terminated from EM by: ether successfully completing the program by remaining on minimal supervision status for four months, or by being revoked for any cause.

The Harris County Board of Pardons and Paroles is also involved in a Pre-Parole Transfer Program (hereafter referred to as PPT). This program also uses EM. The PPT program is designed to place inmates in residences in the community in order to offer a humane, real-life situation that provides opportunities for self-improvement. The goal of this program is to assist inmates in developing good working attitudes, habits, and marketable skills as well as a lifestyle necessary to reintegrate successfully into society.

The operation of the PPT program requires coordination between community services, parole staff, the Texas State Department of Corrections (TDC), and the EM service provider or vendor. Community services staff of the TDC at Huntsville, Texas, screen all cases for EM eligibility, and the community resource officer at the PPT facility interviews and approves or disapproves the selection of inmates for admission into the program. The community service staff at Huntsville also contacts Program Monitor, Inc., and arranges for the inmate to be attached to the EM devices prior to his/her release. The emphasis of the PPT/EM program is on control and reintegration primarily because the clients are still considered to be in the custody of the TDC. His/her freedom is restricted to verified employment, verified job search or job readiness programs, and other absences approved in advance by the PPT/EM officer. The PPT/EM officer makes six face-to-face visits each month with every inmate, and makes a visit a week to their residences.

If PMI reports a violation, the officer must, within one hour, attempt to verify the escape. If the officer cannot reach the inmate by telephone, then he/she must call local law enforcement authorities in order to make arrangements for them to accompany the officer to the residence. The officer must make visual verification of the inmate's absence. If the client is not there, the officer must notify the TDC of an escape.

The inmates in the PPT program must complete 30 days of intensive counseling and orientation in an approved community correctional facility prior to transfer. If the inmate is eligible for release to a halfway house, the officer must then provide a security package which consists of 3" x 5" photograph of the inmate; the inmate's correspondence and visiting list; his/her record summary; a record of the inmate's prior residences and employment; and any other pertinent information in the inmate's file.

When screening private residences certain conditions are followed. The residence must comply with certain specific criteria which include:

1. A stable family of some duration; no ex-offenders in the residence.

2. Liquor not sold or distributed on the premises.

3. Illegal drugs not known to have been consumed, sold, or possessed on the premises.

4. Other illegal activities are not know to have occurred in the residence.

5. No adverse family situations present.

6. Adequate transportation available, and/or telephone communication is easily accessible.

The PPT/EM officer is required to visit the inmate six times per month; once a week at the residence, and also make contacts with the client's employer when necessary.

A progress report is conducted after 30 days of supervision and 30 days prior to the inmate's parole date. If an inmate tries to escape, the officer: verifies the facts of the escape; notifies the administrator of the PPT by phone; files a complaint with the local justice of the peace; obtains a warrant; delivers it to the local law enforcement office; and, advises the administrator of the warrant number, issuing authority, precinct number and county. If an inmate is arrested locally, the officer contacts the administrator, completes an incident report and delivers the report to the inmate 24 hours prior to the hearing. A hearing is conducted unless waived by the inmate.

PROBATION AND PAROLE OFFICERS' SATISFACTION WITH THE MONITORING

In order to obtain information about the probation and parole officers' satisfaction with electronic monitoring as it was used in their agencies, the researchers developed a "private vendor satisfaction survey questionnaire" in order to examine the levels of their satisfaction with EM in general and with EM as provided to their department by a private vendor previously discussed, PMI. A sample of 30 probation and/or parole officers completed the questionnaire. All of these officers were working with electronically monitored offenders in either Dallas or Harris counties.

The survey instrument consisted of a 25-item questionnaire which included forced choice questions concerning the effectiveness of EM, PMI, the equipment, as well as open-ended items that solicited specific suggestions in re to improving the system. The majority of the respondents were parole officers (80%). Fifty-seven percent of the parole officers were from Dallas County and 23% were from Harris County. The remaining 20% of the respondents were probation officers from both counties. Sixty-seven percent of the probation officers were from Dallas County and 33% were from Harris County.

Questions 1 and 2 were directed at determining how the officers rated EM in comparison to regular probation/parole and intensive supervision. More than two-thirds (66.7%) of the total sample of officers rated EM as more effective than regular probation/parole, while the remaining 33.3% of them rated it as less effective or about as effective as regular probation/parole. Approximately seventy-two (72.4%) of the officers also rated EM as more effective than intensive supervision, whereas the remaining 27.6% of the officers felt it was less effective or about as effective as intensive supervision. Thus, probation/parole officers seem to view the effectiveness of EM as approximately the same for both regular probationers/parolees and intensively supervised offenders (72.4% and 66.7% respectively).

The total sample of officers was subsequently divided into several different types of groups in order to further analyze the responses to Questions 1 and 2, as well as to enhance the scientific quality of the survey. These analyses sought to determine if any significant differences existed in the ratings by officers across agencies and regions. A t=test was used to measure the statistical significance of differences between the mean responses. No significant difference was found to exist between the parole officers located in Dallas and Harris counties regarding their ratings of the effectiveness of EM versus regular parole (T=1.2; P=0.24) or intensive supervision (T=0.80;P=0.43). However, the extremely small size of the samples of Dallas and Harris county probation officers makes the use of this particular type of statistical analysis problematic. Therefore, any inferences that are drawn from these data should be considered as preliminary. However, visual inspection of the data suggest a similar distribution of responses among probation officers.

By subdividing the total sample into two other groupings: (1) probation officers; and, (2) parole officers, and again employing a t-test for statistical significance, no significant statistical difference was found to exist at the .05 level between probation officers and parole officers concerning their ratings regarding the question of whether or not EM was more or less effective than intensive supervision (T=1.90; P=.068). However, probation officers were found to more often rate EM as more effective than regular community supervision than were parole officers (T=3.14; P=.004). One possible explanation for this significant difference in attitudes may be related to the fact that restricted confinement (confinement to their residences as part of EM) is novel to probationers in general. It may, therefore, produce a more apparent impact on this population than it does on parolees who have experienced confinement in prison prior to confinement as part of EM.

Questions 3 through 6 inquired about the impact of EM on the probation/parole officers' performance of their job roles. Of the total sample of officers completing the questionnaire, 80.0% stated that EM made their jobs harder. Two specific reasons for this were offered by respondents: (1) EM increases the number of revocations, resulting in more "paperwork" for them; and, (2) the logistical demands of EM require officers to spend more time in direct contact with clients. More than fifty-six percent (56.7%) of the officers stated that, due to EM, there was less time to conduct other duties, while the others 43.3%, indicated that EM resulted in about the same amount of time or an increase in the amount of time available for other duties.

Questions 7 and 8 addressed the benefits of EM for offenders and their families. The majority of the officers sampled (76.7%), indicated that EM was beneficial to their clients. However, only 30% of them felt that EM was beneficial to the families of EM clients. Interpretations of these beliefs are difficult to make, but it seems reasonable to suggest that officers fear that offenders will vent the frustrations produced by home confinement and behave more aggressively at home.

Questions 9 through 12 dealt with the monitoring equipment itself. Of all the officers in the sample, 23.4% had clients who had experience with both continuous and random EM systems. One-third (33.3%) of the officers had clients who had only been on continuous monitoring, and 43.3% had clients whose exposure was solely to random monitoring. Over forty-six percent (46.7%) of the officers indicated that the equipment was dependable, however, the majority (53.3%), claimed that the equipment was unreliable. Two of the specific problems identified by the officers who had indicated that the equipment was unreliable were: (1) ankle straps broke, causing the equipment to cease working; and, (2) any accidental tampering with the equipment caused interference with the telephone, which in turn caused violations to be reported when no violations had in fact occurred. As far as equipment maintenance was concerned, 53.3% indicated that the equipment was adequately maintained, while 46.7% thought the equipment was poorly maintained.

Questions 13 through 16 queried the attentiveness of PMI to the needs of officers and their clients. Their views of PMI's attentiveness to their needs were virtually identical with their views of PMI's attentiveness to the needs of their clients. Half of the officers in the sample thought PMI was attentive to their needs as well as to the needs of their clients, while the other half of the sample disagreed, claiming that PMI was inattentive to both their needs and to those of their clients. Suggestions made by those officers who felt PMI was inattentive to their needs included: (1) more follow-ups on equipment repairs and hook=ups; (2) more attention to the computer printouts with regard to violations; and, (3) more attention to the accuracy of violation reports. Suggestions made by those officers who viewed PMI as inattentive to the needs of their clients included: (1) pay more attention to which type of EM system (continuous or random) the client is assigned; (2) reduce unnecessary telephone calls to randomly monitor clients; and, (3) be neither inconsiderate nor overly cordial to officers and clients.

Questions 17 through 19 were directed at ascertaining the information provided to the officers by PMI about the clients. Of those surveyed 63.3% claimed PMI provided most of the information needed by them, while 36.7% claimed they did not. More than seventy percent (74.1%) indicated that the neglected information was important, whereas 25.9% viewed this information as relatively unimportant.

Questions 20 and 21 dealt with PMI's ability to promptly connect and disconnect clients to EM equipment when requested. More than fifty-six percent (56.7%) indicated that PMI usually honored their requests in a timely fashion, while the remaining 43.3% felt they did not. The time delays in hooking-up clients to the EM equipment after PMI received the request varied from 4 to 8 days in most cases.

The last four questions in the survey, Questions 22 through 25, solicited overall ratings of PMI and the electronic monitoring program. Of all the officers in the sample, 56.7% claimed that overall PMI provided poor or extremely poor service, while the remainder (43.3%) disagreed and claimed that PMI provided adequate to extremely good service. Again, the total sample of officers was subsequently divided into several different types of groups in order to further analyze the results concerning the officers ratings of PMI's service. This was done to determine if any significant differences existed in the ratings by officers from within and across agencies regarding these ratings, and to strengthen the inferences that one might draw from the study. One grouping consisted of the four geographical locations. The t-test results indicated a significant difference at the 0.05 level of significance between the parole officers located in Dallas and Harris counties regarding their ratings of PMI' service (t=2.0; p=0.05). Dallas County parole officers were found to have rated PMI's services higher than did Harris County parole officers. Here again, the extremely small sample size of the Dallas and Harris county probation officers places restrictions upon the nature and type of generalizations that one can draw from the analysis of these data.

The sample was next subdivided to test for differences between probation and parole officers. The results of the t-test indicated no statistically significant difference between probation officers and parole officers concerning their ratings of PMI's service (t=0.00;p=1.00).

When asked what they would prefer to have their department/office do concerning the provision of EM services, 13.3% indicated that they would prefer to have PMI continue to provide EM services under the current arrangements, another 13.3% indicated that they would prefer to continue having PMI provide EM services, but would modify the contractual arrange-ment with PMI, 30.0% indicated that they would prefer switching to another private vendor for the provision of EM services, and the remaining 43.3% indicated that they would prefer to have their own department/office directly provide this service.

The last question (Question 25) inquired as to whether officers would prefer to continue utilizing EM. Approximately forty three   percent (43.3%) indicated that they would strongly insist that EM be continued; 20.0% indicated that they would insist that EM be continued; 26.7% indicated that they had no preference regarding continuing EM or doing away with it; 6.7% indicated that they would insist on getting rid of EM; and the remaining 3.3% indicated that they would strongly insist on getting rid of EM. Thus, at least for this sample, EM appears to be fairly popular among probation/parole officers despite the perceived increase in workload and the logistical problems encountered with the contractor.

SUMMARY AND CONCLUSIONS

This Chapter contains original material derived from a study which was conducted in order to measure the effect of private sector electronically monitored home confinement on adult probationers and parolees and the levels of staff satisfaction with electronic monitoring (Holman, Quinn, Black, & Enos, 1990). Descriptions of EM programs are included from: The Dallas County (Texas) Adult Probation Department; the Harris County (Texas) Adult Probation Department; and, the Harris County (Texas) Board of Pardons and Paroles. This Chapter also contains specific descriptions of the types of clients served by these three programs, details concerning the eligibility criteria for enrollment in the programs, and specifics concerning the operation and technical details of these programs. Quantitative data regarding satisfaction with EM provided by a private vendor was derived from a study of the staff at the Dallas County Adult Probation Department and from the staff at the Harris County Adult Probation Department.

The Dallas County Adult Probation Department exercises a control-strategy probationary method. This approach emphasizes supervision and restitution rather than personal adjustment and rehabilitation. This department does, however, offer both group and individual counseling and makes use of client referrals to various social service treatment agencies for remediation of certain problems experienced by the offenders assigned to their department. This department also uses the Community Control Program which is an option for diversion from incarceration. Electronic monitoring is employed in conjunction with this program.

In Harris County EM is used as a diversion from jail in order to reduce jail overcrowding. The Harris County Board of Pardons and Paroles also uses a control-strategy. In both of the Houston programs the emphasis is, again, on supervision and restitution. As with Dallas County, both Houston departments make a great deal of use of client referrals to social services treatment programs; especially, substance abuse programs.

In addition, the Board of Pardons and Paroles emphasizes special caseload programs structured along the lines of types of offenders, such as: sex offenders, drug offenders, offenders with communicable diseases. In these programs, rehabilitation is emphasized. Electronic monitoring is sometimes used with these populations and, especially, with their more difficult clients.

In conclusion, across the departments studied, the writers noted that one of the most important findings was that most of the probation and parole officers seemed to view the effectiveness of EM as approximately the same for both regular probationers/parolees and for intensively supervised offenders. And, furthermore, that a majority of these officers (43.3%) wanted to continue the use of EM in their departments while only 6.7% wanted its use discontinued.

In the opinion of the writers, continued research studies, such as the one conducted by the writers, need to be implemented so that a database base may be developed that over time will allow for scientific inferences to be drawn concerning the use and effectiveness of this new and important technology in the criminal justice field.

REFERENCES

Dallas County Adult Probation Department. (1987). *Community control program operations manual.* Dallas: Dallas County Adult Probation Department.

Dallas County Adult Probation Department. (1989). *Dallas county community services.* Dallas: Dallas County Adult Probation Department.

Dallas County Adult Probation Department. (personal communication, 1989).

Harris County (Houston, Texas) Adult Probation Department. (personal communication, 1989).

Harris County Board of Pardons and Paroles. (1989). *Specialized caseload procedural manual.* Houston: Harris County Board of Pardons and Paroles.

Harris County (Houston, Texas) Board of Pardons and Paroles. (personal communication, 1989).

Holman, J. E., Quinn, J.F., Black, C.M., & Enos, R. (1990). *A study of the effects of private sector electronically monitored home confinement on adult probationers and parolees.* Denton, TX: University of North Texas, Institute of Criminal Justice.

Patton, S. L. (1988). *Jail diversion - An electronic monitoring program.* Houston: Harris County Adult Probation Department.

U. S. Department of Commerce. (1983). *General social and economic characteristics.* Washington, DC: U.S. Department of Commerce.

U. S. Department of Commerce. (1988). *City and county data book.* Washington, DC: U.S. Department of Commerce.

A STUDY OF THE EFFECTS OF ELECTRONICALLY MONITORED HOME CONFINEMENT ON OFFENDERS AND THEIR HOME ENVIRONMENTS

This Chapter contains a description of a study which was conducted by the writers in order to evaluate the effects of electronically monitored (EM) home confinement on felony offenders and their family environments (members and significant others). The Chapter deals specifically with the research methodology, the survey instruments used in the study to gather the data, and describes, in detail, the socio-demographic and criminologic characteristics of the parolees and probationers who were the subjects of the study.

Electronic monitoring of offenders is essentially so new that it is still in its infancy and literally has no history. The technology is at present experiencing continual growth and development. This is particularly true with respect to the increased computerization of the systems. With something as new as EM, it is perhaps unrealistic at this time to expect the organizations experimenting with the development and implementation of EM in criminal justice settings to be at little more than rudimentary stages of development of the technology. That is to say, the intra-organizational and inter-organizational relationships of the agencies involved in the use of EM have until now faced a plethora of new and unknown problems. These sorts of contingencies are likely to color the immediate future of EM. The analogy that seems most appropriate here is that of EM to open heart by-pass surgery. When open heart by-pass surgery first appeared it was developed and implemented by a few physicians who were confronting the unknown. Today, open heart by-pass surgery is viewed as somewhat common-place. In essence, EM is at the very beginning of its development and many problems continue to present themselves for resolution to the pioneers who are using it as a form of intermediate sanctioning.

Pioneers, such as Program Monitor, Inc., need to be recognized for their role in its development. This is not to say that such pioneers and the organizations that they represent should be exempt from criticism. Instead, such criticism needs to be placed in a proper context. Evaluators must remain salient of the fact that the work of pioneer organizations in the field created the base from which others can build. Thus, it is the hope of the writers that the readers of this Chapter and the Chapter that follows will view the results of the study, and the interpretations of the data derived from the study, in the spirit in which they are offered, that is to say, as an attempt to enhance our knowledge of EM, and which, in turn, should benefit all criminal justice professionals involved with the technology. As with any innovation, errors of judgment, especially in the area of relative priorities, are both inevitable and instructive. Indeed, these errors contribute to both our comprehension of this new area of criminal justice practice and to the sort of development by which innovations eventually become standardized methods.

METHODOLOGY

Several different methodological approaches were used in this study. One approach consisted of the psychometric testing of EM probationers and parolees, and the collection of socio-demographic information directly from EM probationers and parolees themselves. A second approach involved the collection of information directly from significant others living with offenders on EM. A third approach utilized the collection of information directly obtained through the use of a questionnaire from probation departments, parole offices, and the private EM vendor involved with EM in the jurisdictions included in this study. A fourth approach employed interviewing probation and parolee department staff. A fifth, and final approach, consisted of observations made on behalf of the researchers involved in this study. Although each of the methodological approaches used in this study will be discussed separately in the sections that follow, a real strength of employing multiple methods of observations and multiple predictors is that it allows for an empirical synthesis of various observations on a single phenomenon (Rogers, 1981; Denzen, 1989).

All subjects included in this study were adults on probation or parole for felony offenses who resided in either Dallas, Denton, or Harris counties within Texas. Participation was voluntary with a signed consent form allowing information to be used in the final report about the study and for publication. All of the data used in this study was collected in calendar year 1989, with the exception of the pretests conducted in Denton County which were collected in December of 1988. While the primary interest of the researchers was on the effects of EM on these offenders, the study also employed control groups of probationers and parolees who were not on EM. The use of such control groups allowed for a four-group, pretest/posttest, pre-experimental, research design to be conducted (Campbell & Stanley, 1963). The four groups used in this approach were: (1) EM probationers; (2) EM parolees; (3) non-EM probationers; and (4) non-EM parolees.

Dallas and Harris counties were chosen for their relatively large population of EM offenders, while Denton County was utilized in order to include some non-urban offenders. The researchers met with representatives of each of the agencies involved in the study to introduce the instruments being used and establish a logistical format for the administration of these instruments.

Pretest and posttest procedures were identical within individual probation departments and parole offices, however, they were different across departments and offices. Probationers were examined at the local offices to which they were required to report on a monthly basis. The research was conducted on normal reporting days for all probationers included in the study.

Probationers were administered the instruments at the various probation offices by the research staff conducting this study, whereas parolees were administered the same devices at their residences by their parole officers. While this difference in test administration procedures is problematic in that the stimuli associated with the study's instrumentation varies according to whether the subject was on probation or parole, it also provided several advantages. Group testing of probationers was time-efficient and the coordination of testing with routine reporting at the probation office resulted in minimal inconvenience to the subjects. The joint effect of this approach was to maximize the number of completed instruments.

The administration of these study instruments by parole officers was an innovation on the original study design requested by their respective departments. Parolees did not regularly report to any central location as did probationers. Because of their more serious crimes and/or more extensive criminal histories, as well as their recent release from incarceration, parolees tend to live in the least desirable areas of the cities under study and are generally less receptive to socio-scientific examination than are probationers. This seemed to be the best method of obtaining the data in order to assure researcher safety as well as to maximize the number of completed responses.

Logistics required that parolees be administered the research devices by their respective parole officers during routine visits to their homes. This strategy allowed for a much larger number of offenders to be involved in the study thus drastically reducing the cost of administering the testing devices to parolees. The parole officers involved were, of course, first instructed in the proper administration of the instruments and the intent of the study. Similar procedures were followed in both parole offices despite some minor discrepancies in their internal organizational structure.

The method of data collection for parolees also necessitated modifying the Family Environment Scales (FES) questionnaires for use with this sub-sample of parolees. The 90 statement FES was reduced to two FES subscales (18 true/false questions in order to gather data on the conflict and control dimensions of the instrument). The Beck Depression Inventory (BDI) was not altered in any way.

The initial goal of the study was to test a total of 200 offenders and their significant others residing in their households (co-residents). This goal was surpassed in that data were collected on 261 offenders. The initial goal was modified to include the control groups which greatly strengthens the study, and to reduce the significant others in the study, which to a lesser extent, weakens the study. The addition of the control groups is somewhat self-evident in that they allow for comparisons to be made that otherwise could not be made. The modification of the initial goal regarding offenders' significant others residing in their households had to be made essentially for two reasons: (1) the relatively large number of offenders living alone, thus the absence of a significant other to be involved in the study; and (2) the logistics of administering testing devices to significant others. Very early in the study attempts were made, but subsequently discontinued, to either have the significant others accompany their respective probationer or parole when they reported, or to return self-administered testing devices with the probationers or parolees, or to return them by mail.

ASSESSMENT INSTRUMENTS

The main testing instruments used were the Beck Depression Inventory and the Family Environment Scale. The use of EM was evaluated by employing the BDI and the FES in order to determine if the program was successful in facilitating offender mental health status and integration (in the case of probation) or reintegration (in the case of parole) into a law-abiding family and community.

A pretest/posttest design was used with an intervening period of approximately two and one-half months for each subject. The elapsed time period chosen between pretests and posttests was based on the recommendations of the technical staff of the electronic monitoring vendor, Program Monitor, Inc.(PMI), who stated that the average time per offender on EM was approximately three months.

SOCIO-DEMOGRAPHIC QUESTIONNAIRE

Each offender completed a Client Demographic Information Form, which was kept in his/her confidential file, and was assigned an identification number. This form was used to identify and collect the following information: (1) the name of the offender; (2) the agency having jurisdiction over the offender; (3) the county having jurisdiction; (4) the specific type of supervision program; (5) general offender socio-demographic characteristics; and, (6) an abbreviated criminal history of the offender. This form was also used to record test scores and any violations which may have occurred while on the monitoring program.

BECK DEPRESSION INVENTORY

The psychological assessment instrument used was the Beck Depression Inventory. Depression is manifested in many ways and is defined on a continuum from mild transitory affects of feeling low to a severe psychotic depressive state. The BDI was used here to specifically measure dysphoria, as a symptom of depression, rather than depression as a nosologic disorder per se (Beck, 1967; Lehmann, 1959; Kendall, Hollon, Beck, Hammen, & Ingram, 1987). It is estimated that the prevalence of psychological disorders is much higher for correctional populations than it is for the general population. For example, Harper and Barry (1979) suggest that psychological disorders may involve as many as one-half of all male prisoners.

Various correctional populations (i.e., probationers, prisoners, and parolees) are subjected to major psychological stresses and transitions (Masuda, Cutler, Hein, & Holmes, 1978). Many of the stressors that correctional populations are exposed to have been related to the severity of depression, as well as to the severity of various forms of psychopathology. Thus, the utilization of psychological assessment devices, such as the BDI, for identifying dysphoria among correctional populations, such as those included in this study, is an important part of assessing the effect of the correctional setting, in this case EM, on the offender as a component of the correctional rehabilitative process (Scott, Hannum, & Ghrist, 1982).

Reynolds and Gould (1981) employed both the standard and abridged BDI in their study of individuals involved in a methadone maintenance drug rehabilitation program and found both versions of the instrument to be reliable and valid measures for the assessment of depression. In another rehabilitation setting, Scott, Hannum, and Ghrist, (1982) employed the abridged BDI in their assessment of depression among newly admitted inmates to a women's reformatory, and reported that it to be also reliable as a brief reactive depression screening instrument.

The BDI was developed as a method for identifying and measuring depression (Beck, Ward, Mendelson, Mock, & Erbaugh, (1961). However, it is recommended that the BDI not be used for nosological classification of depression without the collaboration of structured clinical interviews (Kendall, Hollon, Beck, Hammen, & Ingram, 1987). Thus, the BDI is a 21 item test which reflects physiological, cognitive, and motivational manifestations of depressive symptomatology such as dysphoria (Tanaka & Huba, 1984). It requires the subject to choose from a set of numbered statements as to how he/she is feeling at the moment. The recommended BDI range of scores 0 to 9 was used to identify normal (non-dysphoric) subjects, and subjects with scores of 10 and above were viewed as suffering from one or more of the levels of dysphoria (Kendall, Hollon, Beck, Hammen, & Ingram, 1987).

The BDI was chosen as the test instrument because the BDI is among the most frequently used instruments for assessing depression in psychiatrically diagnosed patients and for detecting depression in normal populations (Piotrowski, Sherry, & Keller, 1985). Despite the uncomplicated nature of the BDI questionnaire, the BDI compares favorably with other well-researched instruments measuring depression, such as the Hamilton Psychiatric Rating Scale for Depression, Zung Self-Reported Depression Scale, MMPI Depression Scale, and the Multiple Affect Adjective Checklist Depression Scale. Studies have also indicated that the BDI demographic correlates of sex, age, and education for adults is equivocal. However, the relationship of the BDI to race indicates that African Americans tend to score higher than whites (Beck, Steer, & Garbin, 1988).

The BDI is relatively simple to administer. Scoring is based on an additive scale ranging from zero to sixty-three (0-63). This is used as a general indicator of the degree of dysphoria experienced by the subject. This instrument is not so precisely calibrated as to divide subjects into homogeneous groups. Rather, BDI scores are a continuous variable and cut-off points are somewhat arbitrary though nonetheless useful in grouping and interpreting data (Beck, 1967). Traditionally, BDI results are categorized in the following manner:

Score	Interpretation
0 - 9	Normal Range
10 - 15	Mild Dysphoria
16 - 19	Mild-Moderate Dysphoria
20 - 29	Moderate-Severe Dysphoria
30 - 63	Severe Dysphoria

FAMILY ENVIRONMENT SCALE

The Family Environment Scale (FES) measures perceptions of the conjugal or nuclear family, and was used in this study to assess whether the family environments improved, worsened, or remained the same as a result of EM. The FES is a test consisting of 90 true or false statements relating to the subject's perception of his/her family (Moos, & Moos, 1986). It is used to assess the subjects' perceptions of their familial environment and is equally applicable to offenders and their family members. Data were organized to allow comparisons of offenders' perceptions with those of their spouses as well as to measure changes in both over time.

The FES is a relatively simple test and can be administered and scored with minimal instruction. The test is divided into three dimensions which are measured by ten sub-scales. The first dimension, Relationship, is measured by the cohesiveness, expressiveness, and conflict scales. The next dimension of Personal Growth (goal orientation) is measured by the independence, achievement orientation, intellectual-cultural orientation, active-recreational orientation, and moral-religious emphasis scales. The third and last dimension on the FES is System Maintenance. This item is measured in terms of the organization and control scales. Each of these areas, when scored, presents an indication of the perceived family environment based on the clients' answers to the true/false statements.

The 90 items for the FES were originally determined from an early version administered to over one thousand individuals in 285 families, representing church groups, high school parent groups, African American and Hispanic groups, as well as a disturbed clinical group (Dreyer, 1978). Normative data were collected from 1,125 representative families and 500 distressed families. Distressed families were contacted through a family clinic, and probation and parole departments. Additional subjects were from families of alcohol abusers, psychiatric patients, and families with troubled adolescents. Other psychometric criteria for selection of items were: an overall true/false response rate for each item close to 50-50, items correlated more highly with their own sub-scales than with any other, and each of the sub-scales had an approximately equal number of items that scored true and that scored false (Lambert, 1985).

The final distributions of six of the sub-scales are close to a 50-50 split (mean ranges around 5.5). Only the mean for conflict is low at 3.3. The internal consistency measures for the ten sub-scales range from .61 to .78. The eight-week test-retest reliability coefficients ranged from .68 to .86, and twelve month stabilities ranged from .52 to .89. After controlling for socioeconomic factors, age, and education, distressed families were found to score lower on cohesion, expressiveness, independence, and intellectual and recreational orientation, and higher on conflict and control than the "normal" families in these samples (Moos, 1986).

There is extensive support for the construct validity of the FES sub-scales. Many other inventories, tests, and assessments of the family environment support the validity of the FES sub-scales. Moos (1986) found that religious participation is related to the FES sub-scale of moral-religious emphasis (average r=0.62 for an alcoholic and a community sample); family activities are related to the FES sub-scale of recreational orientation (r=0.39); and family arguments are related to the FES sub-scale of conflict (r=0.49). Moos (1985) also reported that families with extensive social network resources scored higher on the FES sub-scales of intellectual/cultural and active/recreational orientation. Assessments of psychiatric outpatients' home environments by professional staff correlated significantly with the individual family member's reports of cohesion, expressiveness, conflict, and religious emphasis (Moos, 1985).

Druckman (1979), in predicting attrition from treatment programs, found that families who completed treatment had higher pretest scores on the intellectual/cultural FES sub-scale. This could indicate that these individuals are more self-reflective, and at the same time, are more aware of the external world. Druckman also found that recidivist families were extremely cohesive. He felt that this may be a dysfunctional factor in these families.

Numerous studies have showed significant changes in pretest/posttest scores for individuals who have gone through crisis intervention and treatment. For example: A group of families was assessed using the FES before, immediately after, and two months after an intensive family therapy program. Significantly increased scores were recorded for cohesion, expressiveness, and independence immediately after the workshop, and additional increases in scores were recorded after two months. A matched, untreated group showed no score change on the FES sub-scales (Bader, 1982).   Garrison and Weber (1981),   and Campbell (1983), reported reduced family conflict after these families completed a crisis intervention program. The literature is abundant with individual interventions that have led to changes in the family environment as assessed and measured through the FES sub-scales.

DESCRIPTION OF THE SUBJECTS BY GEOGRAPHICAL JURISDICTION

Demographic descriptions of the probationers and parolees in this study will now be presented.

DEMOGRAPHIC DESCRIPTION OF THE DALLAS COUNTY PROBA-TIONERS

Pretests for Dallas County probationers were conducted in the months of December 1988, January 1989 and the beginning of February 1989. A total of 48 probationers completed the pretests. Posttesting began in March of 1989 with the majority of the tests completed in May. A few were completed as late as October, 1989. Of the probationers involved in this study, three were taken off probation, seven were revoked, two absconded, two were in jail, and one was in a drug treatment facility before or during posttesting. The rest of the probationers completed the posttests, a total of 33.

There were 27 EM probationers in Dallas County that participated in this study. The majority of these offenders (59.3%) ranged from 22 to 35 years of age, and there were more white offenders (63%) than nonwhite offenders (37%). Male offenders were overrepresented with 85.2%. The majority of these offenders were single (55.6%) and had at least 12 years of education (44.5%). The offenses of the offenders on EM ranged from substance abuse crimes, which was the highest (59.3%), to property crimes (22.2%), to violent crimes (14.8%), to crimes against a person (3.7%). Most of the offenders on EM stated that they lived with 3 or 4 people (29.6% each). The majority of the offenders lived with two adults (55.6%) and/or four+ children (51.9%). Most of these offenders (63%) reported having good family relationships.

Concerning drug and/or alcohol abuse prior to arrest, 22.2% indicated no abuse, 7.4% social drinking, 22.2% social use of drugs, and only 3.7% social use of both alcohol and drugs. Of those claiming alcohol and/or drugs as serious problems, 3.7% claimed alcohol, 29.6% claimed drugs, and 11.2% reported both as serious problems. For the majority of the probationers their current alcohol and/or drug abuse usage patterns have drastically changed. By way of illustration, 92.6% reported that they are abstaining from both alcohol and drugs.

Most of this group of probationers had full time employment (59.3%) and worked at unskilled jobs (40%). Of the offenders who were married, the majority of their spouses were unemployed (84.6%). The spouses who did work held jobs that were unskilled (25%) or semiskilled (37.5%).

There were 21 non-EM probationers in Dallas County that participated in this study. The majority of these offenders (47.6%) ranged from 22 to 35 years of age, and there were more nonwhite offenders (52.4%) than white offenders (47.6%). Male offenders were over represented with 71.4%. The majority of these offenders were single (71.4%) and had some college education (38.1%). The offenses of the offenders ranged from property crimes, which was the highest (47.6%), to substance abuse crimes (28.6%), to crimes against a person (14.3%), to violent crimes (9.5%). Most of the offenders stated that they lived with 4 people (28.6). The majority of the offenders lived with two adults (42.9%) and/or four+ children (57.1%). Most of these offenders (61.9%) stated that they had good relationships with their families.

Regarding drug and/or alcohol abuse prior to arrest, 42.8% indicated no abuse, 4.8% social drinking, and 14.3% social use of drugs. Of those claiming alcohol and/or drugs as serious problems, 19% claimed alcohol, 14.3% claimed drugs, and 4.8% reported both as serious problems in their lives. For the majority of the probationers their current alcohol and/or drug abuse usage patterns had drastically changed. Approximately 95.2% reported that they were abstaining from both alcohol and drugs.

Most of this group of probationer had full time employment (66.7%) and worked at semiskilled jobs (31.2%). Of the married offenders, the majority had spouses who were unemployed. The spouses who did work held jobs that were of a clerical nature (50%).

DEMOGRAPHIC DESCRIPTION OF THE DENTON COUNTY PROBATIONERS

The initial Denton County Adult Probation Department posttests began approximately two months after the first pretests were conducted there. Posttests were ultimately completed on twenty-six (26) of the thirty-one offenders. Two significant others were given a pretest. All posttests were completed by March, 1989, except for one of the offenders and his significant other who were retested at a later date due to an illness that required hospitalization. The researchers were unable to obtain posttest scores on five subjects because: three offenders had been taken off probation before posttesting began, one was transferred to the Dallas Adult Probation Department, and the final probationer could not be located.

There were 30 non-EM probationers in Denton County who participated in this study. The majority of these offenders (46.7%) ranged from 22 to 35 years of age, and there were more white offenders (93.3%) than nonwhite offenders (6.7%). Male offenders were over represented with 83.3%. The majority of these offenders were single (56.7%) and had at least 12 years of education (43.4%). The offenses of the offenders ranged from property crimes, which was the highest (40%), to substance abuse crimes (36.7%), to violent crimes (13.3%), to crimes against a person (10%). Most of the offenders stated that they lived with four people (33.3%). The majority of the offenders lived with two adults (43.3%) and/or four+ children (56.7%). Most of these offenders (43.3%) stated that they had good relationships with their families.

In reference to drug and/or alcohol abuse prior to arrest, 17.2% indicated no abuse, 7% social drinking, 13.8% social use of drugs, and only 3.4% social use of both alcohol and drugs. Of those claiming alcohol and/or drugs as serious problems, 10.3% claimed alcohol, 27.6% claimed drugs, and 20.7% reported both as serious problems. For the majority of the probationers their current alcohol and/or drug abuse usage patterns had drastically changed. Finally, 96.6% reported that they were abstaining from both alcohol and drugs.

Most of this group of probationers had full time employment (53.3%) and worked at unskilled jobs (52%). Of the offenders who were married, the majority of their spouses were unemployed (75%). The spouses who did work held jobs that were unskilled (80%).

DEMOGRAPHIC DESCRIPTION OF THE HARRIS COUNTY PROBATIONERS

Pretesting of Harris County probationers took place during the end of January, the beginning of February, and in the beginning of April of 1989. A total of 67 probationers took the pretest. The majority of the posttests were completed in April of 1989 with the last posttest finished in October of 1989. Of those probationers who completed the pretest, 48 completed the posttest. A total of nineteen posttests were unable to be obtained for various reasons, including: one probationer was taken off probation before posttesting began; two probationers were at a restitution center; one was placed on regular probation and transferred to another office; two offenders absconded; four were in jail, and three had their probation revoked at the time of posttesting. One of the probationers only finished half of the test. The researchers were unable to locate the last five probationers.

There were 66 EM probationers in Harris County that participated in this study. The majority of these offenders (53%) ranged from 22 to 35 years of age, and there were more nonwhite offenders (56.1%) than white offenders (43.9%). Male offenders were over represented with 81.2%. The majority of these offenders were single (56%) and had at least 12 years of education (43.9%). The offenses of the offenders on EM ranged from substance abuse crimes, which was the highest (53%), to property crimes (36.4%), to violent crimes (6.1%), to crimes against a person (4.5%). Most of the offenders on EM stated that they lived with three people (24.6%). The majority of the offenders lived with two adults (53%) and/or four+ children (51.5%). Most of these offenders (47%) stated that they had good relationships with their families.

In so far as drug and/or alcohol abuse prior to arrest is concerned, 37.9% indicated no abuse, 9.1% social drinking, 12.1% social use of drugs, and 13.6% social use of both alcohol and drugs. Of those claiming alcohol and/or drugs as serious problems, 7.6% claimed alcohol, 7.6% claimed drugs, and 12.1% reported both as serious problems. For the majority of the probationers their current alcohol and/or drug abuse usage patterns have drastically changed. Also, 91% reported that they were abstaining from both alcohol and drugs.

Most of this group of probationers had full time employment (53%) and worked at manual jobs (27.5%). Of the offenders who were married, the majority of their spouses were unemployed (78.9%). The spouses who did work held jobs that were clerical in nature (28.6%).

DEMOGRAPHIC DESCRIPTION OF THE DALLAS COUNTY PAROLEES

Subjects for this study were selected exclusively from the EM specialized unit of this office. In addition to the parole officers administering the study instruments to clients on EM, they were also responsible for administering the study instruments to other parolees who had not been recommended for EM, and who subsequently made up one of the control groups used in this study. Those who were not placed on EM were usually those who refused to participate or who lived with a non-offender who refused to allow the monitoring equipment to be set up in their homes. This control group is thus wholly equivalent to the treatment group except for their (or their family's) attitudes toward EM.

The pretests (a total of 73) were administered during the month of April, 1989. The posttesting began in August of 1989 with only 21 parolees completing the test. A total of 19 parolees were unavailable for posttesting because three were in jail, one refused to take the test, five absconded, four were discharged, and six were sent back to the penitentiary. In addition, there were 33 parolees that the researchers were unable to locate.

There were 35 EM parolees in Dallas County that participated in this study. The majority of these offenders (68.6%) ranged from 22 to 35 years of age, and there were more nonwhite offenders (65.7%) than white offenders (34.3%). Male offenders were over represented with 91.4%. The majority of these offenders were single (48.6%) and had less than 12 years of education (60%). The offenses of the offenders on EM ranged from property crimes, which was the highest (54.2%), to substance abuse crimes (29.2%), to violent crimes (16.6%). Most of the offenders on EM stated that they lived with 3 or 5 people (23.5% each). The majority of the offenders lived with one adult (34.3%) and/or four+ children (42.9%). Most of these offenders (44.1%) also stated that they had good relationships with their families.

Concerning drug and/or alcohol abuse prior to arrest, 29.4% indicated no abuse, and 47.1% claimed social use of both alcohol and drugs. Of those claiming alcohol and/or drugs as serious problems, 23.5% reported both as serious problems. For the majority of the parolees their current alcohol and/or drug abuse usage patterns have drastically changed. In addition, 57.2% reported that they were abstaining from both alcohol and drugs, while 37.1% indicated the social use of both.

Most of this group of parolees had full time employment (45.7%) and worked at manual jobs (40%). Of the offenders who were married, the majority of their spouses were unemployed (77.8%). The spouses who did work held clerical jobs (75%). There were 38 non-EM parolees in Dallas County that participated in this study. The majority of these offenders (55.3%) ranged in age from 22 to 35 years. There were more nonwhite offenders (81.6%) than white offenders (18.4%). Male offenders were over represented with 89.5%. The majority of these offenders were single (73.7%) and had less than 12 years or at least 12 years of education (47.7% each). The offenses of the offenders ranged from property crimes, which was the highest (65.5%) factor noted, to substance abuse crimes (17.3%), to violent crimes (10.3%), to crimes against a person (6.9%). Most of the offenders stated that they lived with six people (22.2%). The majority of the offenders lived with one or two adults (31.6% each) and/or four+ children (50%). Most of these offenders (48.6%) also described their relationships with their families as being good.

In terms of drug and/or alcohol abuse prior to arrest, 32.4% indicated no abuse, and 40.5% social use of both alcohol and drugs. Of those claiming alcohol and/or drugs as serious problems, 27% reported both as serious problems. For the majority of the parolees their current alcohol and/or drug abuse usage patterns have drastically changed. Also, 76.3% reported that they were abstaining from both alcohol and drugs.

Most of this group of parolees were unemployed (64.9%) and those who did work held unskilled or semi-skilled jobs (33.3% each). Of the offenders who were married, the majority of their spouses were unemployed (80%). The spouses who did work held jobs that were clerical (100%).

DEMOGRAPHIC DESCRIPTION OF THE HARRIS COUNTY PAROLEES

The subjects from Harris County were selected for exactly the same reasons as Dallas Parolees were selected. They were selected from the same types of groups and the officers also administered the tests as did the Dallas County Parole Officers.

Harris County Parolees were given the pretests during the months of April, May, and June of 1989. Pretests were administered to 42 parolees. Of these parolees, 21 completed the posttests which began during the months of October and November of 1989. Some of the parolees were unavailable for various reasons, for example: three were sent back to the penitentiary; one absconded; and one had his parole revoked before posttesting began. The researchers were unable to locate 16 of the parolees. There were 35 EM parolees in Harris County that participated in this study. The majority of these offenders (71.4%) ranged in age from 22 to 35 years. There were more white offenders (51.4%) than nonwhite offenders (48.6%). Male offenders were over represented at 88.6%. The majority of these offenders were single (51.4%) and had less than 12 years of education (74.2%). The offenses of the offenders on EM ranged from substance abuse crimes to property crimes, which were the highest (48.4% each), to violent crimes (3.2%). Most of the offenders on EM stated that they lived with 3 to 5 people (20.6% each). The majority of the offenders lived with one adult (37.2%) and/or four+ children (48.6%). Most of these offenders (62.9%) also stated that they enjoyed good relationships with their families.

Regarding drug and/or alcohol abuse prior to arrest, 21.2% indicated no abuse, 21.2% social drinking, and 36.4% social use of both alcohol and drugs. Of those claiming alcohol and/or drugs as serious problems, 12.1% claimed alcohol, and 9.1% reported both as serious problems. For the majority of the parolees their current alcohol and/or drug abuse usage patterns have drastically changed. Furthermore, 85.7% reported that they were abstaining from both alcohol and drugs.

Most of this group of parolees had full time employment (52.9%) and worked at semi-skilled jobs (27.4%). Of the offenders who were married, the majority of their spouses were unemployed (93.7%). The spouses who did work held jobs that were of an administrative type (33.3%).

There were seven non-EM parolees in Harris County that participated in this study. The majority of these offenders (85.7%) ranged in age from 22 to 35 years. There were more nonwhite offenders (85.7%) than white offenders (14.3%). Male offenders were over-represented with 100%. The majority of these offenders were single (85.7%) and had less than 12 years of education (71.4%). The offenses of the offenders ranged from property crimes, which was the highest (66.7%), to substance abuse crimes (33.3%). Most of the offenders stated that they lived with three people (42.9%). The majority of the offenders lived with one adult (42.8%) and/or one or four+ children (42.9% each). Most of these offenders (71.4%) stated that they had good relationships with their families.

In terms of drug and/or alcohol abuse prior to arrest, 66.6% indicated no abuse. Of those who indicated alcohol and/or drugs as serious problems, 16.7% claimed alcohol, and 16.7% reported both as serious problems. For the majority of the parolees their current alcohol and/or drug abuse usage patterns have drastically changed. And, 71.4% reported that they are abstaining from both alcohol and drugs, while 28.6% claimed to continue to drink alcohol socially.

Most of this group of parolees had full time employment (57.1%) and worked at unskilled or semi-skilled jobs (33.3% each). Of the offenders who were married, the majority of their spouses were unemployed (100%).

The next Chapter of this book contains the logical extension of the study which comprises the statistical analyses and presentation of the findings. That Chapter then concludes with a section which summarizes and draws conclusions about the entire study.

REFERENCES

Bader, E. (1982). Redecisions in family therapy: A study of change in an intensive family therapy workshop. *Transactional Analysis Journal, 12,* 27-38.

Beck, A. T., Ward, C. H., Mendelson, M., Mock, J. E., & Erbaugh, J. K. (1961). An inventory for measuring depression. *Archives of General Psychiatry, 4,* 561-571.

Beck, A. T. *Depression.* (1967). Philadelphia: University of Pennsylvania Press.

Beck, A. T., Steer, R. A., & Garbin, M. G. (1988). Psychometric properties of the Beck Depression Inventory: Twenty-five years of evaluation. *Clinical Psychology Review, 8,* 77-100.

Campbell, D., & Stanley, J. (1963). *Experimental and quasi-experimental designs for research.* Boston: Houghton-Mifflin.

Campbell, P. G. (1983). Sreit family workshops: Creating change in family environment. *Journal of Drug Education, 13,* 223-227.

Denzin, N. K. (1989). *The research act.* Englewood Cliffs, NJ: Prentice-Hall.

Dreyer, P. H. (1978). *The eighth mental measurements yearbook.* Highland Park, NJ: Gryphon Press.

Druckman, J. (1979). A family oriented policy and treatment program for juvenile status offenders. *Journal of Marriage and the Family, 41,* 627-636.

Garrison, C., & Weber, J. (1981). Family crisis intervention using multiple impact therapy. *Social Casework, 62,* 585-593.

Harper, D., & Barry, D. (1979). Estimated prevalence of psychiatric disorder in a prison population. *Abstracts in Criminology and Penology, 19,* 237-242.

Kendall, P. C., Hollon, S. D., Beck, A. T., Hammen, C. L., & Ingram, E. (1987). Issues and recommendations regarding use of the Beck Depression Inventory. *Cognitive Therapy and Research, 11 (3)* 289-299.

Lambert, N. M. (1985). *The ninth mental measurements yearbook.* Lincoln, NB: The University of Nebraska Press.

Lehmann, H. J. (1959). Psychiatric concepts of depression: Nomenclature and classification. *Canadian Psychiatric Association Journal Supplement 4,* S1-S12.

Masuda, M., Cutler, D. L., Hein, L., & Holmes, T. H. (1978). Life events and prisoners. *Archives of General Psychiatry, 35,* 197-203.

Moos, R. (1985). Evaluating social resources in community and health care contexts. In P. Karoly (Ed.), *Measurement strategies in health psychology* (pp. 433-459). NY: Wiley. Moos, R., & Moos, B. (1986). *Family environment scale manual (2nd ed.).* Palo Alto, CA: Consulting Psychologists Press.

Moos, R. (1986). *Family environment scale manual: A users guide (2nd ed.).* Palo Alto, CA: Consulting Psychologists Press.

Piotrowski, C., Sherry, D., & Keller, J. W. (1985). Psychodiagnostic test usage: A survey of the Society for Personality Assessment. *Journal of Personality Assessment, 49,* 115-119.

Reynolds, W. M., & Gould, J. W. (1981). A psychometric investigation of the standard and short form Beck Depression Inventory. *Journal of Consulting and Clinical Psychology, 49 (2),* 306-307.

Rogers, S. (1981). *Factors related to recidivism among adult probationers in Ontario.* Toronto: Ontario Ministry of Correctional Services.

Scott, N. A., Hannum, T. E., & Ghrist, S. L. (1982). Assessment of depression among incarcerated females. *Journal of Personality Assessment, 46,* 372-379.

Tanaka, J. S., & Huba, G. L. (1984). Confirmatory hierarchical factor analyses of psychological distress measures. *JournaL of Personality and Social Psychology, 46 (3),* 621-635.

AN ANALYSIS OF THE DATA CONCERNING THE EFFECTS OF ELECTRONICALLY MONITORED HOME CONFINEMENT

Analysis of the data proceeds through three basic stages. First, the entire sample is described in terms of sex, age, education, household size, county of residence, and type of program (i.e. parole or probation). This description consists of means, standard deviations, ranges, and frequency distributions and provides a source of baseline data to which sub-groups may be subsequently compared.

The sample is divided into four sub-groups along two basic dimensions: parolees are separated from probationers, and offenders on electronic monitoring will be distinguished from those on ordinary community supervision. This scheme results in four principal subgroups which form an ordinal scale of supervision levels: (1) probationers on regular community supervision; (2) probationers on electronic monitoring; (3) parolees on regular community supervision; and, (4) parolees on electronic monitoring. These sub-groups are later collapsed into EM and non-EM groups. The traits of significant others of the probationers are also introduced and compared with those of the parolees. Oneway ANOVA and Scheffe's procedure are used to determine the statistical significance of any differences between groups that are noted in this phase of the analysis.

The four sub-groups of the sample, along with the significant others of the parolees, are described as distinct entities in order to specify a priori differences between these groups that may effect the outcome of inferential tests. This descriptive phase of the analysis is, in part, designed to aid in identifying programmatic distinctions within the sample that are relevant to the interpretation of other findings.

Each of the distinct sub-samples are described and compared with the others with respect to their demographic and criminal history variables. Further description focuses on the client populations of particular agencies within the counties studied. Anomalous distributions are identified at this point in the analysis and the characteristics of the sub-samples are compared.

In the second principal phase of analysis, attention turns to comparisons of the four sub-samples. ANOVA is used to determine if significant differences exist between sub-groups on sex, age, type of offense, employment status, occupational level, education and marital status. These findings facilitate maximum comprehension of the distinctions between these sub-groups on pretest scores.

ANOVA is then used to determine if the family environment of electronically monitored offenders differs significantly from that of controls within the probation and parole sub-groups. ANOVA is then employed to identify the most significant distinctions in levels of dysphoria and perceptions of family environment between the four sub-groups. Regression is then used to specify the most efficient predictors of BDI and FES pretest results within EM and non-EM sub-groups.

In the third phase, attention is focused on the posttest results of the study and their determinants. Beck Depression Inventory and FES posttest results are described for both the entire sample and for each of its sub-groups. The difference between pretest and posttest for the BDI and FES scores are computed for each subject and used as the crucial dependent variable in this portion of the analysis. This analysis will employ the same independent variables as its immediate predecessor but the dependent variable will be the magnitude of individual change on the FES and BDI inventories.

Finally, an additional area was analyzed: The impact of EM on the significant others of the offenders in the study. This additional set of analytical data helped to broaden the inferential picture of the offenders on EM.

DATA COLLECTION

The general problems associated with the collection of original data, such as the collection of data for this study, goes without saying. The data were collected on a voluntary basis on the part of the subjects. There was a heavy reliance on the individual agencies involved to not only make arrangements with the subjects for the data to be collected from them, but also in many instances for these agencies to collect the data itself from the subjects. In addition, the ad hoc nature of continually adding and dropping subjects at any point in time provides a unique research obstacle which in many instances simply can not be overcome.

To highlight some of the difficulties in collecting original data in a study such as this, the Dallas County Adult Probation Department had 44 clients on EM when the pretesting commenced with more EM offenders being added each week. Out of the 44 EM initial clients eligible to participate in the study, 25 (56.8%) volunteered to participate in the study. The Harris County Adult Probation Department had approximately 60 offenders in their EM program when pretesting began there, and 52 (86.7%) of those offenders agreed to participate in the study.

DEMOGRAPHIC DESCRIPTION OF THE ENTIRE SAMPLE

The vast majority of subjects in this study were offenders who had failed to succeed in either regular and/or intensive probation or parole programs. Initially, sentencing and parole guidelines were used in determining which clients had been selected as regular supervised probationers or as released parolees. The selection systems utilized risk assessment and offense severity criterion. Those offenders who rated high were placed on intensive supervision programs, rather than regular supervision. If the offender succeeds on the more intensive supervision programs, he/she is placed on a less restrictive program. If the offender fails on regular supervision and/or intensive supervision without EM, he/she may be placed on EM. Therefore, the EM clientele is predominately made up of those individuals who have failed at other programs. In essence, EM becomes the last resort next to prison (Grinter, 1989).

A total of 261 offenders were administered the test instruments. Fifty-three (53) subjects were on regular probation, 93 were on EM probation, 45 were on regular parole, and 70 were on EM parole of one sort or another. Overall, 85.0% of the subjects were males. Males constituted 76.9% of the subjects on regular probation, 82.8% of those on EM probation, 91.1% of those on regular parole and 90.0% of those on EM parole. Thus, females are slightly more likely to be found under traditional probation supervision than on EM or parole.

The majority of these 261 offenders (58.2%) ranged from 22 to 35 years of age, and there were more non-white offenders (53.1%) than white offenders (46.9%). The bulk of these offenders were single (59.2%), and most (44.8%) had less than 12 years of education. The offenses of the offenders ranged from property crimes (43.8%), to substance abuse crimes (41.7%), to crimes against the person (14.5%). Twenty-three point four percent (23.4%) of the offenders stated that they lived alone, 39.8% with one other person, and the remaining 36.8 with three or more persons. Forty-one point eight percent (41.8%) of those living with children lived with from one to two children while the remaining 58.3% lived with three or more children. The preponderance of offenders (83.5%) professed to have a good relationship with their family.

Regarding drug and/or alcohol abuse prior to arrest, 31.1% indicated no abuse, 7.1% declared social drinking, 8.3% social use of drugs, and 21.3% social use of both alcohol and drugs. Of those claiming alcohol and/or drugs as being a serious problem, 7.1% claimed alcohol, 9.4% claimed drugs, and 15.7% reported both alcohol and drugs as a serious problem. For the majority of this population their current alcohol and/or drug abuse usage patterns have drastically changed. Eighty-four point two (84.2%) reported that they presently are non-users of both alcohol and drugs.

Most (50.8%) of these offenders had full time employment, and the majority (74.6%) reported working at unskilled jobs (i.e., unskilled, semi-skilled, or manual). The vast majority (83.8%) of the spouses of married offenders were unemployed. Thirty-five point seven percent (35.7%) of the spouses who were employed held clerical jobs, with the majority (42.8%) of the remainder holding unskilled ones.

DEMOGRAPHIC DESCRIPTION OF THE SUB-SAMPLES

The mean age of the sampled offenders was 27.9 years, with a standard deviation of 8.141. In all sub-groups the modal category was 22 to 35 years of age. This age group accounted for 48.1% of the regular probationers, 54.8% of the EM probationers, 60.0% of the regular parolees, and 70.0% of the EM parolees. Overall, 63 subjects were under 21 years of age, 152 were between 22 and 35 years (58.2%), and 44 were over age 35 (16.9%). Regular probationers had a mean age of 27.6 years, EM probationers averaged 26.9 years of age, regular parolees had an average age of 28.0 years and EM parolees had a mean age of 30.0 years. Oneway ANOVA results indicate that the EM parolees were, on average, significantly older than subjects in the other sub-group (F=4.48; P=0.012).

The sample consisted of 122 whites (46.9%), 108 African Americans (41.5%), 28 Hispanics (10.7%) and two of other races, i.e., American Indians and Asians (.8%). Regular probationers were disproportionately white (73.1%) with only five Hispanics (9.6%) and nine African Americans (17.3%). Forty-nine point five percent (49.5%) of the EM probationers were white, 39.8% African Americans and 9.7% Hispanic. The ratio of whites to African Americans changes radically when parolees are examined. Sixty-eight point nine percent (68.9%) of the subjects on regular parole were African American while only 17.8% were white. An additional 13.3% were Hispanic. Forty-two point nine percent (42.9%) of the EM parolees were African American and 44.3% were white with an additional 11.4% Hispanic. This distribution corresponds, albeit roughly, to the distribution of ethnic groups in the general correctional population of Texas. Oneway ANOVA results indicate that race was a significant predictor of the type of supervision under which offenders were placed (F=11.271; P=0.000). The same data were also analyzed with race coded dichotomously as white or non-white and oneway ANOVA was again significant (F=14.455; P=0.000). Scheffe's procedure indicated that traditional probationers were distinctly more likely to be white than were members of any other sub-group. EM probationers were also significantly more often white than were those on regular parole supervision.

The average educational level of the total sample was just under 12 years (X = 11.134; S = 2.639). Regular probationers had an average educational level of 12.1 years (S = 1.987) while probationers on EM averaged 11.8 years (S = 1.871). Parolees on regular supervision had a mean educational level of 10.8 (S = 1.995) years while those on EM averaged 9.9 years (S = 3.358), 42.5% of the subjects had not completed high school, 37.9% were high school graduates, and 17.2% have had at least some college. Thirty-two point seven percent (32.7%) of the regular probationers did not have a high school diploma, while 30.8% had some college and 36.5% were high school graduates. Probationers on EM showed much the same distribution with 31.2% not having completed high school, 44.1% high school graduates and 24.7% having had some college.

When parolees are compared with probationers, the educational deficits traditionally associated with incarcerated offenders become prominent. Only 4.4% of subjects on regular parole had some college while 51.1% are high school drop-outs and 44.4% had twelve years of schooling. Sixty point zero percent (60.0%) of the EM parolees had not completed high school while 27.1% had a high school diploma, and only 5.7% had acquired college credits. The educational differences between parolees and probationers were statistically significant (F=13.425; P=0.000) with the parolees having more frequent deficits than the probationers.

The majority of the sample (59.0%) was single with only 27.2% married at the time of the study. Another 13.4% were separated, divorced or widowed (this group is hereafter referred to as "other" in terms of marital status). Probationers followed this pattern with 63.5% of the regular probationers and 55.9% of those on EM being single. Twenty-one point two percent (21.2%) of the regular probationers and 31.2% of the EM probationers were married, while 15.4% of the regular probationers and 12.9% of those on EM were classified as other on this variable. Parolees under regular supervision were even less likely than probationers to be married. Seventy-five point six (75.6%) of the regular parolees reported that they were single. However, only 50.0% of EM parolees were single while 31.4% were married, and 18.6% were widowed or divorced. Oneway ANOVA indicated that no significant differences in marital status existed between sub-groups (F=2.115; P=0.099).

When demographic variables were used to explicate the variance in type of supervision, the main effects (F=2.729; P=0.017) were statistically significant.

However, the main effects or linear model was significant due only to the effects of sex (F=6.647; P=0.011). Women were more likely to be probationers than parolees and less likely to be on EM than males. Education (F=2.465; P=0.090) was nearly significant. Neither age (F=1.657; P=0.196) nor marital status (F=0.646; P=0.423) had any discernible effects.

The study also examined the number of persons residing in the same household as the offender. The overall sample had an average household of 3.3 persons (S = 1.746). There was little difference across groups on this variable. Regular probationers had an average of 3.0 (S = 1.260) co-residents while those on EM had a mean household size of 3.4 (S = 1.695). Subjects under regular parole supervision had a mean of 3.6 (S = 2.156) while those on EM averaged 3.4 co-residents (S = 1.794). There were no significant differences in overall household size between the four sub-groups (F=0.214; P=0.887).

The typical household in this study had an average of 2.3 adults (S=1.079) and 1.1 children (S=1.282). Among regular probationers the typical household had 2.3 adults (S=1.126) and 0.7 children (S=0.875) while probationers on EM averaged 2.3 adults (S=0.938) and 1.1 children (S=1.374). Regular parolees lived in households with an average of 2.2 adults (S=1.506) and 1.4 children (S=1.470) while parolees on EM had a mean of 2.2 adult co-residents (S=1.358) and 1.2 children (S=1.227). There were no significant differences between subgroups on the number of adult co-residents (F=0.554; P=0.646). However, persons on regular parole supervision had significantly more children in their homes (F=3.238; P=0.228) than did members of other sub-groups.

Employment was measured on a three point scale ranging from unemployed to employed part-time and employed full-time. Fifty point two percent (50.2%) of the sample was employed part-time and 16.1% were employed full-time. Fifty-nine point six percent (59.6%) of the subjects on regular probation were employed part-time while another 21.2% were unemployed and 19.2% were employed full-time. Probationers on EM were similarly distributed with 28.0% unemployed, 54.8% employed part time and 17.2% employed full time. Fifty seven point eight percent (57.8%) of the subjects on regular parole and 34.3% of those on EM parole were unemployed at the time of the study. This discrepancy is likely due to the fact that many of the EM parolees were on pre-parole transfer status in which employment is mandatory for inclusion in the program. Only 8.9% of those on regular parole and 17.1% of those on EM parole were employed full time while 33.3% of the regular parolees and 48.6% of the EM parolees were employed part-time. The greater likelihood of employment among probationers, regardless of the type of supervision they were under, was statistically significant (F=5.537; P=0.004).

Occupational status was measured on Hollingshead's seven point scale which is comprised of ranges from the unskilled through executives (Miller, 1977). The mean occupational level of the sample was 1.9 (S=2.05) or semiskilled (2.0). Probationers tended to have occupations of a skilled nature whether on regular supervision (X=2.034; S=2.14) or EM (X=2.38; S=2.192). Parolees on regular supervision had the lowest mean occupational levels in the sample with a mean of 1.0 (S=1.69) while EM parolees had a mean level of 1.7 (S=1.741). Of the employed probationers most were in unskilled (31%) or semi-skilled (15.5%) positions. Probationers on EM, however, tended to have either unskilled (16%) or skilled manual jobs (19%) when employed. White collar occupations at the level of management and administration accounted for 3.4% of the regular probationers and 4% of the EM probationers.

Among regular parolees with jobs, most were in unskilled (10.9%) or semi-skilled (10.9%) positions. Only one (2.2%) parolee claimed to hold a clearly white collar position. Nine point one percent (9.1%) of the EM parolees held unskilled positions and another 10.6% held semi-skilled jobs. However, 24.2% of the EM parolees were in clerical or sales positions and 13.7% held managerial positions or better. The average occupational level of EM probationers was significantly higher than that of the other three sub-groups (F=5.439; P=0.001).

The study also queried respondents as to their substance abuse and criminal histories. Substance abuse was classified as drug and/or alcohol oriented. Subjects were asked to describe their use as social or serious. The sample was distributed in a tri-modal fashion with most subjects claiming not to have been drug or alcohol abusers (33.3%), but over one-fifth (20.7%) admitted to social use of both drugs and alcohol while 15.3% admitted to serious problems with both drugs and alcohol. Thirty point eight percent (30.8%) of the regular probationers claimed to be non-users prior to their arrest while 13.5% admitted to the social use of drugs and 5.8% to the social use of alcohol prior to their arrest. Twenty one point two percent (21.2%) of this group admitted to serious drug use histories while an additional 13.5% claimed to have had serious alcohol problems, and 13.5% claimed to have abused both alcohol and drugs in a serious fashion. In comparison, EM probationers seemed somewhat more likely to be social rather than serious users of psychoactive substances. Thirty-three point three percent (33.3%) of this group claimed to be non-users while 15.1% admitted to social drug use and 8.6% to social use of alcohol. Ten point eight percent (10.8%) used both in a social manner. Fourteen point zero percent (14.0%) of the EM probationers admitted to having had a serious pattern of drug use prior to their arrest but only 6.5% admitted to a serious drinking problem. Eleven point eight percent (11.8%) had used both alcohol and drugs in a serious fashion.

Persons under parole supervision were more homogeneous in their distribution on this variable than were probationers. Forty point zero percent (40.0%) claimed not to have used either type of substance prior to being incarcerated. An additional 33.3% admitted to using both drugs and alcohol in a social manner and 24.4% admitted having had serious problems with both prior to incarceration, and only one parolee on regular supervision admitted to an alcohol problem (2.2%). EM parolees were equally homogeneous but somewhat more likely to have been substance-involved than their counterparts on regular supervision. Twenty-eight point six percent (28.6%) claimed to be non-users but the majority (40.0%) admitted to the social use of both types of substances. Only 15.7% of this group admitted to having had serious problems with both prior to incarceration. However, differences between sub-groups in admitted substance abuse patterns were not statistically discernible from zero (F=0.397; P=0.755).

The offenses for which the subject was currently under sentence were coded as substance abuse, property crimes or crimes against persons, in ascending order of relative seriousness. The sample mean was 1.6 (S=1.05) or midway between substance abuse and property crimes. The modal category was property crimes (39.5%), closely followed by substance abuse offenses (37.5%). The remaining 13.0% had been convicted of crimes against persons. Non-EM probationers appeared to more often be involved in serious crimes (X=1.885, S=1.114) than their EM counterparts (X=1.581, S=0.981). This distinction was statistically significant (F=4.634; P=0.004). Among regular probationers the majority were property offenders (42.3%) or had committed offenses related to substance abuse (34.6%). Twenty-three point one percent (23.1%) of this sub-group had been convicted of crimes against persons. The majority of EM probationers were substance abusers (54.8%). Property offenders accounted for another 32.3% of this group and crimes against persons involved only 12.9% of these subjects.

Regular parolees had much the same pattern of offense types as those on traditional probation. The majority were property offenders (51.1%) but substance abuse offenses were more common (15.6%) than were crimes against persons (11.1%) in this sub-group. Missing data was more frequent among parolees and, along with unclassifiable responses, accounted for 22.2% of the data in this group. Missing data was also common among the parolees on EM (21.4%). Property offenders were again the modal category (40.0%) followed by substance abuse charges (31.4%) and then crimes against persons (7.1%).

PRE-BECK DEPRESSION INVENTORY (BDI) RESULTS

The study employed two psychometric instruments: the Beck Depression Inventory (BDI) and the Family Environment Scale (FES), to measure the relative well-being of the subjects. Each of these instruments were discussed in detail in the previous Chapter. The BDI and the FES were given to the offenders and their spouses at two different points in time in this study. The first tests, here identified as Pre-BDI and Pre-FES, were given approximately at the time the offender was placed on (hooked-up to) EM; and the second or subsequent tests, here identified as Post-BDI and Post-FES, were administered approximately 90 days after the pretests.

The BDI is scored in a cumulative fashion with a range of possible scores ranging from zero (0) to fifty-one (51). The overall sample had a mean BDI score of 9.345 (S=7.850) which is just beyond the normal range. Subjects on regular probation had the lowest average score (X=7.731; S=6.704) while EM probationers averaged 10.032 (S=8.119). Regular parolees had a mean BDI score of 8.644 (S=8.345) while EM parolees averaged 9.914 (S=7.838). There were no significant differences between sub-groups on the BDI (F=0.859; P=0.463).

The great majority of the sample fell within the normal (58.2%) or mildly depressed (25.3%) range of the BDI. Five point seven percent (5.7%) were classified as "mildly to moderately depressed" and 7.7% were "moderately to severely" depressed. Only eight subjects (3.1%) were severely depressed according to the initial BDI results. These severely depressed offenders were spread throughout the four sub-groups. One was on regular probation, three were on EM probation, one was on regular parole and two were on EM parole. The same pattern was found in each sub-group except for EM parolees where 15.8% (N=11) reported being moderately to severely depressed.

PRE-FAMILY ENVIRONMENT SCALE (FES) RESULTS

As discussed previously, the FES is divided into three dimensions which are measured by ten sub-scales. The first dimension, Relationship, is measured by the cohesiveness, expressiveness, and conflict scales. The next dimension of Personal Growth (goal orientation) is measured by the independence, achievement orientation, intellectual-cultural orientation, active-recreational orientation, and moral-religious emphasis scales. The third and last dimension, System Maintenance, is measured in terms of the organization and control scales. Each of these areas is scored and gives an indication of the perceived family environment based on the clients' answers to the true/false statements.

Complicating the FES analysis is the fact that because of administrative and logistical difficulties, probationers were administered the entire FES but parolees were asked to complete only two sub-scales: those measuring control and conflict within the home. The conflict sub-scale assesses the amount of anger, aggression and conflict among family members; and the control sub-scale measures the extent to which rules and procedures are used to run family life (Moos & Moos,1986). Precedents for using selected subscales of the FES can be found in Ford, Bashford, and DeWitt's (1979) work with marital communication training in which they utilized FES Cohesion and Expressiveness subscales, and Boss' (1977) use of six of the FES subscales with families of missing servicemen.

It should be noted that some of the following interpretations of the statistics provided in this report are based on the scoring nature of the FES subscales. Unlike many psychometric tests the FES utilizes a mean score as the ideal or best score, rather than the more conventional use of a low or high score, as the ideal or best score. The FES subscales have a scoring range of 0.0 to 9.0. These scores are subdivided into continuum range scores of 0.0 to 5.0, with a score of 0.0 indicating the largest amount of under control/conflict and 5.0 indicating a normal amount of control/conflict. Similarly, subscale scores range from 9.0 to 5.0. A score of 9.0 indicates the largest amount of over control/conflict while a score of 5.0 indicates the normal amount of control/conflict. Thus, subscale scores near 5.0 are interpreted as the normal amount of family control/conflict to be found in normal families. In the analysis which follows the writers have elected to interpret subscale scores below 4.0 and over 6.0 as indicating a dysfunctional amount of intrafamilial control/conflict. In essence, 0.0 to 4.0 is the scoring range being used for identifying too little or too much intrafamilial control/conflict, and 9.0 to 6.0 the scoring range indicating progressively higher amounts of over control.

Pretest results show that this sample of offenders averaged a raw score of 2.452 (S=2.142) on the conflict scale. Among subjects on regular probation supervision, conflict sub-scale scores averaged 2.3456 (S= 2.057) while EM probationers had a mean conflict score of 2.527 (S=2.104). Those on regular parole supervision had an average conflict score of 2.956 (S=2.153) while EM parolees averaged 2.043 (S=2.156). Thus, all four sub-groups show a lower than normal amount of conflict within their families, with EM parole families having the least and regular parole families the most. These differences, however, are not statistically significant (F=1.795; P=0.148).

Control scale scores averaged 4.828 (S=1.856) for the entire sample, 4.769 (S=1.906) among regular probationers and 5.043 among EM probationers (S=1.654). Subjects on traditional parole supervision had a mean control score of 5.000 (S=1.523) while those on EM averaged 4.486 (S=2.225). All four subgroups were found to be exerting the normal amount of family control, with EM probationer families exerting the most and EM parole families the least. However, oneway ANOVA indicated that there were no significant differences between the subgroups within our sample on the control scale (F=1.358; P=0.256).

Attention is finally directed at three dimensions of the FES: Relationship, Personal Growth, and System Maintenance. These dimensions serve to summarize overall FES scores but are available only for probationers. The relationship dimension is composed of the cohesion, expressiveness and conflict sub-scales. The sampled probationers had a mean of 14.510 (2.821) on this dimension. Those on traditional supervision averaged 14.865 (S=3.036) while those on EM had a mean of 14.312 (S=2.690). The personal growth dimension is composed of the independence and achievement-orientation sub-scales. This sample of probationers had an overall mean of 29.110 (S=5.849). Those on traditional supervision averaged 29.346 (S=5.083) while those on EM had a mean of 28.978 (S=6.259). The system maintenance dimension is composed of the organization and control sub-scales. The mean for all probationers was 11.324 (S=2.948) on this dimension with those on traditional supervision averaging 10.769 (S=3.473) and those on EM averaging 11.643 (S=2.578). Oneway ANOVA indicated that there were no significant differences between sub-groups on any of these FES variables. Thus, the sub-groups can be said to follow the same pattern on each of the psychometric instruments employed in this research.

EXPLICATION OF THE PRETEST RESULTS

Complete FES results for the entire ten subscales for the three dimensions of the FES are available only for probationers; therefore, only offenders in these groups are used in analyses of the three dimensions or complete FES. When the effects of demographic variables on the relationship dimension were analyzed using ANOVA, none were found to be of significance (F=1.087, P=.385). Only educational level (F=3.302;P=0.045) attained statistical significance in explicating the variance in responses to the growth dimension (Main effects F=1.607; P=0.145). Since education is one method by which the individual learns to adapt to the surrounding world, the significance of this variable is not surprising. Results for the system maintenance scale were similar to those for the relationship dimension - none of the demographic variables had an effect that was statistically discernible from zero (F=0.737; P=0.641).

Because they are: (1) especially critical to the central question being investigated; and (2) available for all groups of respondents, the control and conflict scales were given much attention at this stage of analysis. ANOVA was first used to estimate the effects of social environment and pretest BDI scores on these two FES scales for all offenders (N=261). Respondents were divided into EM and non-EM groups to create a new independent variable. In addition, the

BDI scores, educational levels, regularity of employment of offenders and the presence/absence of EM supervision were used in this analysis.

Only the BDI score had a significant impact ($F=8.691$; $P=0.000$) on the control scale. The significance of the main effects ($F=4.617$; $P=0.000$) is attributable to the impact of this variable. When the effects of these four variables on the control scale were estimated with ANOVA, the main effects were nearly significant ($F=1.939$; $P=0.058$) as was the impact of the BDI pretest score ($F=2.218$; $P=0.069$). However, the regularity of the offender's employment had an effect that was statistically significant ($F=4.015$; $P=0.047$). One plausible explanation for this finding is that, in general, employment is normally viewed as influencing the level of control within households by helping to establish an economic hierarchy. Since most of our respondents are males, it is likely that the regularity with which they maintain employment directly effects the degree of control they are able to exercise within the family.

When the conflict scale was examined, only the offender's level of education was found to approach statistical significance ($F=2.682$; $P=0.073$). The main effects were not significant ($F=1.785$; $P=0.110$). However, no other variable even remotely approached significance. The significance of education to the reported level of conflict probably reflects the acquisition of problem-solving skills by the more educated families. An identical analysis of control scale scores indicated that none of these variables had an effect on this measure that was discernible from zero (Main Effects: $F=0.924$; $P=0.481$.

Regression, a more powerful analytical procedure, was used to explicate the joint effects of nine independent variables on control and conflict pretest scores. Two stepwise regressions were required, one for each dependent variable, using sex, age, education, marital status, number of adults and children in the home, employment, pre-BDI score and the type of supervision the offender was under (i.e., EM or non-EM) as independent or predictor variables. It can be noted in passing the R^2 indicates the amount of variance in the dependent variable that is explicated by the independent variables; F tests the hypothesis of no linear relationship between independent and dependent variables and is associated with the R^2. Beta or standardized regression coefficients suggest the importance of each independent variable in explicating the dependent variable while controlling for all other independent variables. T values test the hypothesis that there is no linear relationship between the independent variable and the dependent variable and thus clarify the significance of the Beta weights.

When conflict pretest scores were examined, the first variable entered into the equation was the offender's pre-BDI score (F=24.167; P=.000). This variable explained nearly ten percent of the variance in conflict scores (R^2=0.082). Age was entered on the second step and increased the explanatory power of the regression equation to 14% (R^2=.137, F=21.556; P=0.000). On the model's third iteration, the offender's substance abuse history was entered to produce an R^2 of 0.177 (F=19.664; P=.000). The final variable to achieve significance in this equation was the type of offense for which the offender was last convicted (R^2=.196; F=16.821 P=.000). Thus the model presented here can be said to have explained nearly one-fifth of the variance in conflict pretest scores with these four variables. In the final model used to explain conflict scale scores the offender's BDI score was the best single predictor with a Beta weight of .276 (t=4.899,P=.000). Age was nearly as powerful, however, with a Beta weight of -.246 (t=-4362;P=.000) though it appears to operate in the opposite direction as the BDI score. Substance abuse history is the next most important variable in this model (Beta=0.211; t=3.793; P=.0002) followed by the type of offense for which the offender was convicted (Beta=.142; t=2.632; P=.009). Since depression can be interpreted as either a cause or result of conflict within the home, its significant impact on this FES sub-scale is not surprising. Ageing is, usually, viewed as increasing personal identification with the family unit and to assist in establishing an appropriate perspective on the relative importance of various aspects of life. Therefore, its inverse association with conflict is also to be expected. The fact that conflict increases with substance abuse is also to be expected, since a history of substance abuse implies that chemical dependency has eroded the offender's loyalty to the family and left a history of aberrant behavior that can only be overcome with time and positive behavior. The more serious the crime committed by the offender, the more dysfunctional that person can be assumed to be. The presence of dysfunctional persons, especially in positions of power in the family hierarchy, is more likely to increase the conflict in the home.

The first variable to be entered in the parallel equation for control scale scores was the offender's sex (R^2=.017; F=5.375; P=0.021) which explicated just over 1.0% of the variance in the dependent variable. The offender's educational level was next entered and increased the R^2 to 0.032 (F=5.337; P=.005). Abuse history was then entered into the equation (R^2=.047; F=5.246; P=0.002) followed by the offender's employment status (R^2=.06; F=5.062; P=.001. The offense that resulted in the offender's last conviction was the last variable found to have a significant impact on control scale scores. This linear model explained 7.0% of the variance in the dependent variable (R^2=.070; F=4.921; P=.000.

While the model of control scale scores included more variables than that for the conflict scores, its explanatory power is much less. This model's reliance on demographic variables raises suspicions of collinearity between independent variables which is likely to be moderately high and renders causal interpretation highly problematic (Norusis, 1983). The offender's educational level (Beta=-1.68; t=-2.761; P=.006) appeared to have the most explanatory power followed by sex (Beta=-.161; t=-2.661; P=.008), substance abuse history (Beta=-2.216;t=-2.216; P=.028), employment status (Beta=-.128; t=-2.144; P=.033) and type of offense (Beta=.123; t=2.028;P=.044). The same explanations offered for the results of the demographic variables on conflict scores would appear to also apply here.

POSTTEST RESULTS FOR THE BDI

The mean score for the entire sample on the BDI was 3.9 (S=7.030). The great majority of offenders were not dysphoric according to this measure (85.8%). Seven point three percent (7.3%) had BDI scores indicating mild depression, 1.9% fell into the mild-to-moderate category, 3.1% were in the moderately dysphoric category and the remaining 1.9% were classified as severely depressed.

Among offenders on traditional probation supervision the average BDI score was 5.8. Again, most of these subjects were not dysphoric according to the BDI (78.8%). Eleven point five percent (11.5%) were mildly depressed, while only 1.9% were in the mild-to-moderate category and 3.8% were in both the moderate and severe categories.

Probationers on EM were similarly distributed. They had a mean BDI score of 5.6 (S=8.020) and the great majority did not appear to be dysphoric (79.6%).

Ten point eight percent (10.8%) were classified as mildly dysphoric with only 1.1% in the mild-to-moderate group and 2.2% in the severely dysphoric category. However, 6.5% were classified as moderately dysphoric by this instrument.

Parolees on traditional supervision averaged 3.1 on the BDI (S=7.285). A lack of dysphoria was somewhat more common among these offenders (88.9%) than among the probationers. None of these subjects fell into the moderately dysphoric grouping but 4.4% were categorized as mildly dysphoric or mildly-to-moderately so. Only 2.2% of these offenders were severely dysphoric. Parolees on EM had the least dysphoria of any group examined (X=0.686; S=2.635). Virtually all (97.1%) of these subjects were in the non-dysphoric category with only 1.4% in the mild and mild-to-moderate groupings.

Oneway ANOVA indicated that the type of supervision an offender was under had a significant effect on his/her BDI posttest score (F=9.040; P=.0000). Scheffe's procedure clarified this distinction by identifying the significant differential between both categories of probationers and EM parolees. This procedure indicated that parolees on traditional supervision were not statistically different from either probationers or EM parolees. However, the EM parolees had a posttest BDI mean that was significantly lower than that of either group of probationers. Since EM parolees are in most cases considered marginal candidates for release from prison, this finding is not particularly surprising.

Stepwise regression was used to explicate the effects of offender demographics, type of supervision, presence of EM, type of offense, and substance abuse history on posttest BDI scores. The type of supervision was the first variable to be entered into the equation and produced an R^2 of .083 (F=24.613; P=.0000). The offender's age was the next variable entered and its addition to the model resulted in an R^2 of .113 (F=17.448; P=.0000). Type of offense was the last variable to be successfully entered and produced an R^2 of .125 for the model (F=13.297; P=.000). One can conclude from this that knowledge of an offender's type of supervision, age, and type of offense explained 12.5% of the variance in BDI posttest scores.

The type of supervision had a Beta weight of -.308 (t=-5.156; P=.000) while the Beta for age was -.184 (t=3.156; P=.002) and the Beta associated with type of offense was -.127 (t=-2.126; P=.035). None of the other variables had an impact on posttest BDI scores that was discernible from zero. The negative sign associated with these Beta weights indicates that post BDI scores were most likely to decrease as type of supervision became more rigorous. The fact that parolees were less depressed than probationers is logical since they have recently been released from institutional custody whereas probationers have, for the most part, not previously experienced direct legal controls on their lives. Younger offenders are also logically associated with higher levels of dysphoria because they are less likely to have encountered the criminal justice system and because of the fewer responsibilities they have encountered in life. Since offense type and type of supervision are causally related in an obvious fashion a collinearity problem exists in that the effects of type of crime and type of supervision cannot be estimated independent of one another. Thus, the same factors used to explain the effects of type of supervision can be applied to the offender's age.

POSTTEST RESULTS FOR THE FES

The overall posttest sample mean for the conflict scale of the FES was 1.1 (S=1.822). Eight-one point six percent (81.6%) had scores in the lowest third of the possible range. Only 1.6% of the offenders reported levels of conflict in their families that were in the top third of the possible range of scores. The sample mean for the posttest control scale scores was 2.3 (S=2.811). Fifty-seven point nine percent (57.9%) of the offenders had control scale scores in the lowest third of the possible range, 32.9% were in the middle ranges of the scale and the remaining 9.2% were at the high end of this scale.

Traditional probationers had a mean conflict scale score of 1.8 (S=2.168) while EM probationers averaged 1.419 (S=1.820). Non-EM parolees averaged 1.0 (S=1.989) on this measure while their EM counterparts had a conflict scale mean of 0.243 (S=.875). Oneway ANOVA indicated that the differences between the means of the four groups under different types of supervision was significant (F=9.220; P=.0000). Scheffe's procedure demonstrated that EM parolees had an average conflict scale score that was considerably less than those of both types of probationers. Familial conflicts undoubtedly pale in comparison with those encountered in prison. Thus, the parolee's with the greatest likelihood of returning to prison are likely to see conflicts at home as less severe than others. It may also be the case that they make a greater effort to avoid conflict, either as a "holdover" survival strategy from prison or as a method of partially insuring successful completion of parole.

Control scale scores among probationers not on EM averaged 3.3 (S=2.871) while EM probationers had a mean of 3.4 (S=2.801). Parolees on traditional supervision had a mean posttest score of 1.6 (S=2.589) while EM parolees averaged 0.5 (S=1.421). Oneway ANOVA indicated a significant difference (F=24.689; P=.0000) among group means on this variable. Scheffe's procedure showed that significant differences between probationers and parolees were discernible on this variable regardless of the presence or absence of EM within these categories. Because they are older parolees are less likely to fall easily under familial control and this is apparent in their FES scores on this sub-scale. The lower level of reported familial control is also a likely contributor to the extremely low conflict scores of this group.

Stepwise regression was used to estimate the effects of EM, BDI posttest scores, age, sex, education, employment status, marital status, and household composition variables on posttest conflict scores. The first variable to be successfully entered into this equation was the BDI posttest score (R^2=.258; F=91.077; P=.000). The employment status of the offender was entered next and increased the model's R^2 to .270 (F=48.908; P=.000). The presence of EM supervision was the last variable to be successfully entered into this regression equation and resulted in a final R^2 of .281 (F=34.674; P=.000). Beta weights for both the BDI score (.514; t=9.20; P=.000) and employment status (.129; t=2.453; P=.015) were positive, indicating a positive linear relationship. The Beta weight for the presence of EM supervision was negative (-.116; t=-2.184;P=.031) indicating that conflict scores were, on average, higher in non-EM families.

The fact that dysphoria had a direct and positive effect on familial conflict is to be expected although these data do not allow us to speculate as to whether dysphoria is a cause or an effect of conflict. The positive association of the regularity of an offender's employment with conflict in the home is difficult to explain. Indeed, quite the opposite direction was expected for this Beta. It may be that the more an offender works, the more he/she expects in terms of obedience and gratitude from the family. Since offenders can be characterized as dysfunctional humans, such expectations would be conflict producing, especially in the context of a history that includes direct or indirect abuse of family members and/or responsibilities by the offender. The impact of EM on reported perceptions of family conflict is noteworthy in this context since the analysis indicates that presence of EM is associated with low levels of friction within the family. Because this relationship did not attain significance when pretest data were analyzed the data suggest that EM may have a positive effect in this regard.

When the same regression procedure was used to explicate the variance in control scale posttest scores somewhat different results were obtained. The BDI post test was entered first with an R^2 of .128 (F=39.031; P=.000). Marital status was entered into the equation on the second and final iteration resulting in an R^2 of .141 (F=22.337; P=.000) for the model. The Beta weight for the BDI post test (.374) was significant (t=6.474; P=.000), indicating the presence of a direct linear relationship between dysphoria and perceived control by the family. The Beta for marital status (.130) also indicates a significant, direct linear relationship (t=2.243; P=.026) of less magnitude.

High control scores, in conjunction with correctional supervision, could be expected to result in dysphoria due to the offenders's perception of being over-controlled. Such dual-controls may not always be congruent in their demands on the offender and the assignment of supremacy to one set will, in most cases, lead to conflicts with the other. The direct relationship between marital status and control was expected since spouses are more likely to be intimate with and dependent upon each other than would parents or other co-habitants.

EXPLICATION OF PRE-TO-POST TEST SCORE CHANGES

The crucial variable in this study was the change in psychometric scores between the pretest and posttests. The mean change for all subjects on the BDI was +2.2 (S=6.734). In the overall sample 0.4% of the subjects's BDI scores dropped by four points, 2.3% dropped by two points and another 2.3% decreased by one point. Sixty-two point eight percent (62.8%) of the sample showed no change in BDI score. Twenty point seven percent (20.7%) had an increase of one point on this measure while 3.8% showed an increase of two points, 6.5% increased by three points and 1.1% increased by four points.

Offenders on traditional probation showed the largest net increase of 4.3 (S=7.275). The scores of EM probationer rose an average of 3.9 (S=7.438) while parolees on traditional supervision showed an increase of only 1.5 (S=6.904) and those on EM exhibited a decrease of 1.1 (S=2.981). Oneway ANOVA indicated that EM parolees were statistically discernible from both groups of probationers.

Stepwise regression was used to estimate the impact of demographic variables, household size, and employment status on the amount of change between the pretest and posttest scores of the BDI. The offender's age was the first variable to be entered in this equation (R^2=.037; F=10.043; P=.002). Education was the next and last variable to be successfully entered (R^2=.057; F=8.817; P=.000). The change in R^2 that resulted from the addition of education (.027) was significant according to the associated F-ratio (F change=7.345; P=.007). The Beta weight associated with age was -.201 (t=-3.329; P=.001), indicating that as the offender's age increases, dysphoria tends to decrease over time during community supervision. Much the same relationship exists between education and (Beta=.164; t=2.710; P=.007) change in dysphoria over time, though to a lesser extent. The fact that increases in age and education are associated with better, or quicker, acclimation to home confinement is not surprising since both lead to improved comprehension of social limitations and the value of the family as a social unit.

The difference between pretest and posttest control scale scores were analyzed next. The overall sample showed a decrease of 1.3 (S=2.390). Three point eight percent (3.8%) of the sample had posttest scores that were three to four points lower than their pretest. Twelve point six percent (12.6%) showed decreases of one to two points. Twenty-three point four percent (23.4%) showed no change. Thirty-three point four percent (33.4%) showed an increase in conflict scores of one to two points, another 16.2% showed an increase of three to four points, and 10.8% showed an increase of five to nine points.

Probationers on traditional supervision averaged a decrease of 0.6 points (S=2.060) on the conflict scale while their EM counterparts had a mean decrease of 1.1 points (S=2.487). Parolees on regular supervision had an average decrease of 2.0 (S=2.374) while those on EM averaged 1.8 points less on the post test than they had on the pretest (S=2.357). Oneway ANOVA indicated that differences between these four groups were significant (F=3.955; P=.009). Scheffe's procedure indicated that probationers on regular supervision were statistically distinct from both groups of parolees on this measure of change in perceived familial conflict over the testing period.

Stepwise regression was used to explore the effects of demographic and household size variables on changes in conflict scale scores. Changes in BDI scores and the presence of EM were also included in this analysis as independent variables. Change in the BDI score was the first variable to be entered into this equation and it produced an R^2 of .106 (F=31.556; P=.000). The offender's age was the next variable to be entered and resulted in an R^2 of .140 (F=21.994; P=.000). The offender's marital status was the last variable to be successfully entered, resulting in an R^2 of .150 (F=16.228; P=.000) for the final model. The Beta weights for each of these three significant independent variables were positive. The change in BDI score had the most apparent impact (Beta=.337; t=5.881; P=.000), followed by that for age (Beta =.152; t=2.507; P=.013) and finally by the Beta for marital status (.124; t=2.038; P=.043). It can be inferred from this analysis that increases in the level of reported familial conflict are associated with increases in dysphoria, age, and marriage in offenders. Marriage probably increases conflict because of the greater intimacy and investment it implies relative to other types of relationships. The predictive value of age may be due to the realization that much of one's life has been wasted on criminal, or at least deviant, pursuits.

Changes in control scale scores were the last to be analyzed. The sample had an overall decrease in control scale score of 2.5 (S=3.136). Five point four percent (5.4%) reported a decrease of three to four points on this measure, 14.1% showed a decrease of one to two points, while 10.3% reported no change. Twenty-one point four percent (21.4%) showed an increase of one to two points, 16.5% showed an increase of three to four points, 23.0% increased by five to six points, and 9.2% increased by seven to nine points.

Probationers on regular supervision showed an average decrease of 1.2 (S=3.098) while those on EM had a mean decrease of 1.7 (S=2.987). Parolees on regular supervision had an average decrease in control scale score of 3.4 (S=2.904) while those on EM averaged a decline of 4.0 (S=2.659) points.

Oneway ANOVA demonstrated that the differences between group means were significant (F=14.083; P=.000) and Scheffe's procedure indicated that the difference between those offenders on EM and those under traditional supervision outweighed distinctions between probationers and parolees.

Stepwise regression was again used to explicate the impact of changes in the BDI score and demographic and household variables on changes in control scale scores. As with the conflict scale changes, the BDI pretest-posttest change was the first variable to be entered into the equation (R^2=.084; F=24.665; P=.000). The employment status of the offender was the next, and last, variable to be entered into this equation, producing an R^2 for the final model of .108 (F=16.664; P=.000). The presence of EM did not appear to have a significant impact on control scale changes but its effect may have been masked by collinearity with other, more powerful, predictors of changes in perceived familial control. The role of employment status and dysphoria in predicting familial control is likely similar to that in predicting conflict.

In closing the discussion of pretest-posttest changes, it should be noted that the effects of EM are notably absent. Age, marital status, employment status and prior imprisonment seem to play a role in predicting changes in psychometric test scores over approximately three month periods of time but EM does not appear to have any discernible effect.

PREDICTION OF SUCCESSFUL COMPLETION OF COMMUNITY SUPERVISION

In the Table that follows, the distribution of offenders across combinations of EM and Success categories is displayed. With Yates' correction for a two-by-two table, EM's effects approach statistical significance (Chi Square=3.201, P=.073). Examination of cell frequencies indicates that offenders on EM had a high rate of success (76.3%), however non-EM clients were more frequently successful (87.7) than those on monitoring. This is best attributed to the fact that the vast majority of clients assigned to EM have had problems in complying with the conditions of their initial release on regular community supervision. Thus, EM clients, as "difficult" clients who have failed on regular supervision, when compared to "non-difficult" clients who have not failed on regular community supervision, appear almost as likely to succeed.

TABLE 9.1
DISTRIBUTION OF SUCCESS ACROSS TYPES OF SUPERVISION

	Non-EM	EM	
			Row
	.00	1.00	Total
Unsuccessful	8	22	30
	26.7	73.3	19.0
	12.3	23.7	
Successful	57	71	128
	44.5	55.5	81.0
	87.7	76.3	
Column	65	93	158
Total	41.1	58.9	100.0

In order to further analyze the predictive utility of the psychometric results found on the successful completion of community supervision two major constraints on the analytical technique had to be dealt with. First, many of the preceding analyses indicate that differences between parolees and probationers are of greater import than those between offenders on traditional community and those on EM. For this reason three analyses, one for each category of supervision and one for the entire sample, were required. Secondly, the dependent or outcome variable in this case is a dichotomy - offenders were either successful in their completion of community supervision or they were not. Standard regression cannot be interpreted with any certainty when the dependent variable is coded in such a fashion. Therefore we have elected to use logistic regression which was designed to deal with just such a contingency.

The first logistic regression addressed the success of probationers using the difference between the pretest and posttest scores on the BDI, the control and conflict scales of the FES and the presence of EM as independent variables. This model made correct predictions of success in 91.27% of the cases. Three point one percent (3.9%) of the offenders were erroneously predicted to be failures when, in fact, they had successfully completed community supervision while 4.8% of the offenders were misclassified as successes when they had failed to complete community supervision successfully.

The pretest to posttest change in control scale score had the most predictive power (R=.326) and indicates that chances of success are directly related to the decline of perceived family control during electronic monitoring. The change in the BDI score was also significant in the same direction (R=.126). The impact of EM was next in importance and explained nearly 5.0% (R=-.042) of the variance in failure. Changes in conflict scale scores (R=.000) did not appear to have any measurable impact on successful completion of community supervision. Overall measures of this model's goodness of fit indicate that these predictor variables, taken together, have an effect that is statistically significant (Model: Chi Square=55.128; P=.000).

The reported decline in family control over the period of the study, accompanied by the significant impact of EM, is of great substantive significance. These results imply that EM may serve to relieve the family of some of its control responsibilities. This may explain the decline in dysphoria since the replacement of controls associated with the family by correctional authorities (i.e., EM) provides the offender with a highly structured lifestyle but keeps the responsibility for its imposition outside the family unit. Thus, the effects of EM may well be beneficial for the offender as well as for the family with which he/she lives.

The same model was used to explain successful completion of supervision among the parolees in this sample. As has been previously noted, data for parolees is less often complete, resulting in a smaller number of cases amenable to multi-variate analyses. This diminution of the sample is likely to introduce selection biases that cannot be predicted. Therefore, analyses of parolees are much more tentative than those for probationers. For this group of subjects the model's fit is much weaker (model Chi Square=25.318; P=.000) but still significant. The model made correct predictions in 90.63% of the cases. In addition, 6.3% of the offenders were erroneously predicted to be failures when, in fact, they had successfully completed community supervision while 3.1% of the offenders were misclassified as successes when they had failed to complete community supervision successfully. One fourth of the parolees were correctly predicted to be failures and 65.6% were correctly predicted to be successes by these variables. However, only the change in control scale score had an impact that was discernible from zero in this model (R=-.2541). Thus, it would appear that, for these subjects, the reduction of perceived familial control predicted success on community supervision, though to a smaller degree than for probationers. Although EM was not significant in this regression, its effects may be indirect and biases in the sub-sample due to missing data may be responsible for its lack of statistical significance.

When the entire sample is examined in this fashion, the predictive power of the independent variables falls to 89.87%. In addition, 4.43% were falsely classified as failures when in fact they successfully completed community supervision while 5.70% were classified as successes when they in fact were terminated before the end of their sentence. Changes in control scale scores were most prominent among the predictor variables (R=.3584) but the presence of EM (R=-.0733) and changes in dysphoria (R=.0250) also had a measurable impact. These results are virtually the same as those for the parolees but the strength of the relationship between reduced perception of familial control and successful completion of supervision is stronger.

SUMMARY AND CONCLUSIONS REGARDING SIGNIFICANT ANALYTICAL RESULTS

In terms of differences between the analytical sub-groups within the sample several distinctions must be initially noted. Parolees on EM are significantly older than members of the other three groups. Probationers not on EM are significantly more likely to be white than members of any other group. Parolees, regardless of the type of supervision they are under are less well-educated than probationers of either type. Parolees, as a group, also have significantly more children in their households than do probationers. Probationers of both types are more likely to be employed than are either type of parolees. However, EM probationers show a significant tendency towards better jobs than do probationers under traditional supervision or either group of parolees.

None of the offender background variables examined predicted noteworthy differences in pretest BDI scores. The same is true of all the FES pretest measures examined except the growth dimension in which the subject's educational level had a significant impact. This finding is of little consequence however, since it was to be expected and is of little relevance to the efficacy of correctional treatments.

The subject's BDI score, age, substance abuse history, and type of offense had significant predictive power in regard to pretest conflict scores. The sex, educational level, substance abuse history, employment status and type of offense also had significant predictive power with regard to pretest control scores. None of these relationships was particularly surprising and virtually all of them could have been predicted from past research. None of them can be used to imply a problematic selection bias in the use of EM. As would be expected, differences between parolees and probationers are often greater than those between EM and non-EM groups. EM did not appear to have any predictive power with regard to any of the psychometric pretest measures. Thus, it can be inferred that the psychological states measured by these instruments (i.e., the BDI and FES subscales) are not a significant fact in selecting offenders for EM.

When posttest results are surveyed, EM parolees report significantly less dysphoria than do probationers of either type. Non-EM parolees are intermediate between these two groupings. Electronic monitoring, along with the offender's age and type of offense, had an effect on posttest BDI scores that was statistically discernible from zero. The effect of EM in this context is suspected to be attributable to the fact that EM allows convicts an earlier release from institutional custody than would normally be expected. Thus, members of this sub-group feel less restricted and community supervision does not lead to dysphoria as quickly among them.

Control scale posttests were significantly lower for both groups of parolees than for the probationers. This seems best attributed to the fact that parolees tend to have weaker family ties as a result of incarceration and are a less controllable group as a result of their relatively higher level of criminal involvement. Parolees on EM reported significantly less conflict on the posttest than any other group. Conflict post tests follow much the same pattern but no distinctions between EM and non-EM parolees can be made with regard to this variable.

Regression analysis indicated that BDI posttest scores, employment status, and EM supervision had significant effects on posttest conflict scores. The direct and positive effect of BDI scores on familial conflict is not surprising but these data do not allow speculation as to whether dysphoria is a cause or an effect of conflict. The association of the offender's employment status with conflict in the home is difficult to explain. Indeed, quite the opposite direction was expected for these variables. It may be that the more an offender works, the more power he/she expects within the family. Since offenders frequently have relationship problems, such expectations could, in the context of a history that includes direct or indirect abuse of family members and/or responsibilities by the offender, be conflict-producing. The impact of EM on reported perceptions of family conflict is noteworthy in this context since the analysis indicates that the presence of EM is associated with low levels of friction within the family. Because this association did not attain significance when pretest data were analyzed, the data suggests that EM may have a positive effect in this regard.

The most crucial analyses are those concerning differences between pretest and posttest scores since these changes in the subjects' perceptions reflect the impact of EM supervision. Changes in BDI scores were the first to be analyzed. As in earlier analyses, EM parolees were significantly less dysphoric than probationers on either type of supervision. Regression indicated that the offender's age and educational level were significant predictors of changes in dysphoria. Younger and less-well educated offenders were more likely to report increases in dysphoria over the study period than were older or better educated offenders. Younger offenders are less likely to have encountered the criminal justice system and tend to have fewer responsibilities than older, more established persons.

Analysis of the changes in conflict scores over the study period indicated that changes in dysphoria, along with the offender's age and marital status, had significant predictive power. Dysphoria is logically related to conflict but, as has been previously mentioned, the causal relationship between these two variables is unclear and may indeed be reciprocal with each contributing to the other. Marriage was found to be directly related to reported increases in conflict. This is thought to be a result of the greater intimacy and investment implied by such unions, relative to other types of relationships. Age was also directly related to increases in conflict scores. The predictive value of age may be due to the realization that much of one's life has been wasted on criminal, or at least deviant, pursuits.

Analysis of control scale scores indicated that only changes in dysphoria and the offender's employment status had effects that were discernible from zero. Both of these relationships were of a direct (i.e., positive) nature. Thus the data indicate that increases in dysphoria are associated with increases in perceived family control and the more regular the offender's employment, the more likely the perception of increased familial control over time. Neither of these findings are especially surprising, particularly in the context of a population of felony offenders.

The final set of analyses were, in fact, the most crucial to the study because of their focus on determinants of successful completion of community supervision. Because of the aforementioned differences between the probationers and parolees these two groups were analyzed separately before the entire sample was examined. Among probationers three factors were found to predict success: (1) decline in perceived familial control as measured by the FES; (2) decline in reported dysphoria as measured by the BDI; and, (3) the presence of EM. It seems apparent that perceptions of family control may be effected by the use of EM in a positive manner. That is, the use of EM constitutes a control mechanism that replaces the family as a monitor of the offender's activities and whereabouts. Thus, when EM is used the imposition of structure upon the offender's life is firmly linked to the decisions of the probation/parole officer rather than a family member. Therefore, the family ceases to operate as the overseer of the offender's movements but the offender is simultaneously forced into a more structured lifestyle by the demands of EM supervision. By relieving the family of some of its control functions, EM facilitates the establishment of more functional patterns in the offenders' lifestyle, and that of the family, thus serving a role that has, at the very least, some rehabilitative potential.

SIGNIFICANT OTHERS

The information that follows concerns the testing devices and the characteristics of the significant others of the offenders in this study. This is followed by an analysis of the results.

TESTING DEVICES

Each of the significant others completed a Client Demographic Information Form, a pretest for the Control and Conflict subscales for FES, and a pretest BDI. The client Demographic Information Form was used to collect and identify the following information: (1) the name of the significant other; (2) the agency having jurisdiction over the offender; (3) the county having jurisdiction over the offender; (4) the offender's specific type of supervisory program; (5) the general significant other's socio-demographic characteristics; (6) the offense committed by the offender; (7) an abbreviated criminal history of the offender; (8) an abbreviated substance abuse history of the significant other; and, (9) an abbreviated family environmental history of the significant other.

SOCIO-DEMOGRAPHIC AND ADDED CHARACTERISTICS OF THE SUBJECTS

There were a total of 29 significant others that participated in this study. The majority (60%) of these subjects were between the ages of 22 to 35, and 51.7% were nonwhite. Slightly more (58.6%) were males than females (41.4), and 56.7% had not completed high school. More (37.9%) of the subjects were married than single (34.5%), while 27.6% were either separated, divorced, or widowed. Forty-eight point two percent (48.2%) had full time employment and 14.8% were employed part time. Of those for which the type of employment could be identified, 84.6% worked at what would normally be classified as blue collar jobs. Sixty-eight point nine percent (68.9%) stated that they lived in a 3 or 4 member family household with 100% having at least one child living with them. Only 6.9% of the significant others claimed to be living with more than two children.

The offense history of the offenders of the significant others ranged from property crimes, which was the highest category (68.8%). This was followed by substance abuse crimes (25%) and by crimes against a person (6.2%).

The significant others' alcohol and drug abuse or use histories in regard to their own usage prior to their offenders' arrest indicated that 67.8% abstained from both alcohol or drugs; 17.9% used both alcohol and drugs socially; 10.7% only used drugs socially; and only 3.6% identified themselves as serious abusers of both alcohol and drugs. The survey indicated a decrease in their current usage over that prior to their offenders' arrest. Eighty-nine point three percent (89.3%) claimed to be now abstaining from both alcohol and drugs, with the remaining 10.7% stating that they used both substances socially. None of these persons claimed to be a serious abuser of either substance. The vast majority (93.1%) stated that they had a good relationship with their families.

The significant others were subsequently divided into two groups. One group, significant others of offenders on EM (hereafter referred to as EM significant others), represented 62% of the total sample while the other group, significant others of offenders not on EM (hereafter referred to as non-EM significant others), represented the remaining 38% of the total sample.

In both groups the majority of subjects were found to be between the ages of 22 and 35 (61.4% for EM significant others and 63.7% for non-EM significant others). The EM group contained 72.2% males whereas the non-EM group contained only 36.4%. There were more non-whites than whites in both groups (61.1% for EM significant others and 63.6% for non-EM significant others).

Each group contained about the same number of married subjects (EM group 38.9% and non-EM group 37.9%). They also had approximately the same educational levels (EM group had 55.6% with less than a high school education and the non-EM group had 56.7%). The overall employment patterns for both groups were similar; however, there was a difference between the groups with respect to full or part time employment. Twenty-seven point three percent (27.3%) of the non-EM group were employed full time while only 6.3% of the EM group were, and 62.4% of the EM group held part time jobs while only 27.2% of the non-EM group did. Both groups had approximately the same number who were unemployed (45.5% for the non-EM group and 31.3% for the EM group). For those whose type of employment could be established,

74.9% of the non-EM group and 88.8% of the EM group held what would normally be classified as "blue collar" jobs.

Both the EM and non EM groups lived predominately in three or four member family households (66.7% and 72.8 respectively). All (100%) members of both groups lived with at least one child. Also, all (100%) of the non-EM households contained less than three children, whereas 11.2% of the EM households contained three or more children. The histories of offenses committed by the significant others' offenders had a somewhat similar pattern: property offenses accounted for 72.7% of the offenses in the EM group, and for 60% of the offenses for the non-EM group; substance abuse offenses for the EM group totaled 18.2%, whereas it accounted for 40% of the non-EM group; and, 9.1% of crimes against a person were noted for the EM group compared to 0.0% for the non-EM group.

Both groups had approximately the same alcohol and drug abuse or use histories concerning their own usage prior to their offenders' arrest. The data suggested that 80% of the non-EM group and 61.1% of the EM group abstained from both alcohol and drugs; 10% of the non-EM group claimed to use only drugs socially as did 11.1% of the EM group; 10% of the non-EM group and 22.1% of the EM group reported using both alcohol and drugs socially. None (0.0%) of the non-EM group claimed to seriously abuse either drugs or alcohol; however, 5.6% of the EM group claimed serious abuse of drugs or alcohol. The survey indicated a decrease in both groups in terms of current usage compared to their usage prior to their offenders' arrest: 100% of the non-EM and 83.3% of the EM group claimed to be abstaining from both alcohol and drugs. Sixteen point seven percent (16.7%) of the EM group indicated that they currently were using both alcohol and drugs socially.

There was a slight difference between the two groups regarding how they viewed their family relationships. All (100%) of the non-EM group indicated that they had good family relationships, whereas 11.2% of the EM group did not feel that they had good family relationships.

ANALYSIS

Due to the relatively small sample of significant others, Pearson Product-Moment Correlations (Pearson's r) and t tests were used to test the significance of the relationships existing between the socio-demographic, psychometric, and background variables for the available data. The matrices of correlation coefficients for the socio-demographic variables (age, race, sex, family, employment, marriage, education, household, adults, and children) indicate that only four of the variables were significantly correlated at the 0.01 level. The correlation between subjects' level of education and the type of offense (r = -.4770) was significant. The number of adults in these households was also closely related to the total number of persons living in households as could logically be expected (r = .5354). However, the correlation coefficients for these two pairs of variables indicate that the relationships are only moderate at best. Generally, only correlation coefficients that are greater than 0.70, and that reach statistically significance at the .05 or .01 levels of significance, are interpreted as having a dependable relationship with each other. In short, our interpretation of the correlation coefficients across all of the demographic variables is that no strong relationship exists between any of the variables with respect to the significant others.

The sample of significant others was next divided into two groups: those associated with offenders who were on electronic monitoring and those associated with offenders who were not on EM. A series of t-tests were then employed to test for significant differences between the means scores of these two groups on the conflict and control subscales of the FES. A t-test was also used to determine if differences in mean levels of dysphoria as determined by the BDI were statistically discernible between these two groups of subjects. Neither of these t-tests revealed statistically significant differences between the EM and non-EM groups: The t level equaled 0.23 (P=0.83) for the two groups on dysphoria (EM group mean score=1.24, non-EM group mean=1.30); t equaled 0.33 (P=0.71) for the two groups on family conflict (EM group mean score=2.15, non-EM group mean=2.38); and t equaled 0.64 (P=0.56) for the two groups on family control (EM group mean score=5.41; non-EM group the mean=5.73).

In essence, no discernible differences appear to exist between EM and non-EM family environments as perceived by significant others of offenders residing with them, nor does there appear to be any discernable difference in the level of dysphoria between significant others of EM and non-EM offenders. In summary, although the extremely small t values found indicate that no such relationships exist, this conclusion cannot be sustained in this analysis because of the small sample size used.

REFERENCES

Boss, P. (1977). A clarification of the concept of psychological - father presence in families experiencing ambiguity of boundary. *Journal of Marriage and the Family, 36,* 141-151.

Ford, J., Bashford, M., & DeWitt, K. (1979). *Prediction of outcome in marital communication training: An empirical investigation.* Van Nuys, CA: San Fernando Community Mental Health Center.

Grinter, R. C. (1989). Electronic monitoring of serious offenders in Texas. *Journal of Offender Monitoring, 2 (4),* 1-14.

Miller, D. (1977). Hollingshead's two factor index of social position. In D. Miller (Ed.), *Handbook of research design and social measurement (3rd ed.),* (pp. 230-238). NY: David McKay.

Moos, R., & Moos, B. (1986). *Family environment scale manual (2nd ed.).* Palo Alto, CA: Consulting Psychologists Press.

Norusis, M. J. (1983). *Introductory statistics guide: SPSSx.* NY: McGraw-Hill.

CRUCIAL ISSUES IN THE FUTURE FOR ELECTRONIC MONITORING PROGRAMS

As Vass (1992) notes, the prison system "is actually *expanding* and the belly of the beast is constantly being enlarged to absorb and process more and more people than ever before. But as happened so often . . . the prison is currently going through another 'crisis' " (p. 17). This crisis has to do with many issues, including the rising costs of imprisonment, prison overcrowding, increasing crime rates, and demands of the public for government agencies to be tough on crime. The use of alternative sentencing has increased partly as a reaction to these concerns, and it seems likely that electronic monitoring (EM) and other non-incarcerative measures will continue to be implemented in the future. It is helpful when examining the future prospects of EM to consider several major issues which impinge on that future. In this Chapter, we will discuss several of these major issues. These issues include: ethical concerns; the structuring of the programs; the organizational management of the programs; and, the impact of external social, economic, and political pressures and influences on EM.

ETHICAL CONCERNS

There are a number of important philosophical, moral and ethical concerns with respect to the use, and abuse, of EM. Technological advances always hold the promise of bringing about marvelous changes in our society and in our culture. Concomitantly, technological innovations often have latent characteristics which can pose serious problems as well.

PROPORTIONALITY

The issue of proportionality is the first, and perhaps the most important, of the ethical concerns with respect to EM. The issue of proportionality, or the relationship between the gravity of the offense and the degree of punishment, has historically been of concern in criminal justice at least since the time of Beccaria (1963). Von Hirsch (1998), has identified several major ethical concerns relevant to community corrections in general. By extension a concern about proportionality can easily be applied to the specific case of the use of EM. For example, assessments of community-based corrections have mainly been made on the basis of whether or not the programs are effective in terms of lowering recidivism, while the potential negative impact of the sanctions on the offender's life may not have been considered thoroughly on a case-by-case basis. In assigning punishment to an offender, it should not be assumed that community-based sanctions automatically represent a lenient treatment of the offender. Rather, due consideration should be given to the fact that community-based corrections sometimes place a severe burden on the offender, for example, home detention/electronic monitoring drastically restricts freedom of movement for the individual. Ball, Huff, and Lilly (1988) note that while many researchers have expressed concern about how home incarceration's potential for turning homes into prisons might develop, generally, little evidence has been available on the issue, and they "strongly recommend the use of specific guidelines as a means of reducing any such tendency" (pp. 97-8). Although noncustodial sanctions may be considered less harsh when compared to imprisonment, the deprivations community-based programs inflict should not be overlooked. Care should be taken to determine whether the sanction is proportionate to the offense committed. Community corrections must not become a blanket response to all less serious offenses, or the result will be net widening. Recent cases have been cited in which an offender who might previously have been only fined is placed on house arrest and electronic monitoring. In this regard, Von Hirsch (1998) admonishes that it would be helpful for reformers to ask themselves two questions in determining the proportional punishment for a particular offense: How serious is the crime, and how severe is the proposed punishment?

Another issue regarding proportionality stems from the fact that there seems to be inequity in terms of fitting the punishment to the crime for certain groups of people. It is often the case that more exacting correctional means are used almost exclusively with the poor and, especially, with ethnic minority offenders. This has become a clear consequence of the "war on drugs." By way of illustration, a recent sentencing study found that African-American offenders were two times as likely as white offenders to receive habitual offender sentences even after controlling for the offender's crime and prior criminal record (Irwin & Austin, 1997). Questions also arise as to the reason for the much longer sentences for possession or dealing of crack cocaine, whose users are more often African American, as compared to the much shorter sentences imposed for possession or dealing of the powder form of cocaine, which is more commonly used by whites (Inciardi, 1992). In short, it is our view that attention needs to be given to the sentencing of offenders to electronic monitoring, house arrest, and other community-based programs to ensure fairness in regard to race, economic status, and other factors.

INTRUSIVENESS

In determining the degree of intrusiveness that is ethically responsible to administer in a given punishment, it becomes important to ascertain if the judicial sanction can stand on its own and be justified in its own right, rather than by making invidious comparison with other sanctions. This argument is similar to the one applied to the issue of proportionality; for example, rather than assuming that community-based corrections are tolerable because they are less burdensome than prison, reformers need to be mindful of the specific burdens that noncustodial sanctions themselves impose.

By contrast, however, the idea that technology-based methods of control, such as electronic monitoring, are de facto more intrusive than traditional methods, such as home visits, is also fallacious. The aspect of intrusiveness can only be determined by the extent to which the method affects human rights to privacy and dignity. Thus, EM itself, may not necessarily be intrusive. It is the interwoven nature of the legal and ethical concerns regarding intrusiveness that presents the interesting challenges. In our society, ultimately, legal and political interpretations of The Fourth Amendment to the U.S. Constitution will provide the baseline for considering the issue of intrusiveness:

The right of the people to be secure in their persons, houses, papers, and effects, against unreasonable searches and seizures, shall not be violated, and no warrants shall issue but upon probable cause, supported by oath or affirmation, and particularly describing the place to be searched, and the persons or things to be seized.

Ball, Huff, and Lilly (1988) note that the courts have ruled that offenders are not entitled to the same rights that ordinary citizens enjoy. In the specific case of electronic monitoring, the consent of the offender has usually been given. Nevertheless, consenting to comply with a community corrections program such as electronic monitoring or house arrest must not mean that the offender gives up all right to privacy. In this same vein, Von Hirsch (1998) maintains that when developing a new program, reformers need to ask themselves not only whether the program is constitutionally legal, but also whether there any ethical grounds for considering the program humiliating or intrusive to the offender. These issues will continue to shape the use of electronic monitoring and other methods of community corrections.

DIGNITY

Von Hirsch (1998) believes that, while punishment must necessarily inflict shame on the perpetrator so that he or she understands that the crime is not socially acceptable, there is however, no need to strip the offender of personal dignity. The idea is to use shame or degradation to elicit remorse for the crime rather than to use shame to make the person feel inferior to the general population. In other words, the behavior and actions of the person, rather than the person per se, is bad. This view seems compatible with rehabilitation of the offender, as it separates the identity of the person from the stigma of being a criminal, and allows for the concept of the offender having the free choice to change his or her behavior, rather than submitting to the idea that he or she is simply an inherently "bad" or flawed person. In contrast to working in a chain gang, for example, performing compulsory labor, such as community service, is a penalty that does not deprive the individual of dignity, while still punishing the offender, and, perhaps, instilling a moral lesson.

THIRD PARTIES

Community-based corrections, more so than incarceration, directly affect the daily lives of the family or anyone else living with the offender. Traditional probation techniques for control, such as home visits, affect the entire household more than electronic monitoring and house arrest do, as the latter are inflicted much more closely on the offending individual. However, the rights of others who may be affected by the sanctions to the offender, must be addressed, and as yet has not been. According to Ball, Huff, and Lilly (1988), "there is practically no information on the impact of home confinement and electronic monitoring on . . . the inmate's family" (p. 97). There are, however, some exceptions about the impact of EM on family members and significant others, such as our study (Chapter 9), and the notation by McShane and Krause (1993). They comment that "many families may resent the intrusion of the electronic equipment and their reduced access to phone service during the sentence" (p. 134). The issue of net widening is of direct concern here, as well. The circumstance of applying the judicial sanction to the offender should not be viewed as an opportunity or as an excuse for criminal justice authorities to practice surveillance upon other members in the household. Nor should it be used for vicarious purposes. In fact, the impact on others should be considered by authorities when choosing the type of control to be imposed upon the offender. For example, home visits would be quite an imposition on the entire household, whereas community service for the offender would not.

On the other hand, electronic monitoring programs have the potential to uphold family relationships. Because they can stay at home, offenders can continue to contribute to the support of the family and can maintain their roles within the family. This may be of particular importance in preserving relationships with children; often these relationships are severely damaged or broken when a family member is incarcerated (McShane & Krause, 1993).

Many evaluators of house arrest have expressed concern about the fact that offenders are usually returned to the same environment that was conducive to their original offense. Some have expressed fears that the same influences and habits which contributed to the committing of crimes will undermine the offender's ability to be rehabilitated and that the fact that the offender is being electronically monitored only means that there is a greater likelihood that the crimes will be detected. This problem has recently been addressed by a California program that provides offenders with foster or surrogate homes in which to serve their sentences of electronically monitored house arrest (McShane & Krause, 1993). In elaborating about this innovation, Williams, Shichor, and Wiggenhorn (1993) explain that:

> The surrogate homes were selected to match, as far as possible, the individual needs of the offenders. In addition, the areas in which the homes are located were purposefully located outside of the offender's previous environment. Homes were located either through word-of-mouth or through advertisement placed in local newspapers. Owners were paid $16.00 daily for room and board and almost universally provided other services such as transportation, employment leads, and guidance to the parolee. (142)

Preliminary reports have shown positive results for the surrogate home project. Of special note is the fact that the surrogate family seems to provide good role models for the offender, possibly contributing to the rehabilitation or reintegration of the offender. Additionally, the family acts as an impartial party in questions of the offender's whereabouts or activities, thus the family helps to offset any technical failures or inconsistencies in the electronic equipment. The two-fold advantage of both increasing surveillance and accountability and decreasing contact with negative influences may be a powerful combination in the rehabilitation of offenders. However, a full evaluation of the program needs to be done in order to assess the actual potential of this type of approach. Experiments and innovations such as the foster family program may lead to the improved effectiveness of electronic monitoring, house arrest, and other community sanctions, but this remains to be seen.

PROGRAM STRUCTURE

An evaluation of the effectiveness of community corrections programs to date shows that there is reason to believe that the best strategy for structuring future community corrections programs may be to utilize a combination of intensive supervision and rehabilitation (Gendreau, Cullen, & Bonta, 1998). One of the advantages of electronic monitoring is that it can be used in conjunction with treatment such as counseling, therapy or self-improvement groups, thus the client can benefit from the rehabilitative potential of these treatments, whereas an incarcerated individual could not. In this manner, it can be argued that a sanction such as EM appeals to general public outcries for punishing the offender, while simultaneously providing a setting in which the rehabilitative needs of the offender can be more easily facilitated. In this sense, EM does the politically impossible: it appeals to conservative desires for punishment of offenders and to liberal desires for rehabilitation.

Program structure also needs to be considered with respect to matching offender risk profiles and treatment approaches. According to Gendreau, Cullen, and Bonta (1998), the risk principle states that "treatment will more likely be effective when treatment services are matched with the risk level of the offender" (p. 199). In other words, recidivism may decrease when high-risk offenders are matched with more intensive controls and low-risk offenders are matched with less intensive controls (Enos & Southern, 1996). However, we emphasize these controls need to be combined with rehabilitation. Clear and Braga (1998) agree, noting that:

> Since both the RAND evaluation and an earlier evaluation of Massachusetts' IPS reported significantly lower recidivism rates when offenders received treatment (for substance abuse, employment, and family problems), an emphasis on treatment seems to be a promising avenue for crime control in the community. (p. 216).

In this same vein, Lipsey (1992), after evaluating 443 studies of the effectiveness of rehabilitation programs, found that programs which worked were found to have the following attributes:

1. Intensive services that are behavioral in nature are provided to higher risk offenders.

2. The goal of treatment is the reduction of criminogenic needs (offender's attitudes toward employment, peers, authority, and substance abuse).

3. The type of treatment and the therapist is matched to the personality and type of offender.

-215-

4. Consequences are enforced in a firm yet fair manner.

5. Therapists are fully trained and evaluated periodically.

6. Program structure disrupts the criminal network.

7. Services applicable to offenders must be provided and assessed in an objective manner.

Electronic monitoring is often a part of intensive supervision, and as such may be combined with rehabilitation. For such future programs to be successful, Gendreau, Cullen, and Bonta (1998) suggest that program developers become familiar with relevant literature, and that the programs be applied judiciously to the appropriate offenders. There are several problems with their suggestions, however. To begin with, law enforcement professionals are not always ideologically predisposed toward rehabilitative strategies. In addition, they are not usually trained with respect to performing in rehabilitative roles. The potential for role confusion, role strain and role conflict may become exacerbated. Another difficulty with these suggestions is the cost factor. It would take a major monetary investment and expenditure to train law enforcement staff to assume these new kinds of roles and to learn new skills. Of course, corrections already has high employee turnover and replacement rates, this might simply contribute to those problems. By way of contrast, Ball, Huff, and Lilly (1988) point out that one of the specific advantages of home confinement is the fact that the complexity level, in terms of developing and implementing the method, is quite low. The legal research and administrative tasks required are not complicated and are certainly no more difficult than what is required in most areas of criminal law. Hopefully, this simplicity of design will be advantageous in developing and implementing programs which combine community corrections and rehabilitative techniques.

ORGANIZATIONAL MANAGEMENT

Corbett (1998) asserts that the current state of community corrections is so bleak that programs must either change or perish. He proposes applying the business practice of "reinventing" to the management of community corrections operations in order to improve the programs' efficiency and cost-effectiveness. A prerequisite for reinventing is the development of a mission or strategic-driven plan for the community corrections program. This means that the management arm of the program must make the initial effort to establish a true mission statement, including the goals and philosophy of the program. This is an exercise that should not be taken lightly; the goals and philosophy, once agreed upon and established, must then inform all later decisions and practices. Any action taken by the organization must flow from and conform to the mission of the group. Corbett (1998) illustrates the importance of this point by presenting the statement of the Georgia Department of Corrections, an organization well known for its innovations in community corrections. It reads as follows:

> The mission . . . is to protect the public and staff by managing offenders either in a safe and secure environment or through effective community supervision according to their needs and risks. In collaboration with the community and other agencies, we provide programs which offer offenders the opportunity to become responsible, productive, law-abiding citizens. p.209.

Historically, the field of corrections itself has lacked a clear mission. This is particularly true with respect to the structure and function of community corrections. The field would have to at least come to a general consensus concerning the goals, priorities and outcomes expected of community-based correctional programs and services. It is especially important to come to some sort of consensus before new approaches or innovations in programs or services are launched. Perhaps a national professional organization, such as the American Correctional Association, could provide the impetus for change in terms of this issue.

Clearly, EM was launched, developed and implemented without any policy consensus. Offenders want fairness and assistance, the public wants protection from and punishment of offenders, and government agencies, such as the courts, want cooperation. In addition, radical shifts in the political and cultural climate during the last few decades have left corrections with a mixed bag of purposes ranging from rehabilitation to stiff mandatory sentencing. Further, the corrections system is not only unorganized within agencies, but also among agencies. The process may be described as divided among itself to the extent that "jails, prisons, probation, and parole all struggle with one another; the practices of each become contingencies for the others" (Clear & Cole, 1997, p.556). This occurs because there is only so much jail space, and agents such as courts, law enforcement, and probation/parole in a sense compete for the use of this space. Each agency jealously guards its own power and is reluctant to reduce it by coordinating or planning with other agencies. However, some steps have been taken toward ameliorating this situation. A recent trend is the formation of high-level task forces composed of heads of various agencies, such as correctional, justice system, judicial, and executive branch agencies. The purpose of these commissions is to improve coordination among the various agencies.

A results-driven orientation, which is common in business, is of great use in a community corrections agency. Having specific outcomes as goals, and being able to measure whether or not these goals have been met, is crucial in evaluating the success of an agency. Unfortunately, many agencies are unable to state what their performance goals are, and thus are unable to determine if they are achieving any success. Results-driven strategies depend upon describing goals in clear and unambiguous terms. In addition, the outcomes of the goals must be stated, a priori, in behavioral terms. These are prerequisites for any kind of social science evaluation methodology. Unfortunately, today most correctional agencies state their goals in general and ambiguous terms. For example, what does a goal such as "to reduce prison overcrowding" mean? This lack of a results-driven focus among agencies is due to the fact that they are funded based on inputs, such as caseload, rather than on outputs, such as effectiveness. In other words, competition is non-existent; unlike private companies, government community corrections agencies have a monopoly on the services they provide and thus have no need to compete. In some states, this problem has been addressed by creating a marketplace for "out-sourcing" or privatization of services. In the future, the trend toward privatization could mean more results due to the competitive nature of private business. With recidivism as the main goal, and recidivism rates as the measure of success, community corrections programs could set moderate reduction targets each year. Competition could possibly fuel a great upsurge in the innovations of methods and practices of community corrections. However, privatization may have a down side in that it may result in private agencies "creaming off" only the least serious offenders, who can be most efficiently processed, going through the private system, while the government-run part of the corrections system is left with having to manage only the most costly and difficult offenders on a reduced budget (Clear & Cole, 1997). Whether or not this situation will occur remains to be seen.

Similar to the results-driven orientation, another business success strategy that community corrections organizations could utilize in the future is a customer-oriented approach, whereby the needs of the client (the person or organization paying for the service) are met. The client may include legislators, taxpayers, and the government. In this view, community corrections organizations would be made accountable to their clients' needs, wants, and opinions. A further suggestion made by Corbett (1998) is that community corrections should be prevention-oriented rather than merely reactive. However, this kind of thinking represents a great paradigm shift for courts and the corrections community, therefore funding for preventive measures may be difficult to obtain. Eventually, the public, legislators, and courts must realize that it costs less to prevent crime than to treat it.

OUTSIDE PRESSURES AND INFLUENCES

Clear and Braga (1998) note that external pressures, such as crowded prison conditions, insufficient funding, the continually increasing substance abuse problems of offenders, and declining job opportunities for offenders, will continue to influence community corrections. In addition, cost is always a major impediment to change. However, in examining rates of recidivism for different types of offenders in community corrections, it is clear that:

1. Intervention programs are promising when applied to higher risk offenders.

2. Expanded use of community corrections does not necessarily result in expanded criminal behavior, if low-risk offenders are diverted from prison.

3. The relaxation of stringent program requirements for low-risk offenders does not necessarily mean increased criminality; and,

4. As gauged by the number of arrests, the level of criminality in traditional community programs is low in most cases (Corbett, 1998, p. 217).

Based on these findings, it can be anticipated that increased investment in community corrections may lead to an increase in public safety. In addition, according to Ball, Huff, and Lilly, (1988), there is ample evidence that alternative sentencing costs less than incarcerative sentencing. However, it is noted that, "the savings involved in the use of home confinement will really depend upon the extent to which it is used as an alternative to more expensive alternatives such as secure facilities" (p. 141). In other words, the number of offenders involved in and complying with community-based sentences must be great enough to impact significantly the overall cost of corrections.

Generally, alternative sentences have been used on a small number of individuals, making cost savings difficult to assess. Also, the increased use of alternative sentencing must be associated with a decrease in the number of people incarcerated in order for savings to occur. If the same individuals who are electronically monitored end up being incarcerated, this will only add cost to the system. In addition, if electronic monitoring is applied to large numbers of offenders who would previously have been neither incarcerated nor sentenced to community-based methods, costs will rise. In reality, even the most successful EM programs enroll only a small number of offenders who would have otherwise been incarcerated or placed on traditional probation. Usually, offenders are placed in prison first, then released into the community. This practice needs to change if community-based programs are to make a serious impact.

On a positive note, in considering the cost of electronically monitoring offenders, it should be noted that most programs require the offender to contribute to the cost of supervision and equipment. Payments may be deducted from the offender's paychecks and may be on a sliding scale or fixed-rate basis. Commonly, the fees range from two dollars to ten dollars per day. Unlike incarcerated offenders, those offenders sentenced to house arrest with electronic monitoring can be gainfully employed and contribute to the cost of their sentence (McShane & Krause, 1993).

Another benefit inherent in electronic monitoring has to do with the population of inmates who require expensive medical care due to AIDS, cancer, heart disease, or simply being elderly and disabled. As the incidence of AIDS and other health problems increase, and the elderly population grows, releasing these people to their homes under an electronic monitoring program could save a great deal of money for the corrections system. This should be the case since the relative costs of EM are rather low compared with other probation services which must use probation staff in a more labor intensive manner. This fact and others that contribute to the lower cost of alternative sentencing will prove to be strong factors in the continued adoption of these types of programs.

Clear and Braga (1998) ponder whether in the future the concept of justice will include making amends to victims, maintaining family ties and roles possibilities, and the opportunity to contribute to society rather than the current tack of discipline and harshness. They state that only when the politically popular idea of criminal justice loses its mean-spiritedness can . . . "community-based methods . . . have the potential for a sustained importance and a central place in the scheme of policymaking" (p.218). Ball, Huff, and Lilly (1988) are more optimistic. For them, public reaction may have a serious influence on the potential impact of community corrections. We note that both the media and the general public have reacted very favorably to home confinement, thus the future of alternative sanctions may be very bright.

SUMMARY AND POSTSCRIPT

In summary, in this Chapter we directed our discussion at certain issues which impinge on the future of EM. These issues included ethical concerns, program structure, organizational management, and outside pressures. These groupings are not meant to encompass all concerns; however, they remain useful for any analysis of the future of EM. It has been demonstrated that the future of community corrections, and specifically electronic monitoring, rests on many interrelated factors. There is no simple solution to the current crisis in the prison system with respect to overcrowding, however, electronic monitoring, as an alternative to sentencing, offers just that; an alternative. How well this innovation will be integrated into programs and utilized in the upcoming years remains to be seen. However, as noted above, there are many indicators of a positive future for electronic monitoring and other community sentences. Let us hope that future comes to pass.

By way of a postscript, we note that in our culture, the primary general ethical and moral concern about the use of electronic monitoring has to do with the outer limits of its application, including net widening. Criminal justice technological "purists" urge that these outer limits be pursued. They suggest, for example, that this could be accomplished by implanting electronic signaling devices in various parts of the offenders's body, in the manner of implantation of heart pace makers. Others of this ilk, such as those of the "brave new world" mentality, propose scenarios in which electronic technology would be used to "guarantee" that offenders would be deterred from criminal behavior. These proponents are in favor, for example, of high technology voice tracking interactive information management systems to accomplish that aim. These kinds of systems are now available for purchase (Norment/Pacific Voice Track, 1997).

Conversely, criminal justice "romanticists" believe that EM works against offender rehabilitation because such methods stifle the potential for the attainment of psychological self-growth, self-actualization, and social maturity; all aspects of the person that can only flower and develop in the absence of external controls. These opponents of EM see this technology as minimally dangerous, if not altogether sinister and unethical. We venture to say that most professionals in the correctional field struggle with the dilemma of freedom versus authority with respect to EM. Even the most ethical and moral of us are challenged with the fact that all technological advances in criminal justice must be weighed in relation to the "real politik" of current political policies and realistic public concerns and attitudes about safety and security from criminal offenders. In reality, it often comes down to choosing among various possibilities, and either perceiving such choices as predicated upon the best possible good (best outcome available given the conditions and circumstances) to be obtained, or choosing the better of flawed or imperfect alternatives.

When comparing EM with the alternatives of prison, jail or traditional probation, EM seems be the better choice, both morally and from the standpoint of offender rehabilitation. Ethical and moral issues, legal rights, and concerns about surveillance and invasion of privacy must be weighed in the balance of victimization, a safe and secure society, and the ideal of the ultimate good for offenders. Unquestionably, EM has profound possibilities for destructive and ominous uses and "big brotherism," especially in terms of individual freedom, human dignity, intrusion into private and family matters, and social control in general. However, one can make this argument for almost all types of criminal justice services and programs, especially those involving technological means. Ultimately, the use of EM must be considered in the context of the value of each of our human and Constitutional rights, versus the threat to those rights that might loom if programs such as EM were not employed.

REFERENCES

Ball, R. A., Huff, C. R., & Lilly, J. R. (1988). *House arrest and correctional policy: Doing time at home.* Newbury Park, CA: Sage.

Beccaria, C. (1963). *On crimes and punishments.* Indianapolis: Bobbs-Merrill.

Clear, T. R., & Cole, G. F. (1997). *American corrections (4th ed.).* Belmont, CA: Wadsworth.

Clear, T. R., & Braga, A. A. (1998). Challenges for corrections in the community. In J. Petersilia (Ed.), *Community corrections* (pp. 213-218). NY: Oxford.

Corbett, R. P., Jr. (1998). When community corrections means business: Introducing *reinvention* themes to probation and parole. In J. Petersilia (Ed.), *Community corrections* (pp. 207-213). NY: Oxford.

Enos, R., & Southern, S. (1996). *Correctional case management.* Cincinnati, OH: Anderson.

Gendreau, P., Cullen, F. T., & Bonta, J. (1998). Intensive rehabilitation supervision: The next generation. In J. Petersilia (Ed.). *Community corrections* (pp. 198-206). NY: Oxford.

Inciardi, J. (1992). *The war on drugs II.* Mountain View, CA: Mayfield.

Irwin, J., & Austin, J. (1997). *It's about time: America's imprisonment binge (2nd ed.).* Belmont, CA: Wadsworth.

Lipsey, M. W. (1992). Juvenile delinquency treatment: A meta-analytic inquiry into the variability of effects. In T. D. Cook, H. Cooper, D. S. Cordray, H. Hartmann, L. V. Hedges, R. J. Light, T.A. Louis, & F. Mosteller, (Eds.), *Meta-analysis for explanation* (pp.83-127). NY: Russell Sage Foundation.

McShane, M. D., & Krause, W. (1993). *Community corrections.* NY: MacMillan.

Norment/Pacific Voice Track (1997). *Corrections Today, 59,* pp. 43.

Vass, A. (1992). *Alternatives to prison.* London: Sage.

von Hirsch, A. (1998). The ethics of community-based sanctions. In J. Petersilia (Ed.), *Community corrections* (pp. 189-198). NY: Oxford.

Williams, F., Shichor, D., & Wiggenhorn, A. (1993). Fine tuning social control: Electronic monitoring and surrogate homes for drug using parolees: A research note. In M. D. McShane, & W. Krause (Eds.), *Community corrections* (p. 142). NY: MacMillan.